C000133685

Fashioning China

Digital Barricades:
Interventions in Digital Culture and Politics

Series editors:
Professor Jodi Dean, Hobart and William Smith Colleges
Dr Joss Hands, Newcastle University
Professor Tim Jordan, University of Sussex

Also available:

Furious:
Technological Feminism
and Digital Futures
Caroline Bassett, Sarah Kember
and Kate O'Riordan

Shooting a Revolution:
Visual Media and Warfare in Syria
Donatella Della Ratta

Inhuman Power:
Artificial Intelligence and
the Future of Capitalism
Nick Dyer-Witheford, Atle Mikkola
Kjosen and James Steinhoff

Cyber-Proletariat:
Global Labour in the Digital Vortex
Nick Dyer-Witheford

The Digital Party:
Political Organisation and
Online Democracy
Paolo Gerbaudo

Gadget Consciousness:
Collective Thought, Will and Action
in the Age of Social Media
Joss Hands

Information Politics:
Liberation and Exploitation
in the Digital Society
Tim Jordan

Sad by Design:
On Platform Nihilism
Geert Lovink

Unreal Objects:
Digital Materialities, Technoscientific
Projects and Political Realities
Kate O'Riordan

Fashioning China

Precarious Creativity and Women Designers in *Shanzhai* Culture

Sara Liao

PLUTO PRESS

First published 2020 by Pluto Press
345 Archway Road, London N6 5AA

www.plutobooks.com

Copyright © Sara Liao 2020

The right of Sara Liao to be identified as the author of this work has been asserted
by her in accordance with the Copyright, Designs and Patents Act 1988.

British Library Cataloguing in Publication Data
A catalogue record for this book is available from the British Library

ISBN   978 0 7453 4069 2   Hardback
ISBN   978 0 7453 4070 8   Paperback
ISBN   978 1 7868 0589 8   PDF eBook
ISBN   978 1 7868 0591 1   Kindle eBook
ISBN   978 1 7868 0590 4   EPUB eBook

This book is printed on paper suitable for recycling and made from fully managed
and sustained forest sources. Logging, pulping and manufacturing processes are
expected to conform to the environmental standards of the country of origin.

Typeset by Stanford DTP Services, Northampton, England

Simultaneously printed in the United Kingdom and United States of America

For my parents, and Jackie and Chloe.

Contents

Figures

Series Preface

Crisis and conflict open up opportunities for liberation. In the early twenty-first century, these moments are marked by struggles enacted over and across the boundaries of the virtual, the digital, the actual, and the real. Digital cultures and politics connect people even as they simultaneously place them under surveillance and allow their lives to be mined for advertising. This series aims to intervene in such cultural and political conjunctures. It features critical explorations of the new terrains and practices of resistance, producing critical and informed explorations of the possibilities for revolt and liberation.

Emerging research on digital cultures and politics investigates the effects of the widespread digitisation of increasing numbers of cultural objects, the new channels of communication swirling around us and the changing means of producing, remixing and distributing digital objects. This research tends to oscillate between agendas of hope, that make remarkable claims for increased participation, and agendas of fear, that assume expanded repression and commodification. To avoid the opposites of hope and fear, the books in this series aggregate around the idea of the barricade. As sources of enclosure as well as defenses for liberated space, barricades are erected where struggles are fierce and the stakes are high. They are necessarily partisan divides, different politicizations and deployments of a common surface. In this sense, new media objects, their networked circuits and settings, as well as their material, informational, and biological carriers all act as digital barricades.

Jodi Dean, Joss Hands and Tim Jordan

Acknowledgements

I am indebted to many individuals and institutions in the preparation of this book. First, without the participation of the women designers depicted in the book, I would not have been able to write about them. I am grateful that they shared their stories with me, allowed me to participate in their work and lives, and showed me kindness in many different ways. I also thank the other people I encountered in the span of my study, those who put me in contact with others, and those who generously pointed me to the resources I could use; all the chitchats and sharing helped shape my thinking and writing.

Thank you to the coeditors of the book series *Digital Barricades*, Jodi Dean, Joss Hands, and Tim Jordan, Pluto's editorial director David Castle and editorial manager Robert Webb, and two anonymous readers, who made the book a possibility. Tim Jordan from the University of Sussex is such a wonderful colleague and mentor who saw potential in the book manuscript; Tim provided sincere and constructive feedback and review and generously shares his thoughts in theories and academic errands. I also thank my copyeditors James Marks and Elaine Ross, who carefully edited and proofread the manuscript.

My best friend and feminist scholar Jinsook Kim has witnessed the whole process of preparing this book, from initial ideas, term papers, to a dissertation, several conference presentations, and eventually the published book. She knows the good and bad about me and my work but always stands with me. I am also grateful to other close friends and researchers, Karen Lee, Jennifer Kang, Ji-Hyun Ahn, and Ryan Wang, who offered professional and personal guidance, gave thoughtful suggestions about different versions/parts of this book, and cheerfully energized me with their own fields of specialties in the working process of the project. Joann Ching, Christy Poon, and Grace Xia are friends who teach me how to enjoy life; they accept my stupid jokes, awkward multi-language expressions, and, with their love and care, back me at difficult times in my work and life.

I give my heartfelt thanks to the professors and my peers at the University of Texas at Austin, who were among the first to support me as I began the research for this book. My graduate advisor Shanti Kumar, with his wisdom, insightful input, enlightening thoughts, and warm encouragement, is always motivating me to hold my scholarly commitments at critical times. And whatever I can achieve in research and the writing of this book is largely due to the generous sharing, critical feedback, and unwavering support from Joe Straubhaar, Madhavi Mallapragada, Heather Hindman, Chiu-mi Lai, and Yvonne Chang. In addition, the company of friends and allies has been invaluable during the years of research and writing. I miss the conversations and chats, drinks and food, laughter and good cheer, and endless support from Fangjing Tu, Julian Etienne, Jackie Pinkowitz, Lucia Palmer, Bahaa Gameel, Morgan O'brien, Nick Bester, and Saif Shahin.

I thank Julie Chen, Jack Qiu, and Rose Luqiu for kindly sharing their professional experience of academic publishing. I also thank other colleagues and staff working at the School of Journalism and Communication at the Chinese University of Hong Kong. They are always supportive and have created a friendly and efficient working environment enabling me to write, revise, and finish the book on time.

A small section of the book was published as an eponymous journal article in *Communication, Culture & Critique*.

1

Introduction: Fashion Work, Precarious Labor, and Women Designers in *Shanzhai* Culture

Imitation is the sincerest form of flattery.
                    –Charles Caleb Colton, *Lacon: Or Many Things in a Few Words*

One of the traditions for the Chinese celebration of the Lunar New Year is that families gather for a reunion dinner and watch the annual *Spring Festival Gala*, a state-sponsored variety show broadcast on China Central Television (CCTV). The closest American equivalent to this event in popularity is the Super Bowl. For 27 years, the gala has been a dominant cultural force on the government's flagship TV channel, a venue for movie stars and popular singers and the choreography of hundreds of professional performers—and for high-ranking political figures seated in the front rows who will be filmed in close-up against the backdrop of the pageantry. A competing event seemed unthinkable until, in 2009, a strikingly fresh *New Year Show* appeared as if from thin air on the same night as the CCTV event that featured, not celebrities, but ordinary people who had recorded amateur dancing, singing, and other performances with hand-held cameras for broadcast online. The copycat show stood out for its embrace of the improvisational do-it-yourself (DIY) ethic, its creative spirit, and its rejection of authorities and stars, and it gained enormous publicity in China and beyond. The *Wall Street Journal* described the show as a high point of a peculiar kind of copycat culture in China known as *Shanzhai* and as an expression of a certain kind of creativity, ingenuity, rebellion, and resistance to the dominant cultural values associated with the gala, concluding that "imitation is the sincerest form of rebellion" (Canaves & Ye, 2009). In fact, the *Shanzhai* phenomenon is widespread in China early in the twenty-first century, to the point that it can shed considerable light on the country's changing cultural landscape.

A neologism in Chinese, *Shanzhai* literally means "mountain strongholds" and evokes images of treks into the wildness, risk-taking, and even a sort of Robin Hood ethos. *Shanzhai* also carries a strong connotation of subalternity, with the savageness, cruelty, and rebelliousness of the participants serving as symbols of resistance to the dominant group (Hennessey, 2012). In contemporary China, *Shanzhai* is a well-known term for counterfeit goods and copies, having been originally associated with counterfeit cellphones produced by networks of local and regional entrepreneurs (Lin, 2011). These phones come in a variety of colors and shapes and often offer features that even high-end name-brand phones lack, such as mp3/mp4 players, radio and television capabilities, LED lights, dual SIM card support, long stand-by times, and multiple speakers.[1] The distinctive features of these devices, together with their affordability, have made them especially popular among working-class migrants in China. From these practices of copying cellphones, the meaning of the term *Shanzhai* has expanded so that it now covers a wide range of copycat phenomena.

This book explores the *Shanzhai* phenomenon in the context of the fashion world by telling the stories of a group of women who have participated actively in the practices of appropriating name-brand products to create their own designs and selling them at reduced cost on digital platforms to local consumers. The activities of these women constitute what I call "*Shanzhai* fashion," making them "*Shanzhai* designers" dedicated to a very specific kind of copying than the term information technology is often associated with. I use the gendered noun in speaking of these designers advisedly, for *Shanzhai* fashion is largely a women's undertaking. Most of its practitioners can be described as "fashionistas"—devoted followers of fashion—who are eager to share their fashion knowledge and experience with others. Few have any professional training in fashion design; rather, they have learned by practice as they labored to turn a hobby into a profitable business. In producing fashion items that range from low- to high-end, these designers look to a broad range of brands and markets, including Euro-American brands, regional fashion labels from South Korea, Japan, and Thailand, and, on occasion, popular domestic lines.

To be sure, the *Shanzhai* phenomenon has lost some of the novelty that it held in the mid-2000s, when China and the world were stunned by the advent of almost perfect replicas and creative appropriations of name-brand technological devices. However, while *Shanzhai* practices and products have been constantly in the spotlight ever since, most of the existing scholarly work on the subject has considered *Shanzhai* labor largely in regard to men's ambitions, contributions, and precarity. Thus, the dominant overarching discourse has been one of nation-building and nation-branding through technological development, digital expression, innovative resistance, and the creation of a vibrant national culture. Working against this discourse, I foreground the pivotal role of women in *Shanzhai* culture in order to reconceptualize in multiple dimensions the state of crisis and political potentiality with which it is associated. I accordingly focus on the flexibility that women designers show in creating *Shanzhai* fashion products while constantly facing risks and being subjected to regulations while remaining unacknowledged by and excluded from both state ideology and popular discourse about techno-utopias and national development. The fashion work and *Shanzhai* practice of these women is inherently intersectional, for it resides at the boundaries between legitimate and illegitimate and between creativity and imitation; they are interlopers in China's creative industries.

More specifically, the labor of women designers in *Shanzhai* fashion exemplifies the precarious creativity embedded in the ongoing cultural transformation of production and consumption in China. Precarious creativity is a condition in which individuals aspire to acquire a certain level of autonomy over the cultural content and products that they create in the face of constraints of uncertainty and insecurity within the broader cultural environment (Berlant, 2011; Curtin & Sanson, 2016; McRobbie, 2011).

I accordingly conceptualize women's labor in *Shanzhai* fashion here as a specific kind of digital labor or what Tiziana Terranova (2000) has called the "free labor" that individuals contribute to and get pleasure from the digital economy in both material and immaterial terms. *Shanzhai* women designers are versatile; they make fashion copies of clothes and accessories—tangible, material, physical products—and, at the same time, generate and circulate fashion information and knowledge through posting, sharing, instant messaging, and vlogging—all of which are intangible, digital, and immaterial outcomes of *Shanzhai* practice. *Shanzhai* is, in addition, a business for these women, who need to take into account resource management, market competition, and industrial regulations, which in turn call for the input of even more labor in the form of business meetings, factory visits, scouting of locations for photoshoots, infrastructure maintenance, customer service, logistics, and so on—further efforts that, while they do not necessarily generate physical products, remain indispensable to the fashion industry in particular and the digital economy in general. Digital labor, as I approach the phenomenon in this book, is both a significant feature of the digital economy in which short-term work and self-employment often dominate and an important but unacknowledged source of capital accumulation. Particularly, women's digital labor of this sort exemplifies the gendered experience of precarity in creative cultural work. These women, in the active production of cultural artifacts, grapple with the autonomy of creativity while remaining unacknowledged and marginalized both in conventional *Shanzhai* discourse and by the state.

In order to establish the context for my exploration of the work that these women contribute to the larger fashion value chain, I offer a journey through the burgeoning *Shanzhai* fashion industry from their perspectives.

DESIGN AND COPY:
THE *SHANZHAI* FASHION INDUSTRIAL VALUE CHAIN

The production of *Shanzhai* fashion includes several steps. During the initial stages, women designers, working individually, determine the preferred style of potential customers through online voting; then, in light of the voting, they purchase the original product that will serve as a template and research the material and aesthetic design. They solicit down payments from interested consumers that serve to estimate the demand and entitle the consumers to a small discount when purchasing the finished product. Next, the designers make several sample versions and modify them until they arrive at the production models, a single batch of which usually runs to several hundred. At this point, the consumers are asked for full payment and the finished product is shipped to them. The whole process usually takes around a month, though in some cases longer (especially for winter clothing); occasionally, nothing is produced owing to difficulties in obtaining the necessary materials. Notably, *Shanzhai* fashion does not conclude with the purchase of the product, in that many consumers share selfies and other life photos as a way of commenting on the products after receiving them, a phenomenon that is so prevalent and appealing to both consumers and designers that the latter may offer the former cash incentives to post positive reviews with photos in what is known as a "buyer's show." Armed with these comments and feedback, designers further adjust their designs in response to the market, which in turn leads to another cycle of production, consumption, and circulation. In Chapter 3 in particular, I elaborate on the production culture of *Shanzhai* fashion to illustrate how *Shanzhai* fashion remains highly consumer-centric.

Figure 1.1   The online shop Butterfly Bones' American Apparel knockoff, with a price approximated at ¥49.99

Note: The conversion rate for Chinese yuan to US dollars was approximately 6.4 to 1 at the time the research was done in mid-2016.

To be clear, these designers and their businesses are part of the large and complex *Shanzhai* fashion industry, which forms a hierarchy. At the lower end of the industry are cheap knockoffs produced by apparel original equipment manufacturers (OEMs) or factories that offer OEM services to transnational fashion powerhouses.[2] The brands involved include American Apparel, TopShop, ASOS, and H&M; the online shops sell the products at low prices and expect rapid turnover. Figure 1.1 shows an example of an online shop called Butterfly Bones that is typical of such lower-end operations, selling only factory knockoffs and numerous fakes from so-called "fast fashion" brands, with which it shares a business model based on offering relatively low prices, rapid turnover of designs and styles, and large inventories.

Some stores have advertised their products as what are called in Chinese *yuandan* (原单) or *waimao* (外贸), products that come from the same batch ordered by the established fashion companies. The two terms, often used interchangeably or in combination as *waimaoyuandan*, refer to the leftovers of name-brand products, which are sometimes treated as off-brand fakes or counterfeits with no brand because they have failed to meet quality control standards or were produced from surplus original materials. These *yuandan* or *waimao* products, then, trace back to the originals; they are limited in number and sold at prices slightly higher than those of the "pure" knockoffs but significantly lower than those of the originals. Notably, these self-proclaimed leftovers are sometimes created as part of marketing strategies: they are meant to draw market share from copies and fakes. Figure 1.2 shows an offering in an online shoe store, Huihui Large Size Shoes (HLSS), of Russian *waimao* shoes for ¥29.90.

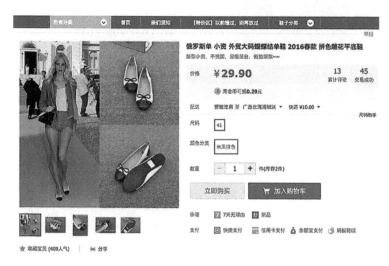

Figure 1.2   Huihui Large Size Shoes' listing for a pair of Russian *waimao* shoes

Moving up the industry, greater creativity is evident as women designers develop their own lines of products rather than marketing goods from garment factories. A general observation of the mid- to high-end fashions makes clear that the prices are proportional to the attention devoted to the design, though all of these goods are the products of similar *Shanzhai* processes.

Figure 1.3 Wanzi's modified version of a name-brand dress

The businesses of some of these designers combine self-designed *Shanzhai* products and fast fashion, in that they sell both their own copies of high-fashion labels and merchandise knockoffs offered by OEMs. Figure 1.3 shows a winter dress that the designer Wanzi ordered from a *Shanzhai*-oriented factory and sold for ¥269. Wanzi told her consumers that the dress was a copy of a luxury brand and that the factory had made several modifications that she demanded, changing the sleeveless design to half-sleeved for a fall-winter wardrobe, enlarging the collar to make it more comfortable, and providing a petite option.

Women designers usually compare the original product to the *Shanzhai* version during the copying process and regularly update their customers about what is new in their copies. Sometimes, though, these designers, rather than juxtaposing the original and the copy or mentioning the *Shanzhai* process in their product description, market their own brands and highlight the creative aspect of their designs. For example, Figure 1.4 shows a shirtdress offered by the online celebrity designer Daxi in her 2015 fall collection costing ¥198. The pattern of the fabric is strikingly similar to Burberry's iconic oversize check pattern, but the design seems to be her own invention intended for a fashion-forward persona.[3] In the product description, she said that she had attempted to convey a feeling of the British aristocracy through the dress through a retro style of gentleness, suaveness, elegance, and femininity.

Figure 1.4 Daxi's self-designed dress inspired by Burberry with its classic oversize check pattern

The category of "*Shanzhai* women designers" is, then, fragmented and multi-dimensional and at times seems to harbor contradictory impulses, for example in the coexistence of the ethics of creativity and copying that is explored in Chapter 4. The unifying theme of *Shanzhai* fashion is the individual spirit of "creating one's own version of things" that endows cultural production with self-expression through the creation of both knowledge and value. *Shanzhai* women designers, especially those selling high-end products and their businesses, represent only a portion of the *Shanzhai* industry, but they serve as its trend-setters. In their practices, they straddle the boundary between creativity in conformity to a legitimate global intellectual property rights (IPR) system and the imitation that is inherent in all fashion design.

Because women designers serve as points of contact for all of the other participants in *Shanzhai* fashion as the crucial link among production, circulation, and consumption, my focus in this book remains on women who have run *Shanzhai* fashion businesses. However, I have also encountered numerous other actors, such as global fashion buyers, shop owners, online celebrities, customer service staff, garment factory workers, retailers, and *Shanzhai* fan bases/consumers in the *Shanzhai* fashion industry. These participants also contribute significant labor and creativity to the booming industry.

The women depicted here ran what were often essentially single-person operations, acting simultaneously as managers, buyers, designers, clerks, retailers, and even, in some cases, as online celebrities. They embraced an entrepreneurial DIY spirit, aspiring to the glamor, fantasy, cosmopolitanism, and status associated with transnational consumerism and fashion awareness. In order to create copies of fashions through appropriation, modification, and innovation, these women actively monitored notoriously fickle global fashion trends, consumed high-fashion products, maintained contacts with garment factories, established and networked with their consumers, sustained their popularity through social media, and remained alert to the political and economic climate, especially with regard to e-commerce policies and rules.

Unlike technological *Shanzhai* products, a *Shanzhai* fashion brand cannot become one of the legitimate brands that are pervasive in daily life because its position in the gray market lacks visibility. *Shanzhai* fashion businesses, then, inhabit a liminal space in a creative industry, a situation that reflects both the gendered and the techno-utopian dimensions of *Shanzhai* culture. While women designers have been pushing the limits of copycat production, engaging in self-branding, and aspiring to the success of such established *Shanzhai* brands as the electronics firm Xiaomi, none has been recognized as a conventional successful business in the digital economy. It is precisely because they are confined to this gray area that these women's creative activities are characterized by great precarity as well as great potential.

SHANZHAI CULTURE, GENDERED LABOR, AND THE CHINESE DREAM: PRECARIOUS CREATIVITY IN FASHIONING CHINA

Studies of *Shanzhai* culture have investigated its historical, socio-cultural, economic and political origins, manifestations, and impacts from various perspectives, recognizing it as a constantly evolving and nonlinear process (e.g., Chubb, 2014; Hennessey, 2012). The bulk of scholarship also approaches *Shanzhai* creativity as that of industrial practitioners and as a set of appropriative practices dedicated to a user-centric consumer market. This mindset appeals to businesses that serve global consumers (Tse et al., 2009); more importantly, it positions *Shanzhai* as a counterfeit, subaltern culture that repurposes nationalism in the name of innovative capacity (Ho, 2010; Keane & Zhao, 2012). The *Shanzhai* phenomenon is peculiar in a time when the government intends to appropriate grassroots creativity to enhance its market economy.

From the establishment of the People's Republic of China in 1949, the country has evolved radically from a socialist planned economy to an effective market-driven one rooted in state control and the official rhetoric of "socialism with Chinese characteristics" (Denton, 2014). Some scholars and political observers have related China's economic and social changes to the Western neoliberal mode of social development and economics since the core practices of deregulation, marketization, and privatization have served as the governmentalities in the Chinese reform era (Harvey, 2005; Wang, 2004; Zhang & Ong, 2008). However, the result of these transformations and changes in the vast terrain of China's social, economic, political, and cultural life has been the liberation and empowerment of some sectors of Chinese society at the expense of others that have been left behind and traumatized and found cold comfort in Deng's famous declaration, "let some people get rich first" (Shawki, 1997).

Amid the paradox between neoliberalism and national solidarity in modern China, *Shanzhai* seems to offer an alternative to the uncritical acceptance of self-discipline, entrepreneurism, privatization, and precariatization. Put another way, in the context of a vibrant ethos of national pride and creativity, *Shanzhai* manifests the affective practice and experience of globalizing China, which should be unconstrained by Western economic, cultural, and political power (Tam, 2014).

Despite acknowledging *Shanzhai* practice and its grassroots creativity, the majority of scholarship on *Shanzhai* culture has fallen short when it comes to providing a dynamic view that transcends the binary opposition between creativity and copying. An exception is the work of Chang (2004), who, while not mentioning *Shanzhai* specifically, in analyzing the production and consumption of high-end copies in East Asia (specifically, fake Louis Vuitton products in Taiwan), drew attention to the fact that copies and counterfeits are subject to a global fashion consciousness while at the same time subverting global capitalism by appropriating its power of dissemination. From this perspective, copying creates not only material value but also knowledge and culture.

Similarly, in analyzing the production and consumption of such cultural artifacts as television programs, films, cellphones, and various petty commodities, Yang (2016) called for an understanding of creativity in *Shanzhai* culture as a social and interactive activity corresponding to the collective imagination of cultural production in *Shanzhai*'s ability both to copy and to produce original work. Yang (2014a), for instance, analyzes a fake Apple store, extending Deleuze's (1992) notions of dispersive capitalism and borrowing from Lash and Lury's (2007) conceptualization of the global culture industry to conclude that *Shanzhai* contains a complex signifying chain, in the context of which "the use of 'Shanzhai' references a nation-specific phenomenon that lies beyond the 'copy versus fake' distinction proffered by IPR" (p. 84). Approached this way, *Shanzhai* culture consists of a multiplicity of imitative activities that echo concurrent worldwide phenomena of participatory culture and counterfeit production that resist attempts to privatize cultural expression (Jenkins, 2004; Sundaram, 2010).

In *Shanzhai* fashion, then, production involves first, the manufacturing of garments for specific markets and second, a meaning-making process that transforms individuals' aesthetic expressions into folk knowledge and feeds both an individual-based conceptualization of creativity and the global system of IPR in the context of the creative industries (Pang, 2012). The proliferation of *Shanzhai* artifacts in China not only rewrites the story of mimesis (Pang, 2008) but also reflects an autonomous mode of modern technological reproduction (Appadurai, 1986) that situates creativity at an uncertain intersection of transnational consumer culture, the state, fashion imitations, and women designers as individuals. What the literature on *Shanzhai* has yet to explicate are the specific life situations and the work praxis of those who are drawn to *Shanzhai* practice, especially women. Thus, while scholars have argued that, from the neoliberal perspective, labor in the digital economy is reconfigured through privatization and entrepreneurism (Neff, 2012; Scholz, 2013), the technomania of *Shanzhai* culture is founded on the assumption that its subjects are creative young men who serve as the source of digital labor. Lin (2011), for example, observed that, in the period since 2006, predominately male Chinese "apartment entrepreneurs," in responding to the preferred modular mode of production in the information technology (IT) industries and the dawn of Internet 2.0, aggressively seized the opportunity to produce and circulate *Shanzhai* cellphones. By contrast, women who have also actively embraced the *Shanzhai* spirit and entrepreneurship and sought to carve out their own spaces in *Shanzhai* culture have been largely invisible. As the following chapters show; their voices have been silenced and their labor has not been viewed as meaningful by either the society or the state for industry or the nation.

Digital labor is rooted in both the production and consumption associated with creative industries, for advanced digital technologies have enticed women with the language of empowerment (O'Reilly, 2005). At the same time, a large group of Chinese middle-class consumers eager for status and elegant styles has emerged (Cheng, 2010; Zhou & Qin, 2010), who have been practicing prosumption (i.e., production by consumers) of transnational symbolic goods, which is emblematic of an ever-tightening global fashion network (Zhang, 2017). Under these circumstances, women have been increasingly captivated by the fantasy of fashion made available largely through digital media and have been enticed to enter the precarious world of self-employment in order to conduct creative labor. Women designers' *Shanzhai* fashion businesses are aspirational in that they tap into the postfeminist sensibility of independence (represented by the availability of some disposable income), freedom (represented by urbanity and cosmopolitanism), flexibility, and an elusive work-life balance—beliefs shared by many other female cultural workers in the creative industries (Duffy, 2016; Gregg, 2008; Weeks, 2007).

Nonetheless, the lexicon of empowerment adopted in the women's workforce in *Shanzhai* fashion is first and foremost one of flexible accumulation (Gill, 2002; McRobbie, 1998), in that it pushes workers into the realm of what Italian *operaismo* ("workerism") theorists called the "social factory," so that the entire content of everyday life becomes raw material for capital accumulation and productivity (Ross, 2013; Virno & Hardt, 1996). As this book makes clear, these women designers' creative work is subject to traditional gender roles, with the result that its exploitation is disguised under the neoliberal ethos of DIY entrepreneurship and the *Shanzhai* ethos of creative copying. Because these women's fashion businesses exist in a legal gray zone, their practice is constantly policed and regulated, and they are, again, denied recognition as a significant workforce that contributes to the popular cultural imagination and the narrative of national branding. These women's very precarity feeds their ability to create and express themselves, and thereby further exacerbates their precarity. Their work and lives are colored by what Lauren Berlant (2011) called "cruel optimism," so that the upward mobility, freedom, prosperity, durable intimacy, and growth that they desire the most actually present obstacles to their flourishing. Their affective attachment to these things is "cruel" since it represents a possibility that can only be realized through an impossibility. This is the paradox of precarious creativity.

The notion of precarious creativity put forward in this book draws heavily on feminist understandings of women's labor and work amid shifting socio-cultural, political, economic, and ideological forces. As alluded to above, many feminist studies have pointed out that the tremendous leap in technology and informatization of work has not brought an end to exploitation, especially for the women who perform the unpaid household work of capital accumulation involved in reproducing life and labor-power (Fantone, 2007; Federici, 2008; Fortunati, 2007; Jarrett, 2014; Ross, 2008). Others have argued that the growth of the female consumer market has enhanced women's self-awareness and individuality, especially with respect to the politics of entrepreneurial activities and feminist movements, even as this market has simultaneously overwhelmed them with intense feelings of precarity owing to the privatization of work and life (Conor et al., 2015; Duffy, 2016; Gregg, 2011; McRobbie, 2011; Wissinger, 2009). Women working in creative industries and cultural occupations are, compared with men, more often called on to privatize themselves and to regulate their conduct so that it is consistent with prevailing work regimes and images in popular culture. The result has been a new precarious subjectivity associated with the creative labor process as the increasingly flexible, agile, mobile, and unspeakable conditions characteristic of the individualist and postfeminist climate have come to valorize creative work using a sophisticated terminology of entrepreneurism, freedom, and agency (Gill, 2014). An understanding of these conditions makes it possible to rethink every aspect of daily life in which women's work remains precarious and under-recognized. In the chapters that follow, I demonstrate that women designers' precarious creativity in the *Shanzhai* fashion industry occupies a liminal space that is a locus of the struggle for existence and decent working conditions and of the social discourses of hierarchy and patriarchy. It is, on the one hand, a space for the accumulation of capital and for reproduction and, on the other, a regime for the practice of individual desires, subjectivities, and relationships rooted in aspirations and hope.

I have referred to women's work in conducting *Shanzhai* fashion businesses as "digital labor," which I mean with respect to both its materiality and its immateriality. These women make such physical products as clothes, accessories, and other fashion items and, in so doing, contribute significantly to knowledge of fashion, the circulation of information, and the exchange of experiences and feelings with fans. Their efforts are emblematic of the immaterial labor that Maurizio Lazzarato (1996) described as producing the informational and cultural content of a commodity. It is one thing to observe that women have the cultural and affective desire for *Shanzhai* creative production and gain real pleasure from it and quite another to argue that the emphasis on knowledge as the main source of added value in information capitalism—and such informal forms of work as makeup, chat, lifecasting, and travel—does not result in the exploitation of their labor. Extending Lazzarato's theorization, Terranova (2000) argued astutely that late capitalism nurtures, exploits, and exhausts free labor. In the first place, the digital economy cultivates cultural and technical workers willing to contribute their labor to "a process of economic experimentation with the creation of monetary value out of knowledge/culture/affect" (p. 36), where the workers pleasurably embrace productive activities. However, the immaterial conditions of cultural and technical production are impoverished when corporations extract wealth from users' interactions on their platforms in ways that diminish the actual quality of the users' participation in the digital economy. The digital economy is over-reliant on massive amount of free labor, "only some of which is hyper-compensated by the capricious logic of venture capitalism" (p. 48). The situation characterizes the double sense of "free" in free labor: not always financially rewarded (unpaid) and willingly given (pleasurable, not imposed). For *Shanzhai* women designers, the promise of independence and prosperity in the *Shanzhai* fashion industry glorifies the work-life balance illusion and fosters a willingness to bear the combination of required domestic work and a precarious digital career. They are striving to carve out an individual dream space in which they fulfill their personal ambitions, experiment with possible life trajectories, and envision futures.

The dream space of *Shanzhai* fashion workers can be understood through both labor and feminist theories but must also be understood in relation to the ideological construct of the "Chinese Dream." This national and state construct allows for the individual pursuit of prosperity and wealth only so long as that pursuit conforms to the official narrative of the rise of a great nation (The Economist, 2013a). Used in a speech delivered by President Xi Jinping on November 29, 2012, two weeks after he took office, the catchy phrase of the Chinese Dream was immediately made popular as numerous government campaigns disseminated the notion that "everybody has a Chinese Dream." The currency of the phrase was due in part to its status as an ideological continuation of a rhetoric of national rejuvenation that admits and encourages individual ideals and imagination (Kuhn, 2013). The government in this way seeks to inspire in Chinese citizens such traditional social moral notions as filial piety, diligence, persistence, and fighting for the greater good in the pursuit of the government's vision of national revival.

The Chinese Dream discourse envisions China as a great cultural power in the world, thereby legitimizing the state's expropriation of *Shanzhai* so as to encourage innovation. For one thing, such a discourse opens up the possibility that women designers can gain recognition for their participation in Shanzhai culture. Yet, for another, the very act of copying and the counterfeit nature of *Shanzhai* fashion products place this work outside the rational system of creativity. The gray market of *Shanzhai* is precarious by nature, sustaining as it does an alternative micro-economy while being an interloper in a larger cultural industry built on a neoliberal apparatus of global capitalism that the dream deems legitimate. The Chinese Dream is an example of the state's reworking of *Shanzhai* culture to suit the vision that it seeks to project globally of Chinese creativity and innovation. While women *Shanzhai* designers may aspire to the Chinese Dream narrative, the very nature of their copying practice and the gray market for their work render them invisible and deny them recognition as contributors to China's growing cultural power. Women designers are, as it were, impossible Chinese Dreamers who experience simultaneously its pull and its elusiveness. They are dreaming individual small dreams. And the multiplicity of their dreams mount up to the very potentiality of the future. The indeterminateness and in-between-ness registered in their *Shanzhai* practice encapsulate the shifting labor terrain in China, where the potentiality and creativity rise within impossibility and precarity.

This dynamic tension extends to the relationship between the power of copying and that of policing. Women designers aspire to the promises of *Shanzhai* fashion in the context of the Chinese Dream and meanwhile are exposed to the dangers inherent in the practices that the dream encourages. Rather than competing with corporate giants in the mass production of fashion commodities, *Shanzhai* designers embrace neoliberal entrepreneurism in the precarious space between danger and promise, crisis and hope, survival and success. In this way, these women both epitomize the ambitions of other participants in *Shanzhai* culture and serve as a lens through which to view China's cultural transformation in the twenty-first century with respect to the digital economy and the global culture industry.

ETHNOGRAPHIC INQUIRY: WOMEN DESIGNERS AT A GLANCE

This book tells the stories of 18 women designers, whom I identify using pseudonyms in order to protect their privacy. I became acquainted with some of them by being a regular consumer of their products for a couple of years, and several were willing to help with this project by sitting for in-depth interviews, allowing me to observe their daily work routines, and/or connecting me with other women designers or business insiders. I conducted the interviews and observations during the summer and winter of 2016. My ethnographic inquiry also took into account the digital dimension of the women's work and life; for while I met some of them in person—women who introduced me to the wholesale markets in Guangzhou and Shanghai where they acquired the raw materials for their *Shanzhai* products—I closely monitored the activities and presentations of all of the women involved in this project on digital platforms. It was on these platforms that their businesses had been built and that an increasing amount of information was available about their lives, fashion knowledge, and businesses. Alongside the fieldwork in 2016, I engaged in many additional informal conversations with and observations of women designers using these digital platforms. Figure 1.5 indicates their geographic locations in China.

As can be seen, the informants were clustered on China's eastern coast, with only a few in inland cities such as Wuhan and Chengdu. There are several key characteristics of the locations in which the women were residing. First of all, most lived in highly developed metropolises with dynamic consumer cultures and an expanding business landscape for e-commerce. Beijing and Shanghai are China's political, cultural, and commercial centers, and Hangzhou is home to the world's most valuable e-commerce company, Alibaba, which includes China's largest online shopping platform, Taobao Marketplace (henceforth, Taobao)—and nearly every *Shanzhai* woman designer sets up shop on Taobao. The social atmosphere of rapid transnational cultural exchange and pervasive digital media nurture the practice of micro-entrepreneurism that is a visible feature of daily life in these cities.

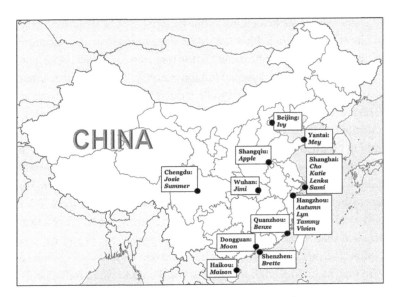

Figure 1.5   Geographic locations of informants for this book

Second, most of the informants were working in places that serve as hubs for domestic immigration and trade and that are close to the materials used to make fashion products. The city of Yantai, for example, has supported a strong export-oriented industry since the reform era began in the late 1970s, and many transnational corporations, especially Japanese apparel companies, have collaborated with the local government to set up factories. An informant whom I call here Mey introduced me to the fact that there were once thousands of garment factories contributing to the economy of Yantai owing to the trade with Japan, but that this trade had diminished since the restructuring of China's economy so that domestic demand became the driving force; an additional factor in this transformation has been the frequent diplomatic tension between China and Japan. Concentrating now on domestic markets, these garment factories have maintained Japanese standards of production and quality control and thereby earned a reputation for workmanship and sophisticated manufacturing. Chengdu and Wuhan are important inland ports along the Yangtze River, and Dongguan and Shenzhen lie in the Pearl River Delta, which is famous for its light industry and a key region in the emerging economy. Quanzhou, a coastal city surrounded by the traditionally pro-business culture of Zhejiang Province, nurtures a vital business climate and offers proximity to the resources for garment production.

There were some exceptions to this pattern—that is, designers living in places that feature neither highly developed infrastructure, a culture of digital economy, nor proximity to the resources, materials, labor, and capital necessary for a *Shanzhai* fashion business. The designer referred to in this book as Apple used to be located in the city of Shangqiu in Henan Province in the center of the country, where her parents owned a textile factory with the capacity to supply her with the materials for fashion production. In early 2016, she moved to Zhengzhou, the capital of the province, opening a beauty salon while maintaining her *Shanzhai* fashion business at a low level because "my consumers do not want me to leave [the field completely], and I do not want to disappoint them. But I have reduced the time and labor invested in making outfits." A practical problem that Apple faced is the limited amount of social and cultural capital that one can amass in such a relatively remote area compared with the possibilities on the coast. This situation is in part a consequence of national strategic planning that has fostered economic and cultural disparities in the development of various regions. Chapter 2 details the impact of geographic location on women designers' business strategies and survival in the *Shanzhai* fashion industry.

Some of these women started out either as salespersons, fashion buyers, or boutique owners and later joined the many entrepreneurs engaged in copying-to-design and selling their products through digital platforms. The fashion work of others began with a *Shanzhai* business. All but one of the informants began their fashion careers and/or *Shanzhai* businesses after 2006, the exception being the designer known here as Cho, who opened (and closed) her first fashion boutique in 1997.[4] It came up in conversation that most of these women were college-educated and in their 20s to mid-30s at the time I interviewed them, though I did not ask specifically about education and age. My only real interests in these respects concerned whether the informants had taken courses relevant to fashion design, and, as it happened, none indicated having had any professional training. The informant referred to here as Katie, for example, began sharing her fashion ideas through blogging while studying abroad in 2006; family wealth made it possible for her to travel abroad frequently and to develop her photography hobby. Her blog received considerable attention, with fans expressing the desire to model her style. She accordingly started to make reproductions of her own clothes, most of which were designer outfits and luxuries, for sale.

With regard to their generally young age, the women discussed in this book were of the generation that grew up reaping the fruits of China's reform era, though in various ways. One of the most common capabilities that they acquired involved, unsurprisingly, digital skills relating to e-commerce. The exception who proved the rule was Cho, the oldest among the informants, who relied on young female salespersons to manage the bulk of her e-business.

Most of the informants were married and had children, and their families, particularly their husbands, were supportive of their fashion businesses, in some cases even giving up their jobs to assist in the operation of the online shops. I further observed that even those who were single were often able to rely on boyfriends for help with the management of the shops or with photography. In either case, the participation of these men served as labor beneath labor in the accumulation of capital by their wives and girlfriends. The following chapters, and in particular Chapter 3, chart the attraction for these women of the pursuit of a desired work-life balance made possible by the potential of new technologies and digital commerce. Their experiments in this pursuit foreground the persistence of the gendered nature of digital work.

While the sample of informants for this project obviously is not representative of all of the women working in the *Shanzhai* fashion industry, their experiences are, I suggest, typical of those of the many women designers with whom they share similar backgrounds, life histories, class status, and social conditions. As is usual with ethnographic research, this project involved not only personal acquaintances but diverse social actors with whom I established a connection in the course of my fieldwork. I am able to base my conclusions on my encounters with, in addition to the designers whom I formally interviewed, receptionists working in some of the online shops, fashion buyers, researchers associated with digital platforms, consumers, and others who helped to fill in the picture of *Shanzhai* culture for me.

When face-to-face conversation was not possible, I communicated with my informants using such social media as Weibo and WeChat, the Chinese equivalents of Twitter and WhatsApp, respectively. These media platforms also serve as major portals for women designers for self-promotion and building consumer relations, which are vital aspects of the survival and success of micro-enterprises online.

BUSINESS OVER THE CLOUD:
TAOBAO, WEIBO, AND WECHAT AS *SHANZHAI* FRONTIERS

I investigated the three major Chinese media platforms mentioned above, namely, the online marketplace Taobao, the microblogging site Weibo, and the instant messaging service WeChat, to trace the production and consumption of *Shanzhai* fashion. These are the main channels through which *Shanzhai* women designers conduct business, follow fashion trends, increase their visibility, maintain their popularity, and interact with other social actors. These three media platforms have similarities and distinct aspects in the context of *Shanzhai* culture.

As already noted, the online shops operated by *Shanzhai* women designers are almost all affiliated with Taobao, which is China's largest online shopping site. Most of the product images reproduced in this book are snapshots from online shops on Taobao. An online shop can be defined as an individual website with its own homepage and sub-pages for various categories of offerings. The homepages usually display a col-

Figure 1.6 The "View All" page of a woman designer's online shop on the Taobao app for tablets

lection of new arrivals and sometimes include a detailed profile of the designer along with store policies (Figure 1.6). Individual items appear on sub-pages that provide basic information about the products and prices, in most cases accompanied by texts and images. These mediated texts and images provide a wealth of details about the production process and significant information about *Shanzhai* production and women designers' work.

Weibo is another key media platform on which these designers conduct business. Most have both a private and a public account on which they post news and feedback, tell personal fashion stories, interact with followers, and generally cultivate their fan base clientele (Figure 1.7). Consumers participate in the *Shanzhai* process through Weibo by recommending their favorite styles, commenting and sharing, and providing feedback on designs. The most common context in which designers and consumers interact is the aforementioned buyer's show, in

Figure 1.7   The designer Daxi's private Weibo account

which a consumer tweets photos of a product, often wearing it herself, and tags the designer on her public or private account or both. Other designers usually re-tweet such posts with compliments. These intensive back-and-forth interactions can be in the forms of texts, emoji, photos, and/or videos. In addition, as noted above, designers frequently receive assistance in running their online shops from their boyfriends or husbands as well as friends and family members, whose private accounts also link to the designers' private and public accounts. Through their participation in the designers' Weibo activities, the various customers and supporters generate a complex web of information and communication. My analysis of Weibo in this book focuses on its interactive nature as I map out these women's social networks.

WeChat is the other critical media platform for women designers and their fashion work.[5] Though Taobao and Weibo have both launched mobile apps, WeChat remains the dominant form of communication between the designers and their customers. Like Weibo, WeChat allows users to maintain separate private and public accounts (Figure 1.8).

Figure 1.8   A woman designer's private account and the Moment feature (left), and public account (right)

Each of my informants had one or both kinds; often, the private one was used for personal communication with consumers and the public one for updates, promotions, sales, and sharing. Through their private accounts, the designers updated their production using a built-in service called Moment, which, like Instagram, allows a limited amount of text and images per post. For the public accounts, the limitation on texts and visuals was much more relaxed, and many designers would write long posts featuring personal anecdotes about the process of making fashion copies or sharing recent beauty experiences and ideas. These posts usually feature a personal touch, stylistic language, and artistic images that combine information about products with promotion.

CHAPTER OUTLINES

I present this story of women designers' work and lives in the *Shanzhai* fashion industry over six chapters, beginning with this introductory chapter. In Chapter 2, I historicize how *Shanzhai* fashion represents an extension of the practice of garment production and imitative fashion in which Chinese designers have engaged ever since the country began to open up to the world at the end of the 1970s. During the reform period, the interests of the state, corporations, and the growing number of consumers coincided, and the result has been the proliferation of domestic e-commerce companies and media platforms. The improving material conditions and glaring disparity within regions and classes as a result of the reform in turn nurtured an internet generation of hard-core media users who at times express anti-authoritarian sentiments in digital space but are also called on to fulfill patriotic consumption ideals. Women designers' creative fashion work takes place at such a conjuncture, through which precarious creativity can be seen as a response constructed and practiced by, rather than given to or originating from, the various digital media users, cultural participants, corporations, and state interests in contemporary China.

Chapter 3 provides a detailed account of the *Shanzhai* fashion production chain, laying out the four essential moments in the process of fashion imitation. I follow a thing, such as clothes and attire, a product, or an image of a desired outfit from the first moment it enters the process of *Shanzhai* through customers' recommendations all the way through its in-house production, consumption, and the feedback offered on it.

I locate the material value of the thing in its social relations (i.e., the immateriality), and in the circulation of these relations identify the women designers as the pivot point in the *Shanzhai* production chain. The digital labor of women designers makes possible the transformation of a thing into a *Shanzhai* fashion product, the changing value systems attached to the product, the digital technologies that marshal various forms of participation, and other complex relations.

Next, in Chapter 4, I elaborate how *Shanzhai* is enlivened through the multiplicity of copies. The *Shanzhai* of *Shanzhai*—that is, the copy of a fashion imitation—opens up an alternative space for women to envision and experiment with various possible futures. I begin with scrutinizing *Shanzhai* offerings of "celebrity styles" related to an emerging class divide between fashionistas as fashion icons and consumers as fervent fans. The production of iconic fashion stars and then appropriation of these icons not only coincide with the multiple concurrent processes of *Shanzhai* fashion production and consumption but also illustrate vividly a Deleuzian articulation of simulacrum as the potentiality of and positivity inherent in the copy of the copy. The *Shanzhai* of *Shanzhai* phenomenon has shown the power to negate any presumption of originality and authenticity and to rejuvenate copying and creativity through internal differences. In this sense, copying becomes the very condition of creativity in *Shanzhai*.

Chapter 5 situates the previous discussion of women's digital labor and the potential space of becoming within the broader social discourse and ideological trappings of the Chinese Dream. In particular, I discuss the encounter between women designers' various *Shanzhai* dreams and the grand Chinese Dream narrative, in which the latter seeks to appropriate the former as a part of an innovative force for nation-building while at the same time excluding them owing to their uncertain legitimacy. Inevitably the Chinese Dream fails to capture fully the sprawling dreaming space of *Shanzhai* fashion. Women designers' precarious creativity in their work and lives showcases a space that is structured by visions of techno-utopia and the profit-driven forces of the patriarchy, on the one hand and, on the other, offers opportunities to fulfill imaginations, desires, and subjectivities, to cultivate intimacy and relationships, and to nurture aspirations and hopes.

The concluding chapter revisits the key arguments as I discuss the significance of my investigation of women's digital labor in an era of precarity. I reiterate my point that women's precarious creativity is produced in and practiced through a socio-cultural, political, and economic conjuncture that creates possibilities for a politics that is intertwined with increasingly subtle and nuanced manifestations of national ideologies and transnational capitalism. The connections among gender, precarity, and copying in China shed light on the unexpected ways in which resistance and liberation develop in digital societies.

2

Shanzhai Fashion and Precarious Creativity in China

In China, fashion designs, particularly ready-made garments that emphasize practicality over the aesthetics, are not covered by copyright law (Ruan, 2016). This means that while fashion trademarks, such as Louis Vuitton (LV) or Prada, are aggressively policed and protected by the various fashion powerhouses globally, the underlying clothing designs can be copied legally.

An illustrative example of the culture of fashion imitation is "Quality-Made in China" (中国质造), a project initiated by Alibaba to promote China-made products. In April 2015, the online retailer teamed up with the government of Fujian Province to release its first "Quality-Made in China" collection of shoes, which were produced in factories in Putian, a prefecture-level city in the eastern part of the province known for producing *Shanzhai* shoes. Alibaba touted the project as "a new standard of manufacturing" that prepared Chinese manufacturers to enhance the quality of their products and to establish their own brands (Dong, 2015). The new standard, however, had a strong *Shanzhai* undertone. The comparison of Putian shoes with name-brand shoes shows that they were strikingly similar to those made by Nike, apart from the logo (Figure 2.1).

The project seems to have represented experimentation with alternative approaches to recognizing *Shanzhai* fashion production and building confidence in Chinese manufacturing. Alibaba's founder Jack Ma celebrated *Shanzhai* production during a conference for investors by asserting that "the fake products today—they make better quality, better prices than the real product, the real names" (Dongge Forum, 2016; see also Clover, 2016). Irrespective of the controversy that Ma's speech created globally (Ramli & Chen, 2016), Chinese consumers' reactions to a project that appropriated *Shanzhai* practice for fashion production was ambivalent. In the Quora-like online forum Zhihu.com, netizens—a term widely used in China describing people who are actively involved

Figure 2.1 A comparison of Siweiqi running shoes from Putian (left) and Nike's Tanjun shoes (right)

in online communities in general—heatedly discussed the quality of the shoes, whether promoting them represented the triumph of fake production (i.e., recognition that it would be preferable and easier to incorporate *Shanzhai* practices into manufacturing standards than to eliminate them), and the differing mentalities of consumers who buy name-brand and Putian shoes (Zhihu, 2015).

While such imitation in fashion production is common and practically legal owing to China's weak copyright regime, the imitation of popular fashion products is a worldwide and ancient phenomenon. Indeed, the situation in the United States (hereafter US) is similar: fashion design is not protected by law, but trademarks are rigorously policed. Raustiala and Sprigman (2012), in their analysis of the knockoff economy, discussed a New York apparel firm called Faviana that offered direct copies of dresses worn by actors on television, in films, and at award shows such as the Oscars. Likewise, the successful "fast fashion" firm Forever 21 has been able to imitate striking and salable designs quickly and at amazingly low prices, thereby keeping consumers coming back on a regular basis. Raustiala and Sprigman came to the provocative conclusion that "fashion thrives due to copying"—which is the underlying logic of the knockoff economy.

The semi-legal practice of fashion imitation has been utilized to increase China's garment production and to lend a cosmopolitan aura to consumption ever since China's reform era. In fact, even before the term *Shanzhai* became common, scholars such as Chew (2010) studied fashion imitation in the context of what was referred to as "pass-off" menswear, a counterfeit trade based on approximating a name-brand product in order to confuse the consumer, and concluded that such copying produces commodities that have distinct uses and appeal for consumers. In current parlance, pass-off menswear would be part of the *Shanzhai* fashion industry, the only difference being that consumers of the latter are well aware that the products are not the "originals" and are attracted by the imitation.

Interestingly, some women's fashion brands in China also use pass-off tactics to construct a global facade that serves as a selling point. An often-discussed case is the leading women's apparel brand ochirly. A popular brand of the Trendy International Group, ochirly was founded in 1999; its official website states that the brand name was derived from Chinese *ou shi li*, "European fashion charm" (ochirly, n.d.). In early 2012, the private-equity fund L Capital, backed by French luxury giant LVMH (Louis Vuitton-Moët Hennessy), spent $200 million to acquire a roughly 10 percent stake in Trendy (Burkitt, 2012). LVMH's investment targeted China's growing consumer base and represented recognition of ochirly's ability to generate profits.

However, discussions of beauty products on online forums have often included criticism of ochirly's guise of global originality. For example, numerous comments under the ochirly page in the Baidu-pedia (Chinese equivalent to Wikipedia) faulted the description of ochirly as a licensed brand from Italy (Baidu-pedia, n.d.). Netizens traced the origins of the head of Trendy to the city of Wenzhou in Zhejiang Province in mainland China, and discovered that he had registered the company in Hong Kong in order to make use of the rhetoric of transnationality in the brand's marketing campaigns (Douban, 2013). In addition, ochirly has frequently been accused of imitating luxury fashion designs. One of my informants, known here as Maison, told me that she had once seen for sale on ochirly a T-shirt aping the "ugly doll" design of Marc by Marc Jacobs. At the same time, the booming domestic fast fashion brand La Chapella imitated the ugly doll design even more blatantly (Figure 2.2).

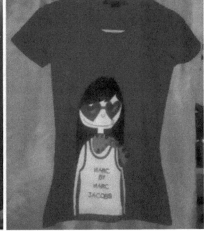

Figure 2.2   A comparison of T-shirts with the ugly doll design made by La Chapella (left) and Marc by Marc Jacobs (right)

Many women designers echo Maison in justifying their *Shanzhai* practice in part by embracing the view of copying as the norm rather than the exception in business. While they grapple with issues of freedom and autonomy in their creative appropriation, modification, and crafting of fashion designs, these designers are nonetheless constrained by the same act of copying that affords them such flexible employment and lifestyles. Working in a flourishing economy amid a confluence of ideological crises, various media practices, and patriarchal and patriotic morality, women designers struggle both with their lived reality and with the dream that they yearn to fulfill. As the meaning and usage of *Shanzhai* has come to transcend copying and piracy, so also has the precarious creativity that these women designers embody become emblematic of the contemporary sense and sensibility of gender, class, labor, and nation.

This chapter presents a conjunctural analysis of the precarious creativity that characterizes *Shanzhai* fashion. Crucially connected with Antonio Gramsci's notion of hegemony and common sense, a conjuncture can be defined as the coming-into-being in a particular articulation of all of the complex social forces operating in a society at a given moment in an effort to hold together a society's specific hegemonic alliance of dominant interests (Davison, 2011). Stuart Hall (1988) expanded Gramsci's theorization with a creative analysis of Thatcherism amid the crisis in Britain during the 1970s, arguing that crises drive history from one conjuncture to the next as the specific forms of hegemonic rules are remade, either by the dominant group or others seeking to create new (or fix old) articulations and political possibilities. Therefore, conjunctural analysis, which Lawrence Grossberg (2010) argued is the real object of cultural studies, depicts the changes and contradictions in and the multiplicity of a fragile and temporary social formation as a field of contestation and (de-)articulation. Grossberg further explained that the unity of the conjuncture is its problematic(s), "which is usually lived (but not necessarily experienced *per se*) as a social crisis of sorts" (p. 41).

Compelling scholarly work has been done depicting the fractured and conflicting practices and processes of Chinese society since the beginning of the reform era, again in the late 1970s. For Wang Hui (2004), the 1989 students' movement precipitated a crisis to the conjuncture that turned China from its socialist path toward a neoliberal one, a crisis that also brought about structural change in the thinking of intellectuals working with the state to enact strategic visions based on common-sense ideas. According to Fan Yang (2016), China's joining the World Trade Organization (WTO) in 2001 also precipitated a crisis to the conjuncture, pushing the country to confront a cultural dilemma in globalization today, in part by rejecting global capitalist forces while building its own national brands and appropriating the exact hegemonic global power in order to disseminate its branding ideologies and activities.

This book advances the notion that *Shanzhai* represents a potential space for change in the context of the crisis in the legitimacy of governance that has led to drastic social inequality in China since the reform era began. I approach *Shanzhai* as practice at the core of contemporary conjuncture that is constitutive of multiple, contesting, and intense forces of politics, culture, economy, and ideology. *Shanzhai* fashion, from this perspective, is a ruptured and inconsistent but also temporarily stable cultural form. Continuing the garment practice of the reform era, *Shanzhai* fashion has boomed due to the government intention to build up technological infrastructure for digital consumption, and the energy and creativity in production and consumption of the rising middle class and young internet users to drive the development of e-commerce industry.

Shanzhai makes a virtue of an anti-authoritarian stance and viral dissemination that reflect the population's cultural, political, and economic disparities. Nevertheless, such a counter-hegemonic seed does not grow to its full potential. Within the potentiality of *Shanzhai*, though, women working in less tech-savvy, less policy-confined, and less rebellious areas of fashion production-consumption find it impossible to gain recognition from the society and the state as a force of change, one capable of contributing to a more liberal form of cultural expression or a more participatory approach to national branding. These women are precarious with increasing creativity emerging from and dedicated to their *Shanzhai* fashion business. In this chapter, I identify precarious creativity as a problematic space for the conjunctural analysis through a consideration of five overlapping, co-embedded, and co-constructed aspects of Chinese society that characterize the rupture and inconsistency, but also the temporary stability, of *Shanzhai* fashion (Figure 2.3):

1. garment production and imitative fashion practice in China
2. the government's technocratic developmental strategies
3. the internet and anti-authoritative cultural practices
4. the success of Chinese e-commerce companies and media platforms in the country's semi-open market economy
5. the propaganda relating to patriotic middle-class consumption ideals.

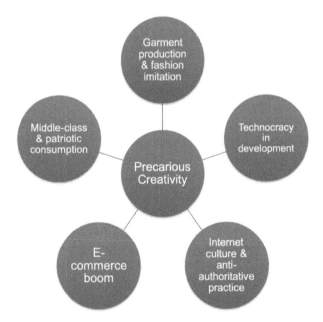

Figure 2.3   The conjuncture of precarious creativity in *Shanzhai* fashion

GARMENT PRODUCTION AND FASHION IMITATION:
"MADE IN CHINA" SINCE THE REFORM ERA

As discussed in the first chapter, the practice of copying in the context of garment production and consumption should be viewed as a stage in the development of the modern fashion industry in China. This history is one of continuities and discontinuities in social values, cultural adaptations, the domestication of fashion production, and shifting market ideologies and labor practices. It is reasonable to argue that the development of the modern Chinese fashion industry took place in conjunction with changes in socio-cultural values. The shifting socio-cultural ethos is compatible with the market economy, and the sweatshop labor exploitation that marked the "Made in China" label and significantly contributed to the export-oriented economy that underwent explosive growth.

The market for fashionable clothing returned to China in the late 1970s with the end of the Cultural Revolution and the beginning of the open-door policy. China has been deeply involved in globalization ever since as a means to boost its domestic economy and engage in cultural exchange. As Finnane (2008) pointed out, "Fashion was one of the many areas in which the opening of a dialogue between China and the rest of the world occurred in the late 1970s" (p. 257). As the Chinese have begun to express themselves through fashion, the proliferation of images of popular culture in fashion parades, magazines, films, and everyday life in China has made consumers aware of trendy outfits, especially young inhabitants of large cities. Fashion-forward urban dwellers then started looking to imported articles for trends in fashion. In like manner, an earlier generation of clothes-dealers in shopping stalls who sold imported seconds (a blend of second-hand and shopsoiled clothes) made a fortune in the 1990s (Sang, 2006).

The government has offered support to the fashion industry. Beginning in 1981, courses, degree programs, and university departments devoted to textile manufacturing and clothing design have been established in various universities (Zhang, 2002). At the same time, hundreds of thousands of clothing factories opened. At the outset, in 1979, French designer Pierre Cardin brought a team of fashion models to put on the first fashion parade in Beijing, thereby opening the door to global fashion trends and professional modeling in China (Yuan, 2006). The thaw in the country's diplomatic relationships with Japan in the 1980s and with South Korea (hereafter simply Korea) in the 1990s brought an influx of

East Asian popular culture to China that served as a kind of cultural code of rebellion for younger generations involving clothing and hairstyles. For example, bell bottoms and red skirts were seen as unconventional and unique in the 1980s, with movies such as *Spectre* (Chen, 1980) and *The Fashionable Red Dress* (Qi, 1984) presenting the leading women actors wearing these fashions as chic symbols of individuality (Finnane, 2008). Such clothes revealed a new social perception of femininity very different from the gender-neutral apparel of Mao's era. The proliferation of fashion magazines beginning in the late 1990s gave rise to numerous practical style guides and collections of tips regarding popular and street fashion. With the current pervasiveness of the internet and social media, fashion information and knowledge have, as noted, been disseminated widely. The concrete material prosperity that resulted from the now 40 years of reform has given at least some Chinese people the buying power to style themselves in an individual and versatile way.

On the other hand, China's fickle fashion trends and its volatile fashion industry have been built largely on the exploitation of labor, particularly that of young migrant women working on assembly lines and in sweatshops (Pun, 2005). The reform required privatization and entry into the open market, for which China relied heavily on direct foreign investment, so that overseas companies were able to set up factories and take advantage of the country's vast resources, especially inexpensive labor, during the 1990s. The concern about economic growth during the reform era was a major force driving the sea change in China's rag trade. China took the lead among the world's textile and clothing exporting countries in the early 2000s, being responsible for 37.4 percent and 39.3 percent, respectively, of that trade globally in 2015 (WTO, 2016). The country's extremely low-cost and seemingly endless labor sources, in particular, proved irresistible to transnational companies. This labor supply, in combination with abundant raw materials for garment production, such as cotton and silk, and rapidly shrinking tariffs and shipping rates made the manufacture of fast fashion items in China both feasible and lucrative. Increasingly, fast fashion retailers began tapping into the global supply chain in order to churn out cheap but stylish articles at a very rapid rate, as has been done by, for example, the Spanish firm Zara, UK-based Topshop, and Swedish H&M (Raustiala & Sprigman, 2012). Twenty years after the open-door policy, the labor-intensive garment industry has continued to grow in China, making massive inroads into retail markets throughout the Western world with labels reading "Made in China."

The discourse of "Made in China" is not only "a marker of *inter*-national job transfers and trade imbalance," as Yang (2016) put it, but also, much more deeply, illustrates "the *trans*-national flow from labor to capital, from surplus value to profit earnings" (p. 37, emphasis in the original). Needless to say, "Made in China" has long been a stereotypical image of manufacturers stagnating at the lower end of the global fashion value chain. The steady supply of cheap labor from world factories churning out clothes labeled "Made in China" has spawned racialized, gendered, and regionally pejorative sentiments in Western countries.

China's indisputable position as the world's hub for the production of clothing aside, the fact is that selling clothes does not necessarily mean designing fashions. In the early stages of its entry into the open market, more often than not, China sought to participate in the world mainly by learning from the West. Generally speaking, the domestic design and production of clothes have long been concentrated on imitating international (mainly US and European) styles and looks for the mass market, such as suits, jeans, swimsuits, mini-skirts, trench coats, and other colorful items of clothing.

In the early twenty-first century, China's domestic fashion industry struggled to come up with creative designs and to cultivate fashion talents so as to compete on the same level with internationally known brands. Most of the time, garment factories adopted the OEM model, with the profit margin coming from subcontracting and exportation. Xintang, a small town in Zengcheng District, Guangzhou, for example, emerged as the world's "blue jeans capital" during the 1980s. Shops, stalls, street vendors, and factories from one end of the town to the other produced export goods, primarily denim garments (Vogel, 1981). The surplus was sold to vendors and buyers elsewhere in China, jeans being an iconic status symbol from Hong Kong and the West (OIOatm, 2015). To this day, Xintang continues to be known for denim production, but most of the factories now recycle designs and styles from off-the-rack foreign brands and produce everyday clothing for the domestic market. These factories employ many patternmakers but not many fashion designers, and few of the region's brands are widely known, partly because of the rampant knockoffs.

In doing the research for this book, I planned to visit the blue jeans capital in the summer of 2016; an informant living in the neighborhood of many of the owners of the town's garment factories tried to put me in contact with some of them. These factories were now producing clothing primarily for online retailers, either copying trendy designs or receiving orders from vendors seeking to imitate various articles. In the end, I was unable to make contact with the factory owners, who kept claiming to be too busy, though my informant suggested that they had refused to be interviewed in part because they considered their own products to be rip-offs and wanted to avoid any unwanted attention.

The situation in Xintang is illustrative of the government's shifting ideology and developmental strategies since the reform era began with regard to the garment industry and the creative industries in general. Indeed, such terms as "creative industries" and "intellectual property" are relatively new to the Chinese lexicon—a topic that I discuss extensively in relation to *Shanzhai* in Chapter 4. The government is increasingly realizing that innovation and creativity in the cultural sphere can enhance a nation's global influence as a form of soft power to be used alongside economic, political, and military hard power. As Michael Keane (2013) pointed out, however, the development of China's creative industries has gone through a unique series of stages or a "cultural innovation timeline" proceeding from standardized production, such as subcontracting in fashion, animation, software, and electronics, to imitation in the production of local versions, and then to collaboration and trade that eventually give rise to creative clusters and communities. The OEM model adopted by garment factories and electronic assembling plants epitomizes the stage of standardized production symbolized in the ubiquitous "Made in China" labels, while *Shanzhai* fashion epitomizes the imitation stage, which is characterized by low levels of risk-taking. As will become increasingly clear, *Shanzhai* as an industrial practice engenders different visions in IT contexts and in fashion contexts. At last, as many of China's arts, media, design, and cultural business have moved up the value chain, part of its fashion industry has also entered the collaboration period, promoted by the government through cooperative conferences, expositions, and the country's International Fashion Week. Nevertheless, the mass market remains preoccupied with domestic fast fashion brands such as ochirly and La Chapella and the myriad of *Shanzhai* garments sold online (Figure 2.4).

The industrial development of fashion is only a small part of China's overall reform program, but it has been crucial for the rapid expansion of online shopping. Fashion in China is intertwined with the technocratic ideologies, the boom in e-commerce, internet popular culture, media censorship, and digital consumerism that have helped to shape and drive the *Shanzhai* fashion industry.

Figure 2.4   A comparison of trench coats made by Burberry (left) and the Chinese domestic brand Five Plus (right)

TECHNOCRACY: BUILDING THE DIGITAL INFRASTRUCTURE

Though *Shanzhai* fashion inherited its imitative practice from the modern global factory and garment industry, its path to digital space and burgeoning markets is owed in large part to the government's technocratic ideologies and the principles that have guided the country's development and modernization. During the long transition period (from 1978 onwards) involving successive generations of leaders, the technocratic narratives of nation-building and nation-branding have not been dismissed or de-emphasized, but they have been finessed through various campaigns and assigned to various policy priorities.

The discourse about technology advancing the nation has always been part of the development of modern China. Historical accounts associated the declining power of the nation with a strong sense of humiliation and loss of the pride associated with the Middle Kingdom at the hands of the technologically advanced nations in the period since the Opium War, a sense that has served as the starting point for Chinese leaders' efforts to restore the country's technical supremacy and its status as a great world power (Qiu, 2004). While the technocratic attempts to build the nation, such as the Great Leap Forward, have not always succeeded, the implementation of modernization policies in the reform era nonetheless reflected the powerful appeal of techno-nationalism, and science and technology policies have played an important role in China's national politics with regard to bolstering the power of the state (Ji, 2015).

In 1978, at the end of China's disastrous ten-year Cultural Revolution, the Central Communist Party (CCP) made Deng Xiaoping the nation's leader, and it was he who soon declared and embarked upon a comprehensive reform program (The Communist Party of China, 1978). This set of policies and campaigns dismantled the state-controlled planned economy, invited foreign investors to promote market-led growth in the country, and, somewhat later, progressively shifted economic policy so as to expand domestic demands and promote consumerism (Gerth, 2010). One of the defining features of Deng's tenure as the head of the party and the nation was his realization of the so-called "Four Modernizations" set forth by then Premier Zhou Enlai in 1964. The basic idea was to strengthen China in the areas of agriculture, industry, national defense, and science and technology so that it would become a great world economic power by the early twenty-first century (P. Li, 2015). Deng's prescient declaration that "science and technology is the primary productive force" served as a guiding principle for a broad set of reforms.

It was, then, in order to optimize its economic structure and pave the road for reform that China throughout the 1980s gradually opened up to the world. The country joined the International Monetary Fund (IMF) and World Bank in 1980, established economic zones, and opened coastal cities to overseas investment throughout the 1980s and 1990s (Tang & Ma, 2008).[6] These new moves and policies facilitated economic and cultural exchange between China and the rest of the world and also propelled Chinese market reform (Wang, 1994). In 1992, after Deng Xiaoping's famous Southern Excursion (during which he made the remarks on science and technology quoted above), China further reaffirmed and adjusted its reform policies regarding the market-led economy (Dong & Peng, 1998).

At the same time, Deng encouraged entrepreneurship, as a result of which numerous intellectuals and professionals opted to "jump into the sea" (*xiahai*), that is, to leave state-owned institutions and join the private sector (Wu & Yu, 2003). For example, former government researcher Chen Dongsheng became an entrepreneur in 1993 and went on to serve as the chairman of Taikang Life Insurance Company. Chen referred to the entrepreneurs who entered the private sector at Deng's prompting in 1992 as the "92 Faction" (Wang & Li, 2014). Some of the women whom I interviewed—including Cho, whose story is told later in this chapter—were among these pioneering entrepreneurs of the 1990s. Alibaba's founder Jack Ma was also among the 92 Faction, having been amazed by the new technologies and the ability of the internet to connect the world during a trip to the US in 1995.

The private sector gold rush at this time was accompanied by a rustbelt in the state sector as an estimated 30 to 40 million jobs were cut and massive layoffs redefined the "iron rice bowls" policy as a financial disaster, particularly in the wake of the Asian Financial Crisis of the late 1990s.[7] The huge number of laid-off workers and rural migrants were absorbed into new urban jobs, most of which involved labor exploitation similar to that in garment sweatshops by information and technology corporations and manufacturers such as Foxconn.[8] Simultaneously, the state has been alleviating unemployment by maintaining consumer demand through the promotion of patriotic consumption ideals, a point to which I return below. Subsequent Chinese leaders such as Hu Jintao consolidated the official policy narrative—the "scientific development concept" and "harmonious society"—during their terms in office. When President Xi took office in 2012 and elaborated his "Chinese Dream" narrative, he was building on the heritage of previous leadership, particularly in prioritizing the Innovative-driven Development Strategy (IDS) as a means to transform and optimize the nation's economic structure.

China has become a world leader in such sectors as advanced military defense, supercomputers, and high-yield rice. The further opening-up to the private sector and the boost given to entrepreneurship has been juxtaposed with China's progressively state-led and market-driven "digital revolution" in the post-Mao era, pursuing the rapid development of information and communication technologies (ICTs) in an attempt to catch up with the West (Zhao, 2007). Although the first Chinese computer was produced in 1958, it was not until the 1980s that China began importing cutting-edge technologies from advanced capitalist countries and developing its own ICTs as a means to promote economic growth (Xu, 1992). The country's full-function connection to the internet began in 1994, when Professor Qian Hualin at the Academy of Sciences in Beijing took charge of establishing the Chinese domain name system. Soon afterward, in 1995, ChinaNet was established to provide the nation's first public internet service (Wilson, 1995), though at the time few in China had even the slightest knowledge of computers, let alone the internet.

Though it has created fertile ground for China's information and technology sector, the government has always been keenly focused on controlling information and media, and has been prompted to act, especially after the dramatic climax of the 1989 Tian'anmen Square protests. Also known as the June Fourth Incident, the set of actions by a massive student-led pro-democracy movement ended with the first declaration of martial law since the founding of the People's Republic of China. The technocratic rationality of economic development was ostensibly at odds with the state's strict control over content and access and its imposition of censorship on media outlets in order to repress political dissent (Zhao, 2007). During the mid-1990s, only state-owned or state-controlled media were accessible in China and their content was tightly restricted. The government issued new laws, regulations, and policies designed both to legitimize use of the internet and to tighten censorship of information.[9] Facing the dilemma of needing to develop its high-tech sector to further drive economic growth while at the same time maintaining control over media and information, leaders sought to accommodate this new technology without allowing it to spawn dissent and so-called counter-revolutionary ideals (Zhang, 2004). At this conjuncture, consumerism provided leeway as a means to avoid backlash because of high unemployment while maintaining staggering economic growth. As Zhao (2007) argued, "China's 'digital revolution' is inspired by a deep-rooted technocratic and techno-nationalist rationality and driven primarily by an overlapping military and industrial imperative and the convergent interests of the domestic bureaucratic and international corporate capital, along with the consuming priorities of China's urban middle class" (p. 101).

While the 1990s witnessed the dot-com boom in the US, as exemplified by the success of eBay and Amazon in establishing models for online retailing and e-commerce, in China, the internet and related industries caught up with the global trend in ICT that had served to boost consumption. This was a double-edged sword for the Chinese government. When Jiang Zemin took Deng's place, he committed publicly to transform China into an information society (Jiang, 2010). The government actively invested in IT infrastructure and established the Ministry of the Information Industry in 1998 (Cartlege & Lovelock, 1999). The population as a whole benefited from economic reform, in the sense that there was an improving material situation with more disposable personal income (DPI). Personal computers and digital gadgets became available and grew increasingly affordable. Internet cafes sprouted up seemingly everywhere to bring the public into contact with the modern technology. The information portals Sina and Sohu, which both debuted in 1999, contributed further to the increase in online traffic in China.

On the flip side of the booming ICT and internet business, the threat to information control and the evasion of state power were increasingly apparent to the government. Jittery about the potential that a great many people saw in the internet for offering new paths to democracy, the Chinese party-state, as noted, has sought to manage this potential and to harness it in the service of economic growth. The government has implemented multi-layered administrative, legal, technical, social, cultural, and economic control measures, exploiting passivity and inertia on the part of the populace regarding the liberalizing effects of the internet to construct a nationwide digital panopticon (Zhang, 2004). The CCP expected the internet, along with modern ICTs in general, to "bring economic prosperity, improved Chinese global competitiveness, enhanced national defense, and heightened efficiency and efficacy of the political system" (Hartford, 2000, p. 261). For an authoritarian country with long experience of press censorship, control of cyberspace was intermingled with economic stimulus and a political agenda.

INTERNET PRACTICES: PARODY, ANTI-AUTHORITY, AND PATRIOTIC CONSPIRACY

China's internet, then, is both a constantly changing playground and a fiercely contested battlefield between the state and media corporations, on the one hand, and netizens, on the other. These latter have, whether spontaneously or deliberately, negotiated their creativity in order to carve out space for free expression. In other words, although the state and market actors have played a vital role in developing China's digital infrastructure and information technologies, the everyday cultural practices of netizens have also shaped the discursive formation of the digital space, usually by making available anti-authoritarian, rebellious imagery in the form of mockeries, parodies, and spoofs under a strict censorship regime. It is in such a political and cultural climate that *Shanzhai* fashion businesses emerged and evolved, in which women designers are part of the tech-savvy generation practicing their digital skills for a living.

Li (2017) found the vernacular online practices of video spoofing and fansubbing led by amateur enthusiasts has been intimately associated with the legacy of piracy in China's pre-internet era but then was later assimilated as a key component of the nascent video industry. The collective production of early parodic videos and fan-subtitles demonstrates the energy and creativity of the grassroots, which, in its strategic appropriation by and absorption into the video industry, came to conform to a professionally oriented and copyright-bound model. However, the early piracy-based vernacular spoof culture remains embedded in the current online video industry.

What Li called video spoofing is also known as a cultural meme, the internet *egao* (恶搞), a sprawling parody culture and practice of audio-visual remixing. Hu Ge pioneered *egao* in his video "Murder by Steamed Bun" (一个馒头引发的血案), which deconstructed elitist myths with the grand narrative and epic style of a blockbuster. Zhang (2009), in her illuminating analysis of *egao* practices, argued that *egao* as parodic resistance represented a continuation of Chinese traditions and folk genres of crosstalk, slippery jingles, hooligan literature, Cantonese *moulitou* culture, and the broader East Asian *Kuso* culture while accommodating a technological breakthrough that disseminated it virally on a mass scale. Such online participatory activities combine humor with a subversive punch, pointing as they do to the complexity and multiplicity of the internet's cultural spectrum, which continues to exacerbate the tension between the state's legitimacy of ruling, on the one hand, and the increasingly hollow socialist promises made to ordinary people, on the other. Although internet *egao* has been discussed as a subversive online culture created and celebrated by younger generations in China as a form of resistance to the mainstream culture, the practice itself, and consequently its products, nonetheless still lack a clear politics and remain confined within mainstream ideology, packaged as commodities to be consumed by the mainstream audience (Cai, 2007; Yu, 2008).

The practices of mockeries, parodies, and spoofs on the internet have animated and anteceded the *Shanzhai* culture. Innovative designers started to integrate parody and spoof into fashion commodities to profit from. For example, the spoofer and fashion designer Su Wukou is known for his fashion collection titled "THE FAKE." Operating his online shop Purlicue, he proclaimed in a statement attached to the tag for each product (usually called a hang tag) in the collection:

> I am plagiarizing. This collection is completed by copying another brands' design directly. However, I originally create[d] the hag [*sic*] tags which are garment paper patterns. They have not been produced to be the real physical garments. Customer could make new garments by copying my pattern design and treating THE FAKE collection as [a] fabric source.

Su's pamphlet clearly articulated the philosophy behind THE FAKE collection (Figure 2.5). Along with the manifesto, his line of products satirized existing branded designs and the aura that attaches to brands'

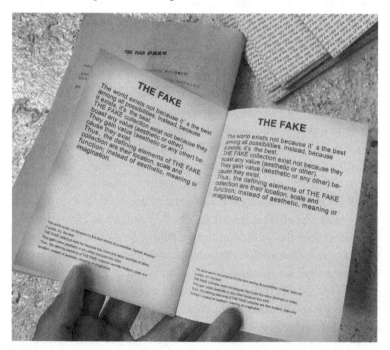

Figure 2.5   THE FAKE manifesto

values. In "faking" a pair of Vans Authentic shoes, he imprinted on them the statement "This pair of shoes is copying a skate shoe brand," erased trademarks to signal concealment of plagiarism, and warned his customers "please wear without care" (Figure 2.5). Technically, Su's fake Vans did not violate any Chinese regulations, unlike many *Shanzhai* fashion products, but rather openly mocked fashion design copyrights in fashion design. Indeed, though the shoes from THE FAKE collection were priced as high at ¥750 (approximately $110), double the average price of the Vans Authentic collection, a couple of hundred pairs were still sold. Further, Su's other product lines have embedded the symbolic anti-anti-copy practice, as shown by the paradoxical copyright warning: "PURLICUE now is a registered brand, and [has] patented the product. Please be cautious before you plagiarize [,] and respect the intellectual input of others. Otherwise PURLICUE will take legal action."

The knotty relationship between internet pop culture and consumerism demonstrates the commodification of cultural production, on the one hand, and the increasingly de-centered practice of production and consumption, on the other—both are characteristics of the sprawling *Shanzhai* culture. The process has been described as a democratic consumption of leisure culture, one that is theoretically egalitarian in terms of the consumer-citizen, at least in comparison with either the socialist

Figure 2.6   A promotional picture of the faked Vans Authentic from Purlicue online shop

or liberal political utopias (Wang, 2001). While consumerism is often associated with political apathy, especially with respect to the generation born in the 1980s into one-child families, the description of this generation as "web-savvy, pop-culture-conscious and decidedly apolitical" (FlorCruz et al., 2009) fails to capture the numerous experiments by young activists who have in creative ways carved out precarious space for pro-democracy and human rights discourse on the internet and in particular social media.

Weibo, for example, is a lively and dynamic space, a site where information about current affairs, critical events, civic engagement, and so on circulates. Users also engage in chitchats, posting of selfies, and presenting their personal lives. The user-friendly interface, multiple interactive functions, and huge traffic on Weibo makes it a popular social media platform among *Shanzhai* women designers to reach their customers, promote their shops and products, and keep alert to the trends and changes in the fashion field. Launched in August 2009 as a copy of Twitter, WeChat cultivates and is nurtured by users' habits, corporate practices, and contingencies of political control. Its subversive potential became clear in March 2015, when the so-called "Feminist Five" were detained on suspicion of "picking quarrels and creating a disturbance" after planning to use the platform to start a campaign against sexual harassment on public transportation in Beijing (Branigan, 2015). They were charged with organizing a crowd with the intention of disturbing public law and order. The incident had domestic feminists and social activists up in arms, and they quickly circulated the five feminists' images along with supportive messages and posters on Weibo and other social media platforms, such as Twitter and Facebook, that are banned in China (but may be available via virtual private networks or vpns). Particularly on Weibo, the discourse of these feminists' advocacy for women's rights—consisting of hashtags with posts featuring their experiments incorporating feminist perspectives into the performing arts, general campaigns and projects emphasizing feminist themes, and joint efforts with other non-government organizations—was discursively constructed and collectively articulated. Their actions were consistently tweeted and re-tweeted on multiple public and personal Weibo accounts and forwarded to other media for cross-posting. The building discontent soon drew the attention of the international community, including human rights organizations and Western leaders such as Hillary Clinton, who condemned the Chinese government on Twitter. When the government mandated that Chinese media platforms filter out subversive content, while many of the Weibo posts about the Feminist Five were indeed removed immediately after posting, users explored creative ways to negotiate and bypass keyword filtering, such as combining linguistic and non-linguistic symbols, posting pictures of subversive texts, generating photos with sensational or playful expressions, and looking for solidarity in foreign media. It has been argued that the ease with which Chinese users can access social media and the internet enables a daily stream of social and political critiques (Yang, 2012).

From video spoofing, faking fashion products, to feminist activism, these internet practices have established a distinctive image of a generation of netizens in China who are creative, rebellious, unobliging, and seeking for self-expression and freedom of choice. These characteristics resonate with the *Shanzhai* spirit in its defiant holdout against authority. However, it is too early to be optimistic about the democratic potential of the internet in China, for the government not only intervenes to strengthen censorship when efforts are made to evade it but also leaves strategic backdoors in the internet and Chinese social media in order to keep the country's overwhelming young, strong, and tech-savvy netizens in the ideological grip of nationalism. On the morning of January 21, 2016, five days after the Democratic Progressive Party (DDP) and its chairperson Tsai Ing-wen won the parliamentary and presidential elections in Taiwan, over 40,000 netizens left critical comments on the president-elect's Facebook page, repeating "a standard Communist Party refrain about how shameful it is to harm the motherland" (Hung et al., 2016). The incident showcased the coordinated effort by Chinese netizens, largely mobilized through a popular internet forum called Li Yi Tieba or Di Ba, to bypass the "Great Firewall of China"—for Facebook was and remains blocked in mainland China—to protest the Taiwan independence movement. Netizens posted comments with a huge variety of emoji and stickers, known as *Biaoqingbao* (表情包), to parody, mock, and caricature the self-ruled island, its political leadership, and cross-strait ties as part of their assertion that Taiwan remains a part of China, thereby demonstrating a nationalist side to the internet generation's political passion and identity.

The incident is an example of the simmering discontent over the growing discrepancy between the economic freedom enjoyed by Chinese citizens, on the one hand, and their lack of real political rights, on the other. In this case, the discontent came to a head in nationalistic nostalgia located outside the party regime, for which the internet was a safe space to exercise citizenship, civic engagement, and freedom of speech without challenging the party-state's political foundation and ruling ideologies. The internet here served as a temporary safety valve for accumulated resentment growing from increasing social inequality, ethnic tensions, failure of the education system, and nepotism and corruption, a resentment further enflamed by natural disasters, breakdowns in the safety of the food supply, air pollution, and other pressures. Similar hot-button issues, such as the international court's ruling on the territorial dispute between China and the Philippines in the South China Sea in mid-2016, also demonstrated the strong allegiance that many in the young generation on social media showed to the party-state. Many of the women designers whom I encountered in the course of my research also eagerly posted on social media to support the government's stance, taking advantage of their large fan bases to support the state's claim of territorial sovereignty over the disputed region (gbtimes, 2016; Tong, 2016).

The participation of these *Shanzhai* designers in the social media "war" against perceived challenges to China's national sovereignty, in this case their political passion in the context of a contentious territorial dispute, is an example of how netizens' activism has been instrumentalized as part of a nationalistic geopolitical campaign. The internet in China allows for economic interests to be fulfilled but is shuttered for political critiques toward its own regime. Women designers are living in such a digital environment to practice *Shanzhai* for profits but being constrained to actualize *Shanzhai*'s political potential for full emancipation and liberation—this is where their precarity grows. Moreover, netizens such as these women designers are hailed to be patriotic subjects, serving the state's purposes in terms of increasing domestic demand and promoting consumption. I return to this point later in this chapter, following an investigation of the online shopping sprees that, with the rise of domestic e-commerce companies, have come to exert an enormous influence on perceptions of what to consume and how to consume it.

E-COMMERCE, ANTI-FAKE CAMPAIGNS, AND THE UNEVEN PROGRESS OF REFORM

As mentioned, the massive unemployment and social resentments of the 1990s were mitigated by the government's efforts to create urban jobs to absorb the surplus workforce and maintain consumer demand. The promotion of consumerism was certainly consistent with the state's interest at the time in moving away from an export-driven mode of economic growth by boosting domestic demand (Kong, 2007). The prioritization of these policies encouraged Chinese citizens to pursue entrepreneurship and careers in the private sector. The "me-generation" that came of age in the context of the social transformation under the one-child policy focused its internet activity on play, entertainment, and lifestyles, seeking a space in which consumers may enjoy freedom of choice— again, in contrast with their freedom as political and moral subjects of the party-state (Liu, 2010). This fluid set of circumstances has fed the practice of online shopping and the growth of e-commerce companies.

In some respects, this was the best of times for budding entrepreneurs, with business opportunities on the internet creating a new kind of worldwide gold rush in the new century. A key moment came in 1999, when China agreed to the tough terms demanded by the US, thereby paving the way to its joining the WTO and deepening the reform and policy of openness (Fewsmith, 1999). This was also the time when e-commerce took off in China. The country's first B2C (business-to-customer) company, 8848.com, was established in the same year (Bai, 2009), as was its first C2C (customer-to-customer) website, EachNet.com. Over 5,000 Chinese entrepreneurs opened businesses on EachNet during the first week of the website's release. In May 2003, Alibaba's chairman Jack Ma led the effort to establish the business Taobao, which registered more than 10,000 users in its first 20 days.[10] Taobao's establishment coincided with the outbreak of SARS in China that year, an illness that led to the shutdown of numerous public schools, department stores, grocery markets, and transportation systems during its peak in 2003 (US-China Economic and Security Review Commission, 2003), which unexpectedly boosted the internet business due to inconvenient public life.

This famous e-commerce company was thus a product of a distinct set of historical, social, and, interestingly, medical contingencies, as the widespread SARS virus in effect brought life to another prevalent contagion in the form of online shopping and e-commerce. In other words, one impact of SARS was that traditional commerce decreased while the new economy and e-commerce grew rapidly (Zhang, 2003). Alibaba and its Taobao platform played a key role in the burgeoning new economy. The government's policies also favored increasing domestic demand through e-commerce, especially during the difficult times of the 2008 financial crisis. The government officially recognized online shops as lawful retailers (Ministry of Commerce, 2004), designated 21 model e-commerce cities in 2011 and 30 more in 2014 (National Development and Reform Commission, 2011, 2014) and 35 demonstrative e-commerce bases in 2012 (Ministry of Commerce, 2012), and established numerous special economic zones and a pilot Free Trade Zone (FTZ).[11] At the same time, with the government's blessing, Alibaba launched its own payment system in 2004 to solve trust issues between sellers and buyers in e-commerce; the effort was later, in 2014, transformed and restructured into the fintech company Ant Financial. Alimama online marketing tech platform was launched in 2007, the Tmall market for name-brand products was launched in 2008, Cloud Computing for data management was launched in 2009, and AliExpress global marketplace was launched in 2010 (US Securities and Exchange Commission, 2014). The success of Taobao has created a great many business opportunities for start-ups, especially in marketing such consumer goods as apparel, beauty, and electronics. *Shanzhai* women designers' businesses are, as observed earlier, inseparable from Taobao as a technological platform and a communicative approach, and they have also benefited from the development of the Chinese internet under the state's technocratic rationale.

However, a severe problem arose as piracy became rampant on the e-commerce platforms. In the case of Taobao, for example, the State Administration for Industry and Commerce (SAIC) announced in January 2015 that, in a sampling inspection, 63 percent of the products sold on Taobao were found to have been fakes, were discredited, or had come through unauthorized channels. Although Alibaba quickly questioned the government's inspection processes, and the SAIC called back the white paper that it had issued a few days previously regulating Taobao's conduct (Huang, 2015; Shao, 2015), the evidence nevertheless indicated that e-commerce platforms were rife with fakes and counterfeit goods. Foreign markets were accordingly wary of China's e-commerce platforms (Tan, 2016), and transnational fashion brands also challenged its digital counterfeiting with lawsuits ("Gucci sues Alibaba over 'counterfeit goods,'" 2015).

To be clear, Taobao and other e-commerce firms in China have been committed to complying with IPR recommendations and to eliminating counterfeits and pirated products from their platforms. Since 2010,

Taobao has collaborated with a dozen other e-commerce companies on numerous anti-counterfeiting campaigns (Taobao, 2010). According to the *2015 Report on China's E-commerce Industry Anti-Counterfeit Campaign* issued by the Policy and Lawmaking Committee of the China Electronic Commerce Association (CECA), the average counterfeit rate of products sold online was 1.58 percent in China, significantly lower than the 10 percent rate for international trade (CECA, 2016). One of the explanations for the low figure reported by the CECA is the working definition of "counterfeit" that it used in evaluating e-commerce, which combined elements from domestic and foreign authorities as well as academics and focused on violations of trademarks and attempts to mislead consumers (CECA, 2016, p. 10).

Such a definition of "fake and counterfeit" excludes the majority of *Shanzhai* fashion products, since they do not necessarily violate trademark laws or suffer from poor quality and functionality. Only rarely do consumers report an IPR violation associated with *Shanzhai* products. One of my informants, known here as Cici, had worked as an intern in Taobao's Department of Risk Management in 2012, monitoring complaints from online shop owners whose products, advertisements, or promotional images had been copied without permission or authorization. According to her, Taobao's consumer protection measures did not cover those who chose to buy what they knew to have been copies, imitations, or fakes, but that, in any case, they only rarely received complaints from consumers of *Shanzhai* products. Even identifying such products can be difficult, let alone taking legal actions against their marketers on e-commerce platforms, and this difficulty in turn has opened up space for *Shanzhai* to survive and prosper.

Nonetheless, copyright enforcement on Taobao has become increasingly stringent, to the point that over time it has come to directly threaten the survival of the *Shanzhai* market. The designers have turned to Weibo, WeChat, or online beauty forums such as Mogujie and Meilishuo, which have relatively looser control over patents and copyrights and allow *Shanzhai* producers to display their products even if they eventually depend on Taobao to complete the transactions because of the protections afforded by Alipay, the mobile paying system Alibaba developed to solve trust between buyers and sellers. Women in *Shanzhai* embrace precarious creativity in the imitative fashion industry while at the same time having to rely on the media corporation's monetization of their work and exploitation of their own digital labor, a point on which I elaborate in Chapter 3.

In addition, although e-commerce platforms promise to provide equal access to everyone, the opportunity to profit from the *Shanzhai* industry is not distributed equally. The imbalance in development and wealth distribution since the reform period in China has resulted in fiercely policed digital production and consumption. In one interview, the designer Maison openly expressed her concern about the lack of e-commerce resources and internet technology know-how. Maison's sales volume and business scale were moderate; she usually updated 5–10 sets of outfits per season. She operated her online shop in her hometown of Haikou on Hainan, an isolated island in South China with an economy that has traditionally relied on agriculture but has recently experienced exponential growth in tourism and real estate. The materials, transportation, labor, and market necessary for light industry such as garment manufacturing have often been difficult to secure there. According to Maison, people often recognized small businesses from *Jiang-Zhe-Hu* (an abbreviation combining Jiangsu and Zhejiang provinces and the Shanghai special administrative region), which are portals of micro-entrepreneurship and online retailing on Taobao and several wholesale platforms. She felt that entrepreneurs in the region could easily find the workers and production facilities necessary to start an e-business and would have liked to find a partner to share the burden, but no one close to her was both interested in such a business and familiar with digital commerce. In addition, the limited number of garment factories in Haikou often refused either to produce or at least prioritize small orders, meaning that the normal production cycle for any product in her shop ranged from two months to three months. Furthermore, the customer service staff that she was able to hire had only limited knowledge of e-commerce, so she had to train her employees to use the AliWangWang instant messaging service embedded in Taobao, change shipping fees and confirm order status, package and ship parcels, follow orders for returns and/or exchanges, and handle low ratings, bad reviews, and customer complaints. "When consumers complain and give the products bad reviews," she observed, "they [the staff] don't know how to respond. I have to call the consumers and explain. And sometimes, you know, you cannot rely on them, because if they do it wrong, it ruins the reputation of my shop."

Most of the women designers with whom I talked resided in coastal cities or metropolises, such as Beijing, Shanghai, Guangzhou, Hangzhou, and Chengdu, that serve as transport junctions, distributing centers for goods and materials, and hubs of migrant and cheap labor and have, historically, been leaders in export-led manufacturing (e.g., Chengdu houses many of the world's leading OEMs for shoes) and crucial for the development of commerce, finance, and culture. It is in part for these reasons that few *Shanzhai* fashion businesses have taken root in China's heartland—the practical challenges of limited infrastructure, geographic isolation, and glaring inequalities in economic benefits from the internet boom. The imbalance in the situation is partially explicable in terms of Qiu's (2004) analysis of "informationalism with Chinese characteristics," that is, the party-state's attempt to construct technology as an entirely economic instrument, an approach that has failed owing to the difficulty of implementing a coherent policy for ICT development across a nation as complex and diverse as China.

Qiu (2004) made the interesting claim that a kind of collective identification has been forming as the internet has developed as a result of the two powerful trends of consumerism and online nationalism. That is, the worldwide phenomenon of "the versatility of consumerism in subsuming other cultural elements" (p. 114) has been conspicuous in China since the 1980s, valorizing as it has the symbols of money-making and pleasure-seeking in cyberspace. Netizens are construed fundamentally as consumers, in which "grassroots nationalism in China's cyberspace remains a short-term political spasm" that reduces "the spectrum of possibilities to a single core identity: that of a Chinese consumer" (pp. 116–17).

THE RISE OF THE MIDDLE CLASS AND PATRIOTIC CONSUMPTION IDEALS

October 17, 2016 witnessed China's advancement in its space capabilities, when the country successfully launched its sixth manned spaceflight, Shenzhou 11, to send two men into orbit. On the same day, the WeChat account of the designer known as Shybyshy tweeted a new post saluting the launch. Written by Shybyshy's husband Airge, the post opened with the lofty declaration that great technologies buttress a great nation, including spaceflight household wares and gadgets for washing faces, brushing teeth, and exercising.[12] The shop run by his wife and himself, he claimed, sought to "create something weird, magnificent, and stylistic to be great ... otherwise it is boring to compete with thousands of homogeneous products at low prices in the Taobao ecosystem." The post then directed consumers to a new suit that the shop was offering made of 100 percent worsted Basolan wool yarns in a "magnificent style" (*Shenkuan*, 神款; Airge, 2016). The suit—based on a Japanese design—was associated simultaneously with a key national event, with technology, and with individual aspirations. For ¥658, the shop promised, the consumer would not only purchase an elegant garment but also buy into a narrative of nationalism. Viewed this way, a Chinese consumer does far more than consume and spend; rather, consumerism is an identity rooted in national pride—notwithstanding the fact that the state has consistently refused to recognize the means by which it is produced. In other words, the worsted suit occupies the uncertain position of being touted as a badge of political correctness in the form of a salute to the power of the nation while itself being a product of the politically incorrect manufacture of knockoffs.

The nationalistic accounts of *Shanzhai* products reflect the interwoven economic and political identities of a Chinese producer-consumer. Although the slogan "buy domestic" and consumer nationalism generally are not new to China (Wang, 2006), the contemporary patriotic form of *Shanzhai* consumption is bound up with the improved material conditions in the country, the associated formation of a rising middle class, and the phenomenon of internet-based consumer citizenship. According to a World Bank report (2016), China's GDP per capita neared $8,000 in 2015, a remarkable 13-fold increase in only two decades (World Bank, 2016). The rise of a middle class in China has been and continues to be nurtured by a consumption-oriented society, in the context of which the embrace of consumer citizenship and assertion of multi-faceted national and international identities on the part of netizens are recalibrating not only the economy but also the media culture under pressure from various political agendas. It is important to understand the middle-class profile in China, as it is constructed through different media outlets to supply imagination and aspirations for women designers and other participants in *Shanzhai* culture, for these participants might come from different social backgrounds but all are yearning for the economic and cultural status associated with the class.

While definitions of the middle class in China have been varied, ambiguous, and at times controversial (Cheng, 2010), the term is there as elsewhere associated first and foremost with household wealth and economic power. According to a study by the consulting firm McKinsey

& Company, more than 75 percent of China's urban population will be considered middle class by 2022, the definition in this case being households earning from $9,000 to $34,000 annually (Barton et al., 2013). Another report, issued by Credit Suisse, which defined middle class as wealth double the annual median national income, estimated its numbers in China at 109 million in 2015—a larger total figure than that for the US (Kersley & Stierly, 2015). Though the country's wealth disparity is significant both across regions and within urban/rural areas, it cannot be denied that its middle class is burgeoning and exercising increasing buying power and that this growth has been associated with that of the digital media industry. Reports also suggest that China's middle class is getting younger even as the whole population is aging (The Economist, 2016). As might be expected, members of this class are more likely than the rest of the population to be university graduates, entitled only children, and of the digital generation that grew up with the internet and expanding horizons despite the intensified media censorship from the government.[13] Most of them are hardcore producers-consumers in the digital culture.

The burgeoning middle class and the formation of a consumer society dominated by digital consumption have been shaped by and have been shaping the social terrain and cultural perceptions of wealth accumulation in the private sector. It was in this context that, as mentioned earlier, with government-encouraged entrepreneurism stimulating the economy by unleashing productivity from the market, numerous Chinese intellectuals and professionals who had worked in government institutions or collectively owned enterprises shifted their career paths and entered the private sector, and many of them went on to number among the early millionaires of the 1990s.

This transition, however, was not smooth. Those who benefited did so through a combination of keen insight into their career prospects, responding creatively to the capriciousness of industry, their ability to endure tremendous precarity, and a bit of luck. China's transition from "iron rice bowls" to entrepreneurship has striking parallels with the shift from Fordist employment, 9-to-5 and stable, to post-Fordist employment, flexible and precarious, in the Western world. The lure of entrepreneurship is economic well-being and middle-class status, but success in the effort to achieve upward mobility has remained contingent upon an intricate web of multivalent forces.

Cho, whom I introduced earlier, owned three shops selling women's clothing, both online and offline, having opened her first store in the late 1990s. Her journey began in 1993, when she moved from inner China to Shanghai through participation in a local government program that offered teaching positions and Shanghai *hukou* to talented migrants.[14] She taught in a local middle school, but the pressure of the job caused her both physical and mental suffering. When, in 1997, she temporarily lost her voice, she took two months' sick leave from teaching, during which time a friend in her neighborhood suggested that the two of them open a fashion shop together and sell newly released ready-made clothes. Cho said that she had always been conscious of her own style and received many compliments about her fashion sense and so agreed to the proposal; her partner would take care of purchasing and inventory, and she would be in charge of sales. Within three days, the tedious and exhausting work drove Cho's partner to give up, but she connected Cho with wholesalers in order to secure stock for the store.

Cho did quite well operating the shop by herself during her sick leave from the school, but eventually the parents of some of her students discovered her business and reported it to the school principal. Her shop was located not far from the middle school where she was employed, in Qibao Township, and the principal and academic director soon paid a visit, surprising Cho at her place of business. In China's current economic and socio-cultural environment, she would be seen as an entrepreneur, a respected and often-discussed occupation encouraged and endorsed by the government and the society. In the environment of the late 1990s, however, the school's principal and director considered a *getihu*, "self-employed person" running a clothing business to be lowbrow and beneath the dignity of a teacher.[15] The principal said to her: "I think it is better that you go to work for another public institution. The things you are doing [i.e., being a *getihu* and taking part in the fashion industry] go against our original intention to give you a residence permit for your talent; it is not right." Cho believed that these officials sincerely and earnestly wished that she would give up the store and remain at her teaching post, and she felt compelled to do so, so she shuttered her business and resumed her teaching career in the middle school for another twelve years.

The reform period has been discussed earlier but here I need to foreground a specific tension between some forward-looking people who embraced capitalist ideas of consumption and entrepreneurialism, the massive population who were not ready to accept jobs other than iron rice bowls, and the government that was still searching for a way to a market economy while retaining socialist control. Cho's story is representative of the ethos of the 1990s, specifically the ambivalence of many in Chinese society toward entrepreneurship. Needless to say, for people like Cho, entrepreneurship was fascinating with the potential represented by promises of flexibility, creativity, mobility, and middle-class-ness. But the discrepancies between individual desires and long-existing public expectations put the temptation of entrepreneurship in a chokehold. Precarity is registered in the inability to realize one's economic aspirations, not owing to any lack of individual capability, but because the neoliberal vision of entrepreneurism has remained inchoate, temporary, fleeting, intangible, and, therefore, elusive. It is not a neoliberal problem, but a problem of lack of neoliberal environment in general.

The aforementioned tension started to loosen as China marched toward a more neoliberal state, tackling global financial crises and the resulting sluggish economy. In concert with the rising number of entrepreneurs and start-ups has been the demand created by expanding domestic consumption. National campaigns in China began to propagandize a "patriotic shopping" movement that framed spending as a way to demonstrate love of country and self (X. Wu, 2009), and was propagated through such measures as extended holidays (creating the so-called "Golden Week" economy) and subsidies, especially of consumer electronics for rural residents. A widely read op-ed from Xinhua News Agency's *Outlook Weekly* magazine declared that "active consumption is patriotic" (Han & Dou, 2009) and encouraged citizens to demonstrate their confidence in the market through spending, regardless of income (Martinsen, 2009). While the strategic move to promote consumption has always had an explicit political agenda—namely, to reduce economic reliance on foreign investment and maintain a strong market—it has since the 1990s nevertheless contributed to the shifting social perceptions of self-employment and small businesses as enterprises that complete the circle of wealth accumulation and active spending and thereby mitigate the tension between public and private economy.

The relationship among economic development, the rise of the middle class, and increased consumption in China is interwoven and complex, being impacted by growing disparities between urban and rural regions and on the basis of class, gender, and ethnicity, among other tensions. To be clear, the middle class in China includes a wide range of individuals working in various areas with a wide range of household wealth and disposable income. Spending choices differ across this variegated group. Even during the campaign to view consumption as a patriotic duty, disagreement surfaced relating to income gaps (Le, 2009). The gray and fertile market for counterfeits and knockoffs is a product of yearning for a place in an urban, modern, acculturated, and cosmopolitan middle class among those unable to purchase transnational luxury goods. In the ferment of digital culture, *Shanzhai* products provide an alternative, sometimes a patriotic one, to a younger audience that makes up the core of China's growing middle class; these products embrace the DIY spirit, micro-entrepreneurism, and participatory and de-centered approaches to production and consumption, representing temporary stability for individuals seeking ways amid the insecurities and uncertainties of multiple transformations and tensions.

LIVING IN THE TIME OF *SHANZHAI*

Shanzhai fashion practice is a focal point of precarity in the current historical, socio-political, economic, and cultural conjuncture, making it an important focus of study at the intersection of gender, class, labor, and nation. As a continuation of the garment practice of the reform era, *Shanzhai* fashion is thriving thanks to the fluid situation with respect to numerous complex governmental, economic, socio-cultural, and ideological forces. The government's intention to develop technologies and science created the technological infrastructure for digital consumption in China, while the middle class and the internet generation have supplied the labor, money, and energy to sustain and propel the e-commerce industry. The accessibility and availability of digital media in combination with anti-authoritarian sentiments have given rise to a multiplicity of imitative activities such as *Shanzhai*.

The work and lives of the women discussed in this book shared many features of the prosumption activities (Zhang, 2017). They primped themselves to create the image of a perfect life, sharing the latest fashion news and knowledge via social media, negotiating feminine gendered roles as girlfriends, wives, and mothers with entrepreneurial inspirations, and operating at the convergence of the public and the private, the personal, and the commercial. The notion of prosumption thus captures the pervasive co-constitution of production and consumption in the rise of Web 2.0 and growing Web 3.0 in contemporary China, necessitating further exploration of the intersectionality of Western conceptions intertwined with contextual differentiations with respect to gender, race, class, and nationality. I view this situation from the overlapping but distinct theoretical angle of precarious creativity, which is emblematic of the contemporary conjuncture of factors including the garment production and copying practices in the fashion industry, the Chinese government's technocratic strategies in the construction of digital infrastructure, the cultural and political practices of the younger generation of internet users, the boom in domestic e-commerce platforms in the increasingly open market, and the rise of the middle class with its patriotic consumption ideals.

While women designers are eager to articulate and de-articulate their copying practices, the Chinese state has formulated its own response to precarity, expropriating *Shanzhai* in a manner that foregrounds the increasingly precarious creativity in its discursive formation and manifestation in terms of the multiple times, locations, and scales of various crises and contradictions. The following chapter continues with Cho's story as a manifestation of this precarious creativity.

3

The Digital Labor and Production Culture of *Shanzhai* Fashion

In this chapter, I explore further the promising but also precarious space of *Shanzhai* production occupied by women and their work and through which they are linked. Consumers, global fashion trend-setters, surrogate shoppers, retailers, garment factories and workers, and sales and service staff members have come to rely heavily on women designers, and in this respect they are interconnected through the dedication of the latter to fashion work and digital labor. In the *Shanzhai* fashion production chain, that which has been produced, distributed, and consumed is always something more than an actual product, for the participants constantly throughout the process negotiate, relocate, and reinvent the commodity's exchange value.

Earlier I have clarified that digital labor is both material and immaterial. On the one hand, it understands labor as increasingly dependent on emotional, communicational, and technological skills and largely encompassing such non-traditional work domains as leisure activities (Hardt & Negri, 2000; Hesmondhalgh & Baker, 2008; Lazzarato, 1996). On the other, I draw on feminist critiques to see digital labor as a double-exploitation to women who carry out the majority of unpaid reproductive work in the domestic sphere (Fantone, 2007; Federici, 2012), and of the exploitation by technology capitalism, which depends on a female and globalized labor force to perform routine and peripheral digital work (Huws, 2003).

The present chapter focuses on the production chain of *Shanzhai* fashion, following women's digital labor as a part of their lives. Here I highlight four moments in the process of fashion copying in order to discern how a commodity, as a thing, a piece of attire, a product, or simply an image of a desired outfit, comes to life and reproduction through the consumer's initiation, purchasing, in-house production, consumption, and feedback. The "thing" in the first moment differs drastically from its instantiation in the last moment; nor does its value remain fixed from the moment of purchase to that of production. Rather, the value of the thing is embedded in its social relations that is beyond capitalist valorization (Appadurai, 1986). In this process, women designers serve as the nodal point that links the transformation of a thing into a *Shanzhai* fashion product, the changing value systems attached to the product, digital technologies that facilitate various forms of participation, and social relations among consumers, purchasing agents, factory workers, service and logistics staff, and their families and friends.

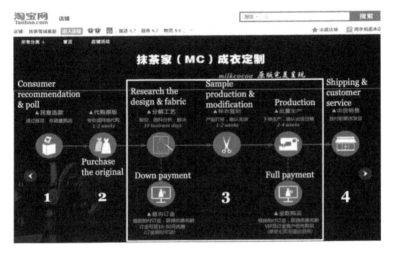

Figure 3.1   VIAN's post of a routine for making fashion copies (the translations in English and numbers are mine)

A post by the designer known here as VIAN of the routine for making a fashion copy on her online shop MC serves to illustrate the *Shanzhai* process (Figure 3.1). To be sure, this process differs among designers, as they add to or reduce the various steps depending on the situation. While I have introduced the *Shanzhai* process earlier in the introduction to this book, here I would like to highlight the four essential moments in the production chain. The first moment is sorting through and selecting images and looks of an item to be copied. The second moment is about purchasing the identified original product. While the third moment focuses on in-house production, the fourth moment of feedback creates a circuit back to the first moment where women designers can again initiate reproduction or a new round of selection-purchase-copying/production-distribution.

As it moves through the production chain, then, the thing—the commodity, the actual product—becomes increasingly spontaneous, temporal, and, to some extent, even autonomous in terms of its remaking and reproduction. In other words, the actual commodity becomes immaterial as digital labor takes center stage in the *Shanzhai* practice.

THE FIRST MOMENT: IMAGE IN EXCHANGE AND SORTING OUT NICHES

Cho was my guide the first time I walked into the Xin Qipu Costume Wholesale Market (henceforth the Xin Qipu). Picking up her story, in 2009, she gave up her teaching position entirely and returned to the fashion business and has since opened three boutiques that offer copied versions of foreign luxury goods, clothes identical to designs by Chanel, Burberry, Valentino, and Thom Browne that are popular among metropolitan fashionistas. In March 2016, she opened a store in the wholesale market on Qingpu Road in order to target retailers. Her store in the Xin Qipu, which opened in 2001, is in a relatively new building on the business circle of the Qipu Road wholesale market, which is the largest of its kind in Shanghai. The Xin Qipu's five storeys feature relatively high-quality products including shoes, handbags, hats, and other forms of women's and men's apparel. There are more than 1,000 stores in the building, most of which do not sell retail.

Cho and I took the subway for about 30 minutes from downtown Shanghai to reach Tiantong Road, where the market is located. We then took a shortcut, passing through the basement of the Xin Qipu, where numerous small shops were located selling such miscellaneous accessories as phone cases, ear pods, selfie sticks, hats, belts, scarfs, necklaces, ornaments, socks, and essential oils. Merchandise was piled up inside the tiny space of each shop or kept in the hallway. I had expected to see a great abundance of goods, but still I was overwhelmed by the enormous number of choices available there.

Cho's shop was on the third floor. Generally speaking, the higher the floor was, the tidier and more organized the shops were. The segmentation of the shops was clear: one half of the space was reserved for women's clothes and the other for men's, with the elevator in the middle of the floor separating them. The hallway was broader on this floor than the lower ones, and each shop was larger, though goods were still arranged in piles within. Occasionally, one or two workmen carted in piles of products packaged in huge black bags and wrapped with chrome yellow tape. Cho walked me around and discussed how most of the stores in the market had benefited from e-commerce:

> You see people there packaging their clothes; they are big on e-commerce. ... There, they are good at touting their goods to retailers through online platforms, and their cash flow in a day can reach ¥60,000–70,000; the average price of one item is around ¥200. ... It is not rare to get a net profit of ¥700,000–800,000 a year.

Looking inside one of the shops at which Cho pointed, I saw a man seated behind a desk in the center of the space surrounded by huge black bags. The shop catered to every kind of clothing, including shirts, pants, skirts, dresses, jeans, blouses, and blazers, most of which were in black, white, and beige, its theme colors. The man was focused on typing entries into the computer in front of him while a printer beside him spat out documents that seemed to be shipping labels.

Most customers of the wholesale markets were, of course, retailers; they were among the first to begin the process of picking and sorting to choose the products that they considered best suited to their specific markets. At one point during my visits, a middle-aged man came into Cho's shop seeking collaboration with her as a supplier in the development of a niche brand and asking specifically to replace trademarks and hang tags on Cho's clothes with those of his own brand. I was surprised at such a frank and overt attempt at this kind of switch, but this is in fact a common form of fashion imitation known as *tiepai* (贴牌), that is, placing the original (either copied or not) trademarks, labels, and hang tags with someone else's brand. Cho answered that, while she was interested in his proposal, she needed to know the particular style or trend he was looking for so that she could check her inventory and meet his needs. The man responded that he had not quite settled on his boutique's style yet, so the two of them traded business cards and agreed to discuss the matter in the near future.

My experiences at the Xin Qipu are illustrative of the first moment of *Shanzhai* fashion practice, when designers sort through mountains of images that they have received from consumers, trend-setters, luxury resellers, and the like to find those that are suitable for specific markets of fashion imitation. To be clear, for a designer to begin to produce a copy of a certain fashion look, an actual product need not be in hand.

The hype and fervor of imitation usually begins with an image of a brand's advertisements, a picture of a catwalk, or a series of street photos of a celebrity with looks that are desirable to both the consumers and the designers. These images serve as intermediary fashion trends and aspirations that appeal to a specific market.

Figure 3.2 Japanese Otome Kei (top left); urban chic (top right); norm-core (middle left); Korean casual (middle right); goth chic (bottom left); bohemian (bottom right)

To understand the selection of images for the next moment in the *Shanzhai* production chain, it is necessary to appreciate how designers create their own niches in order to focus on a particular kind of taste-making, to target a more specific group of consumers, and to sort out looks that they wish to and can imitate. One strategy that the designers adopt to differentiate themselves from one another is decorating the homepages of their online shops in accordance with the styles that they intend to develop. Figure 3.2 features six online shops with distinct personalities in terms of fashion style as reflected in the designs of their homepages. On the top left is the homepage of Double-Summer's online shop, consisting of collections in the romantic and girlish Japanese Otome-kei style emphasizing such details as bold mashup colors, ribbons, embroidery, and ruffles. On the top right is the homepage of the eponymous shop of Little Mushroom, a well-known online celebrity, also known as *wang hong* (网红) in China (Chapter 3 provides a detailed account of *wang hong* and its relation to the *Shanzhai* fashion industry). As the image shows, Little Mushroom's shop had the personality of a well-groomed, sophisticated, and chic urban lady. Sisy's shop (middle left) touted the casual office lady design, adding a bit of a trendy feel to basic attire and leaning toward something safe but stylish. Compared with Sisy's, Rabbit's shop (middle right) offered more streetwear, with lighthearted color and spontaneous layering. Mucha Studio (bottom left) cultivated the look of gothic fashion, with a conspicuously dark-colored dress, heavy makeup, and the theme of the mysterious black cat. The homepage of Flower's online shop (bottom right) presented consumers with a bohemian image in the form of a rich combination of bold and natural colors, casual, hippie, and vintage.

There are many other *Shanzhai* shops that feature, rather than a synthetic personality, a combination of trendy styles to maximize the attraction to potential consumers in search of a variety of looks, resulting in a mix-and-match approach to their homepages. Figure 3.3 showcases an example of this approach through the webpage for the woman designer Ayuan's online shop, which offers a variety of styles ranging from streetwear and prep to modern classicism and casual work.

These designers normally change their styles season-by-season to follow cutting-edge fashion trends closely. Consistency, however, outpaces change. These images of style not only present an engaging look but also develop a personality for the shop itself, telling consumers a compelling story of what they can expect from it. To a certain extent, it is the images that constitute the shop rather than the real products.

Customers play an essential role in building both a shop's image and images of the shop. Thus, the designers try to motivate them to contribute their ideas about what to copy, normally sending a free piece as a gift once a recommendation has been adopted. As a result, customers contribute a large collection of images to be turned into products, usually on

Figure 3.3   The homepage of the designer Ayuan's online shop

social media platforms, where they publicly tag women designers with images of outfits of their interests or privately message pictures to them. The designers, like the retailers sorting out goods in a wholesale market, need to assess the many looks and styles in the images and select a few to produce. This process seems arbitrary, and no common standards can be followed, for each designer is thinking about her own niche, desiring to put her competitors out of business while remaining standing herself.

Another of my informants, introduced above as Mey, had a shop featuring versatile basics, designs that are simple but always in style. She asserted that she did not want to make things that everybody else did and therefore usually did not follow the recommendations from consumers who simultaneously tagged several women designers. Mey produced an Alexander McQueen basic T-shirt in summer 2015 that became a real hit in the shop, being on backorder several times. She said,

> I want to keep things simple, and I like simple designs. My consumers like my stuff because I reassemble the original elements in a nice way, I guess. … I bought one [T-shirt] from another shop—I hate to say it,

but it was so poorly made. I kind of understand how I can and should input [changes] into my own [design].

Some of these designers, then, are willing to make products similar to others that are popular among their customers. In this case, they need to create niches in terms of pricing and marketing, ideally with these customers' participation. A designer may choose a set of images of trendy looks that, first of all, will sell well, second, will correspond to her shop's niche, and third, that she likes to make. As for myself, I never once succeeded in recommending a look to any of the women designers whom I followed. At one point, I recommended through Weibo several dresses from Anthropologie, a boho-chic American brand, to a designer known here as Bunny who normally remakes a variety of styles, most inspired by Korean street fashion. A friend of mine, an English teacher in her mid-20s and a savvy *Shanzhai* fashion fan, informed me that Bunny would never take recommendations from a random customer who makes occasional purchases; her own recommendation was adopted once by a designer with whom she was acquainted, for which she received a free midi floral lace skirt. Although several customers made the same recommendation at the same time, my friend believed that her relationship with the designer contributed to the choice of her posted image for remaking.

This is an enchanting moment in the life of an image—when it is not yet an actuality in the sense of a physical dress. The image is the same for everyone, but, because the relationship between various recommenders and the designer differ, the value of the same image, or of the would-be-copied product recommended by different consumers, is not fixed. The sorting process is self-explanatory regarding the social relation embedded in the images in circulation at this moment of the production chain.

Sometimes, after the designers have sorted through the recommended images, they invite their customers to further select one or several looks that they prefer. This selection usually takes place on social media sites Weibo and WeChat by means of polls and sharing. Figure 3.4 is a snapshot of the woman designer Shybyshy's WeChat public account with an invitation to potential customers to participate in a poll to select their favorite styles for copying; they have the option of choosing all of the items. In these ways, customers continue to exercise freedom of choice, though to a much more limited extent than when they are first invited to

Figure 3.4 Shybyshy's WeChat poll to select products for imitation

offer recommendations. This is more of a step that the designers take to assess taste and demand, estimate the market, and calculate the potential profit from production of a consumer-chosen look. In the end, Shybyshy produced four of the six outfits based on the poll result.

In these first moments of the *Shanzhai* fashion production chain, it is mainly an image of a particular style or look that circulates in the market. I suggest that such images should be understood as commodities themselves, not so much in a classic Marxist sense, in which a commodity only has value for use and exchange, but more as things with lives that are built upon the value for use and exchange as well as social relations, connections, and communications. The volume *The Social Life of Things* edited by Appadurai (1986) pioneered such an approach to commodities. Rather than reading a commodity as a product of alienated labor and the fetishization of goods, this approach calls for attention to objects as living beings with social lives, so that their trajectories can be grasped through the anthropological device of the "life history." The thing-in-motion makes a commodity not so much a type of thing as a type of situation, for which reason the study of it should be processual, meaning "looking at the commodity potential of all things rather than searching fruitlessly for the magic distinction between commodities and other sorts of things" (Appadurai, 1986, p. 13). Treating things as if they are living represents a significant break from the political economist's view of a commodity as being fixed in the moment of production, focusing instead on the thing's trajectory from production and exchange to consumption. Understanding things in social terms also represents a break from the often semiotic analysis of commodities in circulation, such as Baudrillard's (1988) theorization of consumer society that presents the commodity in the context of a signification system as something that has been pre-programmed and predetermined and remains utterly subject to omnipresent power from above. In Appadurai's conception, objects come with a life that grants them spontaneity, temporality, and, to some extent, autonomy. This view subsequently gives life to questions of consumption as production, locating it not so much at the intersection of domination, exploitation, and suppression as at that of signification, opposition, and reciprocity.

Crucial to understand how images as commodities proceed to the next moment in the *Shanzhai* fashion production chain is the fact that these women designers and consumers co-experience the inspiration of a particular style and sort through the various market niches. These images remain the same through their recommendation by consumers, sorting by a designer, and being voted to proceed to the next step of production, but their social relations to both women designers and consumers change dramatically throughout the arbitrary process. There is no guarantee that a recommended image will eventually become a fashion imitation. What is guaranteed is the pleasure of freedom and flexibility experienced through the exchange of images, desires, choices, expressions, and participatory acts. Such an experience of pleasure mandates and enforces free labor (Terranova, 2000), in which context the selection of styles and looks is an ongoing project intertwined with work and play and women designers always have to have something in the pipeline.

These designers frequently place something in their online shops in one season as a result of brainstorming with consumers during the previous season. It is also common practice for the designers to save some of the ideas solicited during one season for production during the next. Their work has been largely enabled by the digital skills and the labor of communicating with their customers along with the proliferation of images and products, through which these women survive in the market and also suffer to maintain an "always-on" mode (Gregg, 2011). For women designers, leisure or hobby is the other side of work. Their pleasure in work and social relations (with their consumers) are commodified and ready to be turned into a profit. The exchange of images, ideas, and looks of yet-to-be-made fashion items also constitute their labor to stay alert to the trends and maintain customer relations during the production cycle. The production in this sense is immaterial, experiential, spontaneous, and temporary, unfolding in an unknown land with possible desirable outcomes.

THE SECOND MOMENT: OBTAINING THE ORIGINAL

Once a particular image has been preferred to others or is favored by a designer, the next step, the second moment of *Shanzhai* production, begins when the designer gets her hands on the original product for copying. Since most of the original attire is from foreign luxury brands, in order to secure the originals, designers follow three main approaches: either traveling to another country to get them, making purchases locally through sites supported by international shipping, such as Amazon in the US (known as *haitao* shopping), or engaging a surrogate shopping agent or reseller.[16] The agent or luxury reseller is a new occupation created by the expanding demand of Chinese consumers for quality and symbolic international goods. It is possible to exploit differences in countries' currency exchange rates for profit, and agents and resellers also profit from the surrogate fees that they charge Chinese customers for overseas products. The purchasing agent can be an individual or a company operating an online shop on popular shopping platforms; most, like the designers, set up shops on Taobao and also maintain public social media accounts on platforms such as Weibo and WeChat. According to market research, from June to November 2015, 58 percent of consumers bought foreign products online from a domestic shopping website through purchasing agents, their prime concerns being the quality of the products and pricing (Mintel, 2016). The market research company iiMedia Research (2018) reported that the Chinese population who did *haitao* had increased to 65 million by 2017, in which year the overall transaction scale (including retail and B2B) of cross-border e-commerce reached 7.6 trillion yuan. Since 2012, the government has introduced a number of policies regarding cross-border e-commerce imports intended to protect consumers' rights and state revenue (Tsang, 2016).

Purchasing agents usually act as buyers and as purveyors of mediated images of cosmopolitanism, taste, desire, and aspiration of working-cum-shopping, though sometimes the sense of working ruins the sense of pleasure in shopping or vice versa. These agents, mostly women, may open their own Taobao shops and recruit buyers around the world to shop for resells or, again, themselves engage in shopping. To maximize their business opportunities, they also frequent many *Shanzhai* women designers' shops and social media accounts to recommend the latest trends and looks, often circulating images of themselves shopping and taking photos of the intended products. As Zhang (2017) has shown, many of these luxury resellers belong to the transnational mobile middle class that exercises its freedom through shopping as a solution to the competing demands of fashioning a feminine self. She further contended that "Fashioning an 'authentic' self—that is successfully annexing individuals' unique personalities and life experiences to commercial products through visual and discursive narratives—is paramount to attracting customers, enhancing 'stickiness,' and increasing profit margins" (p. 11). These transnational resellers become a node of the *Shanzhai* fashion production chain by brokering the imaginaries of a global consumer citizenship and negotiated cosmopolitan lifestyle.

In global reselling, obtaining a luxury product induces an affect attached to Western fashion ideals, middle-class-ness, consumer citizenship, and so on, with contesting narratives of different gender regimes. This affect, which is already conveyed to and appealing to consumers, largely approximates the first moment in *Shanzhai* production. That which has been produced and consumed is not the product itself, for its value transcends simple use and exchange. If the global purchasers are secondary cultural brokers for *Shanzhai* consumers with whom they do not have direct connections, the women designers are the direct intermediaries of their aspirations, desires, and affective sentiments, which are further reinforced and almost coercively encompass consumers through the designers' commodification of their lifestyles and their relationships with consumers during their own overseas shopping trips. They are not only shopping for the original products that they prefer to copy—especially niche brands that can rarely be found in the local market—but can help to build the reputation of a designer's business for exclusivity and uniqueness once reproduced; also, they increasingly act as transnational surrogate shoppers and transfer overseas goods for their customers, which they view as "doing a favor for friends."

The designer known here as Autumn had engaged in this practice many times and often sold a combination of self-created imitations and factory knockoffs in her online shop. She told me that her parents were in the textile business in Hangzhou, Zhejiang, and that she had regularly followed them to work when she was not in school from one wholesale market to another as they negotiated with retailers and contractors, dealt with various batches of textiles and orders, and haggled over prices, quantities, and quality. Especially during summer vacations and winter breaks, for Autumn, almost every day was "take your daughter to work day." Being immersed in this environment, she grew to appreciate her parents' hard work and looked to enter the fashion industry herself. She married a man whose family was also successful in small business and micro-entrepreneurship, and together they opened an online shop targeting 20- to 30-year-old women.

Autumn has a particular taste for Korean and Japanese fashion trends, and her collections project an image of delicacy, freshness, youth, and playfulness. She traveled to Korea annually for inspiration and every time brought back such fashion accessories like rings, necklaces, and headwear and such beauty products as facial masks, creams, and perfumes for her customers—some of the products were random shopping finds and others were requested by them. These products bought from the country of origin not only carried a guarantee of authenticity (in the face of rampant counterfeits and fakes in the domestic market) but also showed Autumn's sincerity to her fanbase-clientele, members of whom quickly placed online orders and purchased the entire stock.

When I first contacted her, Autumn was on pregnancy leave with her second child. When she did not feel well enough to place a call or text message, she would send me emails, and we had several exchanges in this manner. Autumn was very proud of her work as a woman designer and of having developed a good relationship with her customers, whom she referred to as "friends." In my interview with her, Autumn expressed her gratitude to these friends, who, she said, encouraged her when she received a bad review or had a bad day and sent her cards, gifts, and other items from various parts of the country. As she put it, "I just want to do something for them in return for their trust."

"Trust" is a concept that came up frequently during the interviews and chats with my informants. It referred in some contexts to the ingenuousness and sincerity with which the designers managed the visuals, videos, live lifecasts, narratives, comments, re-tweets, likes, and shares on their social media accounts. If their behavior through transactions and interactions with their customers were consistent with the personalities that they projected, these customers came to trust them and became fans of their online personas. Trust can also refer to the reliability and consistency of a designer's products, the reputation of her shop, and its performance in terms of logistics and service. In Autumn's case, during every trip to Seoul, she updated her itinerary several times a day so as to remain in close touch with her fanbase-clientele through visual displays of favorite items that she was interested in copying, videos of her shopping, and narratives of her adventures and the feelings that they invoked. The immediacy, interactivity, and intimacy discursively constructed on social media are enticing and seductive, creating the social dimension of relational and reciprocal recognition and trust. Autumn's customers generally appreciated the mediated experience of shopping for "authentic" products; her trips involved more than simply acquiring original products to be copied in-house in that they also served as ways for the designers to commodify—which is to say, earn a profit from—their lifestyles and social relationships. Trust thus has both a material form and an immaterial social relation that is manifested in the designers' digital labor, as their roles as global purchasers demonstrated.

Autumn's narratives and visuals of her fashion work were further reconciled with her commitment to her family as a good wife and mother, a possibility offered and enabled by technologies and transnational mobility and practiced as digital labor. During the winter holiday of 2016, Autumn and her husband took their three-year-old son to Kyushu, Japan, for a vacation and a celebration of their yet-to-be-born second son. Autumn kept updating her status on WeChat Moments regarding both the family trip and new products for her shop, thereby projecting the image of the perfect life of a well-rounded woman with respect for career and family, work and leisure, and enjoyment of every moment.

Such an ostensible unification of work and play and the work-life balance have been heralded in many creative cultural occupations, especially advertising, as the ethos and a benefit of entrepreneurship. The flexibility, autonomy, and aspiration in their entrepreneurship and creative work under some conditions allow women to be financially independent and to acquire self-esteem while at the same time remaining responsible for childcare, household chores, and other familial expectations that, in turn, demand a young body in both physical and psychological terms. As McRobbie (2002) acutely pointed out,

> Youthfulness is more or less a requirement for participation in the "new work," not because a bodily essentialism kicks in later in life disallowing the "long hours" culture, but rather because the expectation and indeed legitimacy of some degree of struggle and even failure to "make it" reduces with age as other requirements for status and authority replace youthful resilience. (p. 110)

The creative workers' youthfulness, in McRobbie's understanding, is neither stable nor determinative, so that extending the ages that count as young expands the labor available with respect to both time and locations; such kind of labor can be invested fully in productive labor. Further, because youthfulness connotes a social expectation of independence as well as responsibility, creative work or digital labor calls for complete devotion to the job, resulting in the postponement of marriage, parenthood, and familial duties, particularly for women.

Considering that the creative labor time of youth requires indefinitely enforced youthfulness in terms of age, digital labor in China—intertwined as it is with the traditional patriarchal ideals of gender roles and ideologies in its recent manifestations of "leftover women" discourse and the two-child policy—takes place during a paradoxical social time of youth, when women are interpellated into the domestic arena of marriage and motherhood as early as their 20s to perform the majority of the unpaid work of reproduction.[17] The enforced youthfulness in creative work, as it were, wears a Chinese mask in the context of *Shanzhai* fashion production culture. The creativity and social world of youth in China eventually come together, for work in the *Shanzhai* fashion industry allows women designers to have children and have work. Autumn told me during the interview that she was not ambitious but simply wanted to enjoy family life. She always maintained her dignity as both a mother and an independent woman, and she was not alone in this respect. Many other women designers whom I interviewed and/or observed shared a similar point of view, being grateful to have work as well as significant others to support.

The thing being exchanged here is clearly the sentiment attached to the discourse of enterprising women who manifest the glamor and fantasy of creative fashion work, which encompasses shopping for global fashion, promoting consumption and production, conveying picture-perfect lifestyles, and managing the work-life balance. It should be noted in this context that although the second moment is essentially about acquiring the original product to serve as a template for copies, it is also the co-construction and co-shaping of an atmosphere, a structure of sentiments surrounding the working lives of women designers with their fanbase-clientele. That which is offered for exchange and the source of its value transcends the commodity as an actual product, residing instead in a convergence of the material form and affective digital labor.

The story of the woman designer known here as Daxi, who frequently flew overseas to purchase the latest fashion luxuries as inspiration for her creations, is particularly instructive in this regard. She never used a purchasing agent, nor did she act as one; she strictly controlled her own production chain, navigating from supply to production, distribution, and consumption. Daxi was also a high-profile online celebrity and part-time model for digital magazines and studios. Her husband Yan was a professional photographer, or, in contemporary parlance, a "beau-tographer," defined by Fashionista.com as "a man [who] is fully employed by his girlfriend to be her full-time photographer" (Yi, 2014). Yan took most of the photos of *Shanzhai* outfits, which Daxi modeled herself. Pham, in a (2015) study of elite Asian "superbloggers," argued that these individuals played a significant role in developing the core practice of personal style blogging by having a boyfriend photograph outfits for them that showcase elite status in the racially bounded fashion blogging world. Different from Pham's focus on fashion bloggers, the women designers in my study "hired" their boyfriends or husbands to take photos of them, first and foremost as an economical way to operate *Shanzhai* enterprises. Once the business was on track, they might hire another professional photographer for improved scouting of locations and sophisticated lighting and exposure, photo styling, editing, and so on, or, in the case of Daxi and Yan, simply to allow him more time to manage the business.

Daxi and her husband represent a successful "merger" in the world of *Shanzhai* fashion. Together, they have become one of the most popular couples and most-watched figures in the circles of online celebrities who actively present themselves on social media. When interviewed by magazines and news media, Daxi and Yan always recalled that theirs was love at first sight, kindled when Daxi was modeling in Changsha, Hunan, as a college student and Yan was running his own studio in Hangzhou. They fell in love on the internet, specifically through Weibo encounters, and soon after Daxi graduated, she relocated to Hangzhou and married Yan and began to assist him in operating the studio. They moved their shop to Taobao in 2012 and started to sell clothes directly from factories and then some products that they had designed themselves. The story that I tell here is one that Daxi and Yan have recounted to a variety of media while promoting their online shop, Daxi Retro Styling, claiming to share a commitment both to their love and to fashion and style. While their intimacy began with and increasingly came to be built on virtual performances in addition to face-to-face encounters, their mediated love story contributed to the success of their fashion business, which demanded a borderless life in terms of work and play and of public and private. These designers' multiple trips to Tokyo, Paris, New York, San Francisco, Bangkok, and other such destinations presents a disturbing contrast with the real, tedious work of sorting through and selecting styles and looks in one outlet after another, cultivating consumers' trust, constant photography and editing on vacations, and taking direct responsibility for everything at their home base.

Strikingly, women designers tend to identify various types of work as embedding specific masculine and feminine characteristics. A man tends to be in charge of the technological and business operations of *Shanzhai* businesses, while a woman performs the roles of a muse, fashionista, and stylist whose main duty is to be beautiful and to live a picture-perfect, carefree life. The visibility of women designers' personal lives is packaged as a dream and aspiration that can be bought. More often than not, the work-life balance in entrepreneurship has benefited from digital technologies, social media networking, international trips, and other practices that reinforce the patriarchal ideals of women and gender norms rather than challenging them. There is, therefore, the need for considerable reexamination of the gender regimes of digital labor and creative work in *Shanzhai* culture. Such work, as it is often lifecasted by women designers in their overseas trips and daily lives, seems to empower them with the dignity of being independent while maintaining loving relationships with partners and other family members. Though work and play, job and life, and enterprise and family have been in flux for them, they have refused to mount a sustained critique of the patriarchal gendered assumptions underlying infinite working hours, which paradoxically generate "the effect of making women feel grateful for so-called 'flexible' work arrangements" (Gregg, 2011, p. 4).

In this moment of the *Shanzhai* production chain, women designers' work consists of far more than simply getting their hands on an original product to be copied. The value accumulated in this moment takes the forms of desire, trust, glamor, and work-life balance. What has been produced, circulated/distributed, and consumed always exceeds its actuality, its material form as a physical product. Women designers exercise their flexibility and autonomy to make and remake constantly the immaterialities of their yet-to-be-produced fashion imitations.

THE THIRD MOMENT: IN-HOUSE PRODUCTION

The third moment in *Shanzhai* fashion is in-house production, which consists of multiple making steps and manufacturing procedures, including fabric and design research, printing, pattern-cutting, sample-making, negotiating production with a factory, and, eventually, manufacturing. Throughout these steps, the designers feel compelled to display an appropriate personality for and relationship to their work as professional designers and entrepreneurs.

In 2014, my informant Apple, who was introduced in Chapter 1, started her *Shanzhai* business after quitting a stable job at a hospital in Shangqiu, Henan. Most of her relatives on her mother's side were hospital workers, a vocation perceived as prestigious, skilled, and stable, but Apple was eager to quit the hospital job arranged for her by her aunt because she considered the 9-to-5 schedule tedious; she was looking for something more creative and flexible. She went about setting up her own shop as a mid-range designer and copied numerous looks from Korean brands. Her father's small garment factory provided the textile materials and patternmakers to assist in her researching of styles and creation of prototypes along with the skilled workers necessary to produce *Shanzhai* fashion products.

Like many other of the designers mentioned in this book, then, Apple was lucky to have supportive family members who could contribute resources, particularly access to garment factories with stocks of textiles and fabrics, trained patternmakers, and skilled workers. However, after operating her shop for two years, Apple was barely eking out a living, even though she had been gradually building up her consumer base and collections. With the modest seed money earned from the *Shanzhai* business, she went to Zhengzhou, the capital of Henan Province, to collaborate with her friends in opening a beauty salon dedicated to Korean-style microsurgery. In the interview, Apple repeatedly recalled the pleasure of chatting with and befriending her fanbase-clientele and expressed regret that she had not been able to update her collections continually owing to her full-time job in the beauty salon. She told me,

> But it keeps draining me, not only of money but also of energy in searching for designs, monitoring the process, posting and updating, communicating and customer service. … Though I make really good friends, and people buy my stuff because they think I'm fun to be with, and they love to share with me … it doesn't make money, and I have to figure things out. … I can't eat up my parents' investment in me.

It is clear that women's digital labor in *Shanzhai* fashion is not always compensated for with great financial rewards and is often valorized instead in terms of pleasure and the autonomy of creative work, such as the notion that a career in fashion design allows for both freedom of choice and a flexible lifestyle. At the time of our last conversation, in December 2016, Apple still kept her shop operating at minimal expense, creating one new piece every season on average. On her Weibo public account, she listed all of her stock, except the new arrivals, as clearance over that winter, actively promoting on her Weibo and WeChat accounts the sale merchandise at her shop along with her new beauty business.

In traditional garment manufacturing, in-house production normally takes place behind the scenes, with the result that consumers are unaware of it. *Shanzhai* fashion, by contrast, foregrounds precisely the behind-the-scenes labor, putting women designers' work on display for consumers' evaluation, assessment, or pure entertainment. As already noted, the work and lives of other *Shanzhai* participants frequently revolve around those of the designers. For example, and as mentioned earlier, global purchasing agents form one link in the production chain that actualizes partially the fashion images circulated and selected through the coordinated efforts of designers and consumers in the first moment of production. In the second moment, the designers also serve as intermediaries of transnational fashion trends and desirable lifestyles for smart and independent "career+family" women; their appealing and enticing social media personas are a result of their imperative to perform, again, both on the job and in time not officially defined as "work," such as the overseas family vacations that enhanced Autumn's glamor as and pride in being a fashion designer and capable housewife. These sensibilities potentially translate into the designers' *Shanzhai* production, with every offering being a package of the aesthetic, entrepreneurial, and relational manifestations of digital labor.

Many women designers with whom I spoke described their motive for entering the *Shanzhai* fashion business as the desire to provide high-quality but affordable fashion items to their customers, for they were well aware that their customers did not tend to visit European boutiques twice a year and to spend on luxuries, just as "the people on Santee Alley are not the ones who shop at Gucci" (Blakley, 2010). At one point, I made a connection with a man referred to here as Sam who managed the *Shanzhai* shop of his girlfriend, whom I will call Ivy. Ivy and Sam both graduated from college in the summer of 2015 and proceeded to set up a shop together on Taobao. Ivy favored copying Korean street fashion brands, while Sam mostly took on responsibility for technical support, daily maintenance, logistics, and serving as a "beau-tographer," observing that

> She [Ivy] liked *Shanzhai* clothes during college. Many girls just like good-looking outfits, something that's comfortable and pretty regardless of brands. After we graduated, she proposed to make *Shanzhai* clothes together. I wanted to work with her, so I agreed.

It might be thought that *Shanzhai* practices would undermine the aura of established brands by providing cheaper versions; however, the names of these brands are still appealing to consumers. In point of fact, *Shanzhai* practices have pushed the boundary of legality when it comes to attaching trademarks and hang tags of original brands to the imitations, a practice that is considered to boost sales. Nevertheless, most of the designers whom I interviewed and observed tried their best to avoid such tactics in order both to avoid running afoul of the regulations governing IPR infringement and to cater to their customers' loyalty to their own brands.

Arguably, the distinct demographics of *Shanzhai* consumers, differing as they do from those of consumers of transnational luxuries, keep alive the *Shanzhai* industry. Part of the *Shanzhai* routine involves posting a comparison of the original and the copy with a detailed account of the resemblance and any improvements to be found in the imitations. Sometimes, the designers post their acquisition of the original product and emphasize its high price, thereby arguing effectively that consumers can take advantage of an outstanding bargain by acquiring a quality product that resembles the original in all but name at a fraction of the price. For example, a woman designer who referred to herself as Peach tweeted a long post comparing her first version of a Dolce & Gabbana dress with the original, which, she was careful to note, cost ¥12,500 as compared with ¥248 for the copy. She detailed her modifications of the original for her customers, including the use of a different fabric and slight fine-tuning of the color, while affirming that her piece resembled the original in other respects. By making more accessible products that under other circumstances could only be enjoyed by a few elite consumers, the *Shanzhai* product provides an alternative, a means to bypass and de-articulate the division of class that attaches to the high-end fashion industry in a transnational sphere.

Another of my informants, whom I refer to here as Sami, based in Shanghai, replicated only high-end products from such luxury brands as Gucci, Valentino, and Chanel in an effort to carve out her own market niche. Her work featured hand-executed, delicate detail and limited numbers of every item in her shop. Sami described herself in a statement prominently displayed in her shop as the "queen of handmade fashion and high-end tailoring" and that also appeared on the webpage for each product. Following the conventional *Shanzhai* process, once her customers selected a particular look through social media polls or comments, Sami recruited a purchasing agent or luxury reseller to secure the original product for her.

Owing to the emphasis on both the aura of luxury brands evoked by the resemblance of *Shanzhai* products to high-end fashion products and on the customization of each piece, the collection of attire in Sami's shop was on average priced higher than comparable products in other *Shanzhai* shops. For example, she listed one new product, which imitated a wool sweater from Gucci that had been endorsed by some celebrities, at ¥699, significantly higher than copies sold by her counterparts (Figure 3.5).

Figure 3.5 A search of similar copies on Taobao. The product shown on the bottom left, because it involves global purchasing of the original Gucci sweater, is offered at the original price

Note: Taobao search has the function of photo search: by uploading photos to the search window, the system will automatically match the search results with the photo. The snapshot is part of the result page enabled by photo search on Taobao (retrieved February 7, 2017, from https://s.taobao.com/search?q=&imgfile=&commend=all&ssid=s5-e&search_type=item&sourceId=tb.index&spm=a21b0.50862.201856-taobao-item.2&ie=utf8&initiative_id=tbindexz_20170208&tfsid=TB1s6GZPpXXXXbOXpXXXXXXXXXX&app=imgsearch&cat=0).

As a consequence of her pricing strategy, Sami risked losing consumers to the lower-priced clothes with similar designs offered by her competitors; after all, all of these products were "fakes." In order to cultivate customer loyalty, she offered customization. Observing the advertising fees on Taobao in proportion to their capacity to cultivate customers' loyalty to her shop, Sami decided to focus on loyalty marketing and repeat purchases by developing membership and tailoring services. She created an honor program for members of her online shop that was mentioned on the homepage and on every product's sub-page. Under the program, she defined as VIPs those who purchased six or more distinct items for at least ¥5,000 and awarded these customers with a 4 percent discount on every subsequent order, and she defined as VVIPs those who purchased eleven or more items for at least ¥8,000 and rewarded these customers with an 8 percent discount for subsequent orders and custom tailoring as well as expedited shipment of their orders.

As it happens, Sami's practice of fashion imitation in many ways resembled that of haute couture fashion houses. Haute couture is a fashion culture that originated in France, the term itself referring specifically to a form of high fashion that is hand-executed, personalized, and custom-fitted (Haute|Hot Couture News, n.d.). It supports its own philosophy and culture of fashion, in which only a narrow circle of several hundred people around the world can participate (Klaffke, 2003). This industry relies heavily on the loyalty of its consumers and the bond between elite designers and the rich and powerful, creating a dream "of chic cachet, of beauty, desirability and exclusiveness" that is turned into a selling point by haute couture fashion houses through the branding of ready-to-wear products (Thomas, n.d.). It is precisely the imagery of exclusivity created by high-fashion powerhouses and facilitated by multiple forms of media that convinces their customers that they are "chosen ones."

The parallel with *Shanzhai* fashion is close but not perfect; the latter resembles the exclusive culture of haute couture but simultaneously inverts it by de-fetishizing the labor process and de-mythicizing the role of class in the making of garments. Simply put, *Shanzhai* delinks and relinks the privilege and prestige of custom-made clothing to the elite class. As was just seen, these designers frequently emphasize the customizability of their products in terms of special fabrics, printing technologies, sewing techniques, and hand-crafting skills, all of which contribute to the products' resemblance to the original but also to its superiority over the original. For instance, when copying a European designer dress, Daxi (2015) tweeted a video showing how female garment factory workers sewed the buttons on by hand. The interview-style video revealed that workers spent ten minutes sewing each of twelve buttons for each piece. At the end of the video, Daxi declared her diligence in making a proper imitation, which requires considerable time, labor, and skill. The practice of "*Shanzhai*-ing" concentrates a cultural process in which the high-class exclusivity of fashion has been translated into an individual entrepreneurial practice that de-mythicizes its elite nature, since ordinary individuals can access and afford to purchase *Shanzhai* products. Further, unlike fast fashion, most of these *Shanzhai* products are limited in number, usually not exceeding a couple of hundred pieces for an entire run. The relative scarcity reinforces the sense of exclusivity and suggests that it is a privilege to obtain the product.

In *Shanzhai* fashion, the practice of copying and imitation disrupts the established system of fashion and commodities, challenging the myth of authenticity that transnational consumer products tend to possess and with which they enchant consumers. A more detailed account of the politics of copying and creativity in the context of *Shanzhai* fashion culture is offered in Chapter 4. For now, it can be seen that *Shanzhai* production results in opening a plurality of interpretations of luxury products, turning them into something that can more readily be experienced. The various activities associated with *Shanzhai* fashion involve individuals variously as consumers, platform providers, purchasing agents, garment workers, service and logistics staff, and so on. Producing a copy of fashion items involves inviting participation in style selection, cross-border shopping, networking via social media, devoting time and knowledge to blog writing and posting, factory production, shipping, return and exchange, and commenting and critiquing. Sometimes, the end product is essentially the same as the high-end original apart from the removal of logos and trademarks; at other times, it differs considerably in its fabric, design, and style and is more tailored to the needs of individual customers.

Nevertheless, the reworking of exclusivity into something affordable in *Shanzhai* fashion foregrounds the labor process in garment-making. Since the consumer base is potentially massive, designers compete to attract and maintain an audience. As a form of demand-based e-commerce, the *Shanzhai* fashion industry requires designers' dedication to digital fashion work, which gradually turns them into online idols who can monetize their fashion production in both material and immaterial ways. *Shanzhai* designers actively articulate the technological and aesthetic conventions of self-fashioning—shopping, selecting styles, posting outfit photos—and of the *Shanzhai* labor process with respect to designing, appropriating, factory-producing, and retailing clothes.

In contrast with the high-profile life of women designers, other key participants in the *Shanzhai* production chain remain less visible. In the case of Daxi and Yan, for example, as the scale of their shop and revenue grew, the couple invested in their own garment factory in order to integrate further the industrial chain of fashion production. The first time Daxi posted pictures of the factory, she thanked her fanbase-clientele for making it possible to open "Xi's Factory" (Figure 3.6). In stark contrast with the colorful, hard-working, yet fruitful life of Daxi and with her romance with Yan, the images that she posted showed a disturbingly familiar picture of female garment workers keeping their heads down and devoting themselves to the sewing machines, if not to their sweatshop jobs. It seems that the glamorous shots of outfits modeled by Daxi and the exhibitions of buyer's shows in her shop and tags on her Weibo account were built largely on the silent work of these factory workers.

Figure 3.6 Daxi modeling herself in the *Shanzhai* version of a two-piece dress from a high-end Japanese brand (top); workers working in Daxi's garment factory (bottom)

Besides the work of the factory workers in garment production, the visibility of many of these designers' lives and careers is also based on and backed by the invisibility of the salient work done by the salespersons (usually women) and other support staff, such as clerks, customer support, logistics staff, and delivery personnel. Some of the service staff members view these supporting roles as a step to something better; for example, the designer Mey, who was introduced earlier, complained about the difficulty of retaining online customer service and sales staff, many of whom were young migrants from rural areas who came to cities searching for new experiences and excitement and tended to become bored with the tedious work.

By and large, these service staff members aspire to the autonomy and upward mobility that the designers possess. My informant Cho's salesperson, whom I shall refer to as Tang, is a typical example. Tang was hired when Cho's wholesale store was just starting up and not yet reaching the sales volume of other shops that she pointed out to me in terms of customer flow, online orders, and, most importantly, revenue, though it was becoming successful. Cho sold copies but created her own brand, Yi'afan, with which she labeled each of her products. Cho told me that she intentionally gave Tang opportunities to cultivate her own clientele. Tang was around 20 years old, a native of Hunan; witty and ambitious, though she was still learning to operate a fashion shop. Cho said that she would mentor Tang for a couple of years and then turn the shop over to her. Tang worked hard to support the college education of her older sister and younger brother and believed that she would be more financially secure and live a more flexible and better life if she could take over Cho's shop. She was responsible for the wholesale management system and some of the WeChat accounts, ordering products from buyers and garment factories. Tang also constantly updated the new arrivals, discounts, and sales. More often than not, the shop's customers simply browsed through a bewildering array of items on WeChat Moments, asking questions, placing orders, and making payments through the app without ever visiting the physical locations.[18]

It was unclear when or even whether Tang would eventually attain the life for which she yearned, one that embraced uncertainty and self-employment in the search for not only economic rewards but also, increasingly, cultural achievements in terms of taste, lifestyle, and status. The designers' social networks weave a precarious web that situates various participants, from their family members and friends to factory workers and service staff, in the complex and multiple registers of *Shanzhai* fashion. While focusing on the customers' needs and demands, remaining resilient amid the volatility of the fashion industry, mobilizing social networks, and becoming admired and yearned by the other *Shanzhai* participants just discussed, women designers' *Shanzhai* practice remains contingent on the digital platforms that they rely on to circulate their products, create new content, and carve out alternative space for creative business experiments.

THE FOURTH MOMENT: THE FEEDBACK LOOP

Once the fashion imitations are in stock, they are shipped to customers. Finally and equally importantly, *Shanzhai* products are eventually circulated, distributed, consumed, and reproduced. When consumers receive their long-awaited products, they attach various sentiments to them. Again, the product constitutes only part of the mediated experience; consumer-generated visuals and narratives connect those involved in the culture of fashion imitation. Production and consumption intertwine to spread the *Shanzhai* spirit through a multiplicity of physical products and virtual comments, reviews, visuals, videos, narratives, and so on. All of these elements temporarily realize the infinite feedback loop of *Shanzhai* fashion, which is evidence of the practice of the buyer's shows introduced in Chapter 1.

Figure 3.7 shows a consumer's review of the woman designer MarySue's Taobao shop, which included the comment

I looked forward to the flamingo sweater for such a long time and have never regretted buying it. I was amazed by the comfort. A friend got one from another seller for 400 bucks, but the material is not as good as mine. Excellent seller. I am your fan from now on. (November 13, 2016, 12:03)

The buyer's show as part of the customers' feedback in the form of consumer-generated visuals and narratives constitutes a widespread phenomenon. Unlike such similar global e-commerce platforms as Amazon, eBay, and Etsy, which offer parallel review functions, the review of the products on Taobao (which, again, hosts most *Shanzhai* fashion transactions) is only one part of the information loop. A further part consists of thousands of reviews, comments, and feedback on fashion copies

小***香（匿名）

这件火烈鸟期待了好久，收到后果然没让人失望，很惊喜，料子超舒服，朋友别家四百多买来，料子摸起来感觉还是我的舒服，良心卖家，以后就是玛丽苏的粉了

↑ 收起 :: 原图 ○ 向左转 ○ 向右转

2016年11月13日 12:03   颜色分类：粉红色 尺码：S (拍下后15天左右发)   有用 (0)

Figure 3.7 A buyer's review on Taobao. She posted selfies in order to compliment the designer's recreation

through WeChat and Weibo. Through algorithmic mechanisms, such as like, save, share, following, tagging, direct message, cross-post, and re-tweet, and the aesthetic appeals of pictures, emoji, stickers, videos, and live streaming, *Shanzhai* practices and products have proliferated.

Shanzhai fashion, therefore, and especially the entanglement of the practices, experiences, and perceptions of being chic produced and consumed in the process, provides a vantage point for viewing culture as more than "a way of life" (Williams, 1985) and, increasingly, as a way of earning a living (McRobbie, 2002), as "a form of labor—how people actually make a living out of culture" (Ross, 2008, p. 31).The marketing strategy of monetizing customers' labor, or, more accurately, that of the fanbase-clientele, such as the buyer's show, did not originate with the *Shanzhai* fashion business. Naomi Klein (2000), at the beginning of the century, identified a practice that companies such as Nike and Gap had recently developed of paying young people to serve as "cool hunters" and "legal stalkers" by closely observing their friends and peers in order to spot cutting-edge trends. In the context of today's internet culture, these individuals would be superstar "Instagirls"—a term coined by fashion magazine *Vogue* in its September 2015 issue in reference to nine supermodels who each had millions of followers on Instagram (Sharkey, 2015). It is just as common for the fashion powerhouses to pay celebrities to wear their brands and logos. In February 2017, for example, the famed US actor Meryl Streep was accused of participating in a pay-to-wear scheme by Chanel's then creative director Karl Lagerfeld after she opted to wear a gown by another designer to the Academy Awards ceremony (Foley, 2017). Although Streep steadfastly denied the accusation and Lagerfeld later apologized, the scandal suggested that pay-to-wear is not uncommon, though it continues to be viewed negatively.

Taking advantage of this historical and worldwide trend in the monetization of consumer-generated content, *Shanzhai* women designers encourage and motivate their customers to create, post, circulate, and disseminate buyer's shows and other promotional materials for their businesses. It is because a *Shanzhai* shop's customers have the potential to drive further revenue through word-of-mouth channels for popularizing their merchandise (or to diminish revenue through sabotage) that designers eagerly connect with them, often in a humble manner as a friend who shares the secrets of fashion imitation. In order to nurture their fanbases and profit from the cultural input of their clientele, the designers re-tweet or cross-post selfies and other photos of their customers modeling their outfits.

Unsurprisingly, the designers have come up with creative ways of stimulating their customers' interest and eagerness to post reviews with pictures across various digital platforms. Some insert a card in the shipped package with a written message offering a cash rebate for posting a five-star review that includes images of the merchandise. On Taobao, the accumulation of five-star reviews is thought to indicate trustworthiness with regard to the products, shipping, and service. Other designers hold "Best Buyer's Show" competitions on Weibo and WeChat to single out customers who showcase various outfits and receive the most "likes" from onlookers.

The designers themselves often model their production and are featured in their own online shops and social media accounts, making them the embodied agents of a particular kind of "style." The buyer's show, on the other hand, is a participatory experience that seemingly empowers consumers through the use of digital technologies. The images and narratives of consumers are technologically beautified and discursively constructed, creating a living lifecast of the type associated with someone special, a model or star, rather than with an ordinary person. In these respects, a *Shanzhai* product is typically perceived by consumers as an experience, a whole set of feelings, emotions, and messages as well as interactions with other consumers. Production depends on customers taking the initiative and modeling for the designers and serving also as embodied agents and masters of the aesthetic labor involved. In their investigation of the fashion modeling industry, Entwistle and Wissinger (2006) argued that fashion models commodify themselves so as to produce a culturally valued body for the market, investing in styling their bodies, looks, outfits, and attitudes in order to secure work. The circulation of a buyer's show is always a highly mediated encounter that brings together images, videos, and narratives as part of "a trend toward packaging and selling the experience of being 'in fashion' as a commodity in and of itself" (Wissinger, 2009, p. 276).

Shanzhai fashion designers are astute when it comes to exploiting their entrepreneurial skills and cross-posting the buyer's shows. Returning to Cho and her three physical or online shops featuring women's *Shanzhai* fashion, she had two main WeChat accounts, which her sales staff managed, constantly posting the buyer's shows received directly from customers. An example is "Auntie Chanel," a customer of Cho's who was given the nickname by Cho and her sales staff because she often purchased imitation Chanel outfits. Tang showed me some private messages from the WeChat account between herself and Auntie Chanel that concerned the latter's trip to New York, including a picture featuring herself at a subway station leading to Macy's in Herald Square. This satisfied customer declared that she had not found anything to buy at the iconic department store because she already had with her a wardrobe replete with outfits from Cho's shops that fit her elegantly. "Now we are shopping around the outlets, but I'm just looking," Auntie Chanel wrote. "No good bargains here can compete with yours." With her consent, Tang re-tweeted the pictures and compliments on both of their WeChat accounts, after which many prospective customers left comments asking for details about the outfits.

Along with the potential for such marketing successes, these practices carry certain risks. For one thing, the legality of encouraging consumers' input into the *Shanzhai* fashion process through incentives such as cash and money rewards is questionable. For example, when I made a purchase from one designer referred to here as Lyn, she sent a card along with the product explicitly warning her customers not to mention the cash rebate scheme on Taobao's built-in messaging service AliWang-Wang but rather to send a photo of the desired five-star review to her private WeChat account, after which the promised rebate would be deposited in the customer's WeChat Wallet. When I consulted her about this warning, Lyn explained that Alibaba filtered out words and phrases such as "cash rebate" on its various platforms and affiliated applications in order to strengthen its control over financial transactions. This policy could also be considered a means to combat unfair competition and to regulate the market.

Moreover, the fact that positive reviews may be posted alongside ambivalent to negative ones has led to the marketing strategy of "buying" the former for one's own shop and "giving" the latter to one's competitors, thereby exploiting the algorithm used in digital media. A designer may hire the group of ghostwriters known as the Internet Water Army (*shuijun*,水军) to post comments praising her shop and its products as a means to manipulate public opinion and move up the ladder in Taobao's star system. Conversely, a shop's competitors may stoke dissatisfaction with it through resentful reviews, which can be written by the hired Water Army or by the competitor using a ghost account. Indeed, the Taobao platform can be viewed as a battlefield bristling with bayonets, since the review function does not allow sellers to delete comments but only to respond to them. On WeChat and Weibo, sellers have much more autonomy in presenting themselves to their fashion fans, being able to highlight compliments from consumers and remove critical postings. Customers may be aware of both the self-promotion and attempts at sabotage and engage in furious critiques on various online forums and through word-of-mouth communication. During my interviews and field study, almost all of my informants voiced disapproval of such practices as being corrosive to customers' confidence in their shops and the relationship of trust between them and their shops.

The informational and cultural content of *Shanzhai* production, though created collectively and interactively among designers and consumers, is compensated for selectively. As the next chapter makes clear, *Shanzhai* fashion is nurturing a new class division between online fashion stars and fans of *Shanzhai* fashion, since the stars can be easily replaced by new fads and trends. Some high-profile designers have gradually lost their popularity, and some once-popular online shops have shut down because of the fickleness of fashion trends and consumers' shifting tastes or changes in the trajectories of the designers' personal lives. The *Shanzhai* fashion business requires constant investment in the designers' digital labor, for which, as has been seen, the embodied and personified practice of production is as important as the fashion products themselves. Precarity always lingers ghost-like around the reworking of aspirational global fashion trends in terms of local tastes and affordability in the ongoing effort to sustain customers' loyalty. Precarity is also manifested within the actual site of production, in garment factories, after-sale services, and the assistance that designers receive from family and friends who constitute the designers' social network. This social network helps supply the resources to, on the one hand, further their entrepreneurship and life pursuits and, on the other, to be exploited in return for the hope of upward mobility for multiple participants in the business.

DIGITAL LABOR AND SOCIAL FACTORY

Not every woman designer follows exactly each step in the production chain as I explain it here. In order to stand up to fierce competition, designers are eager to release new designs and products at ever greater frequency by shortening the production cycle. Some collapse the first three moments of selecting a style, purchasing the original, and putting it into production and present to their customers only the final product. The fast turnover of products results in, and from, the increasing breadth of choices available to consumers from various designers whose production and collections feature similar styles and apparel. As consumers have become pickier, the designers have been compelled to come up with new ways to maintain their loyalty.

In this chapter, I have analyzed the four essential moments in the *Shanzhai* production chain that has taken shape since China's state-controlled planned economy gave way to the unfettered productivity of manufacturing of the post-reform era. Garment production has come to the party with a creative DIY ethos, broadly available digital technologies, and a spirit of self-reliance and entrepreneurism. Cultural practice as meaning-making "is increasingly disembedded, rapidly disconnected from any notion of vernacular as soon as its potential for commodification is spotted" (McRobbie, 2002, p. 98).

Women have always been at the center of making fashion garments and copies as factory workers and of selling them in their roles as street vendors. However, it was only when men drew attention to the pirated cellphone industry that *Shanzhai* came to be treated as a cultural practice and a locus of creativity. Discussions of these issues have tended to situate male workers, particularly those in the IT sector, at the heart of the young, urban, and creative *Shanzhai* culture. In this hyper-masculine discourse, creative male entrepreneurs with technological know-how are the ideal *Shanzhai* subjects in terms of both value- and culture-making, being contrasted with the implicitly more compliant and less radical figures of women. Compared with those of their male counterparts, women's contributions to the proliferation of *Shanzhai* practice are less visible, adding another layer to their already silent precarity.

This situation has profound resonance with Laura Fantone's (2007) understanding of changes in modern Italy in gender and generational politics. She argued that the shift in living conditions and the blurring of boundaries between work and life that characterizes precariousness have been "largely discussed only at the moment when the western, male worker began feeling the negative effects of the new, postindustrial, flexible job market" (Fantone, 2007, p. 7), despite the fact that women have done the majority of immaterial labor in the domestic space. Women designers' creative fashion work is, from this perspective, emblematic of the immateriality of digital labor, "where labour produces immaterial goods such as a service, a cultural product, knowledge or communication" (Hardt & Negri, 2000, p. 292). Maurizio Lazzarato (1996) defined immaterial labor with reference to both the changes in the industrial and service sectors that have required direct labor to rely increasingly on technological skills and computer systems as well as leisure activities as the formerly bourgeoisie domain has been transformed into labor. These changes are vividly demonstrated in women's fashion work.

In the "informational economy" characterized by the replacement of manufacturing industries with services and information as the main drivers of growth (Hardt, 1999, p. 91), the fashion industry—as an activity and articulation involved in cultural expression, artistic creations, tastes, consumer norms, and opinions formed by trend-setters—has been transformed into "work" in the form of paid creative labor. Simultaneously, the sudden centrality of information to society also has meant that fashion work includes emotional and communicative capacities, in particular with respect to social media networking, and digitized management, even in preference to technological skills. In other words, the meaning of labor has been extended to include normally non-labor space, such as leisure and play, while its nature has come to depend greatly on cybernetics and technological maneuvers. The exponential progression of digital technologies has escalated the deterritorialization and decentralization of labor, so that "the whole society is placed at the disposal of profit" (Negri, 1989, p. 79), thereby reproducing the social world as a factory in the manner described by the *operaismo* theorists.

In *Shanzhai* fashion, digital labor refers to the working processes through which individuals endlessly produce and consume both material and immaterial cultural products in the social factory. On the one hand, women designers make physical products in the form of clothes and accessories; on the other, they regularly update their online shops with trendy products, post photos of themselves wearing clothes that they have made, and share fashion experiences with their customers. What ICTs provide to women designers are the technological breakthroughs that heighten what Gregg (2011) called "work's intimacy" in a telling discussion of office culture in Australia. Gregg's work drew attention to the coerciveness of online technologies in disingenuous representations of the work-life balance and flexible work arrangements. She argued that technologies in practice merely "freed" women from the office so that they could perform traditional childcare and home maintenance in addition to paid work, thereby obscuring the amount of additional work demanded of them.

Through the *Shanzhai* fashion production chain, the meaning associated with any object as a commodity, including that associated with products as fashion authentic or copycats, transcends the object's actuality. The financial value of the commodity lies both within and without the commodity itself as just one of the numerous products of digital labor. During the *Shanzhai* process, the (re)production and consumption of the social relations embedded in women's digital labor is no less than that involved in the production of physical *Shanzhai* products. To these women designers, the form of life is now at the disposal of profit.

4

The *Shanzhai* of *Shanzhai*:
The Politics of Copying and Creativity

In the world of *Shanzhai*, perhaps the sincerest form of flattery is the *Shanzhai* of *Shanzhai*. Daxi, whom I introduced in Chapter 3, is a good example. As she became increasingly popular on social media both as a result of and as reflected in her sales, many other women designers wanted to emulate her success. As shown in Figure 4.1, one of these designers, Lancy, copied Daxi's *Shanzhai* outfit, describing her own work as "Customization of an online celebrity's original design, high-end tailoring, exceptional bargain," that is, a copy of a copy, a clone of Daxi's imitation. Appropriating the latter's marketing language as well, the listing also emphasizes high quality at a lower price—less than half of Daxi's (¥99 and ¥199, respectively).

The investigation of the *Shanzhai* of *Shanzhai* presented here adds further nuance to my account of the politics of copying and creativity in *Shanzhai* fashion culture by demonstrating how this culture is enlivened through the multiplicity of copies. I begin by evaluating the notions of copying and creativity in *Shanzhai* fashion, arguing that *Shanzhai* is an individual yet shared practice of imagining the multiplicities of multiplying cultural expressions while at the same time being conditioned and challenged by its very capacity to copy, appropriate, and create. The dynamic of copying in such a cultural context funnels into the potentiality of the *Shanzhai* of *Shanzhai* as both an alternative to the circulation of global culture and an appropriation of its power. The *Shanzhai* of *Shanzhai* constitutes both a direct threat to women designers' businesses and a creative stimulus for responding to the omnipresent uncertainty and insecurity in the business environment by producing intangible assets, such as social media personas, to prime their customers to be fervent fans loyal to their fashion idols.

I then investigate the formation of a potential new class of fashion icons and fanbase-clienteles, thereby delineating the evolution of the business model of *Shanzhai* fashion amid various challenges and opportunities. I

Figure 4.1   A European designer's maxi (left); Daxi's original *Shanzhai* version (middle); Lancy's *Shanzhai* of *Shanzhai* (right)

focus specifically on the practice of celebrity endorsement as a marketing strategy for brands and its new manifestations in e-commerce, in particular as "celebrity styling" in *Shanzhai* fashion businesses. I found that women designers had seemingly polarized views—being supportive or against—about the practice of copying copies but eventually converged at the point of profitability and capital accumulation. It is their embrace of the celebrity economy that centers *Shanzhai* as a profitable practice and fuels their further transformation of themselves into iconic fashionistas or *wang hong*, groomed to serve as the fulcrum of e-commerce and to monetize their media production.

I next consider the contours of the *wang hong* phenomenon as a contemporary exhibition of the practice of fashion imitation in China that begins with the construction of an appealing persona and a consistent personality designed to sell not just a product but a whole lifestyle package. Although *wang hong* are not necessarily *Shanzhai* designers or vice versa, the overlapping of their marketing strategies, social commerce tactics, and practices nonetheless serve as an index of the tangible performativity of authenticity and sincerity in their production and self-branding. This discussion again leads back to the politics of copying and creativity that have animated *Shanzhai*.

Lastly, I follow multiple versions of a hunter green check-pattern chiffon dress that was originated in an established fashion house, worn by transnational celebrities, reproduced by a Korean popular online brand, and multiplied in *Shanzhai* online shops and in the styling and online listings of *wang hong*. This pattern reveals the becoming of the *Shanzhai* of *Shanzhai* through a Deleuzian theorization of simulacrum. The *Shanzhai* of *Shanzhai* assumes a positivity of its own owing to its power to negate any presumption of "original," "model," or "authenticity" and to rejuvenate copying and creativity through internal differences. *Shanzhai* in this respect operates like a brand, differentiating itself from others by the means of differences, and offering experiences beyond the product through immanent simulation and copying as the very condition of creativity. This, I contend, is the potential that *Shanzhai* holds as a form of culture.

COPYING AND CREATIVITY IN *SHANZHAI*: "EVERYBODY DOES IT"

In my interviews and conversations with women designers, they rarely denied the fact that their *Shanzhai* businesses involve a high degree of imitation. VIAN, for example, said that she had begun cloning branded clothes in 2010 and remained positive about the future of the industry, observing that "Few of us can spend thousands of dollars on a fancy outfit, but the desire for beauty is there." VIAN's business had been thriving in the previous few years in terms of volume, sales, customer loyalty, and steady expansion, and she attributed its success to her early entry into the field and her family's devotion to her operation.

Mey was more explicit about *Shanzhai* practice: "Everybody does it. Those famous brands also copy each other; why can't I?" Mey had at one time been a self-employed fashion buyer connecting garment factories with clothes shops and helping franchise houses to replenish their stock. Soon, however, she realized the hefty profits made by franchise stores and that the managers of these stores sometimes asked for imitations and knockoffs of certain brands, instead of original merchandise directly from fashion powerhouses. As soon as she knew that franchisers at times substituted fakes for the authorized labels, she decided to start her own *Shanzhai* shop, since, again, "everybody does it." She promised her customers that her products were imitations that matched the quality of the originals and delivered on her promise. These views of the practice of copying, insights into consumers' habits, and personal experience may seem random and opportunistic, as women designers conceptualize their success in various ways—some shops grow larger and more profitable; some women emphasize the balance of family and entrepreneurship; some extend the business to other fashion-related fields. Their specific understandings of the idea of "copy" deserve closer analysis.

First of all, "empowerment" is not the proper term to describe the complex dynamics of the *Shanzhai* fashion industry. However, the practice of copying can at least be seen as an alternative to a "normative" and mainstream *Shanzhai* culture. Scholars have already demonstrated that the world of fakes offers the possibility of plural forms of expression (Chang, 2004), and *Shanzhai* fashion can be seen as a repudiation of the democratization discourse of fashion under the reign of global capitalism and also as an effort to seek an alternative cultural intervention within the cultural imagination that emanates, again, from Western imperialist ideology. Creativity in *Shanzhai* is less of an instrument for the globalizing regime of intellectual property and more of a social and interactive practice corresponding to a possibility of cultural production in respect to designers' ability both to copy and produce original work (Pang, 2012). Such an understanding of creativity is not unique to *Shanzhai*, for it applies also to a multiplicity of imitative activities and other concurrent worldwide phenomena of participatory culture, such as remixing audio-visual arts and counterfeit production. All of these practices are examples of a collective form of knowledge production that defies legal or other official claims of "property" that recur in privatizing cultural expressions (Jenkins, 2004; Lessig, 2004; Sundaram, 2010).

Women designers' *Shanzhai* practices highlight the effort to modify, appropriate, and create, which is symptomatic of the power of copying in general. For one thing, industrialized creativity as a function of copying entitles the imitative products of power to partake in the aura of the so-called "authentic" commodity (Benjamin, 1968). For another, the very act of copying again confers the aura of authenticity and exclusivity on the original (Tam, 2014). In many cases, only the legal recognition of official status serves to distinguish the original from the copy (Ho, 2010).

Yang's (2016) illuminating insights into *Shanzhai* culture include the contention that *Shanzhai* is "an object that is formed in transaction—that is, by the act of bringing an object to the online archive of *Shanzhai*" (p. 78). She described this performative character of *Shanzhai* as signifying the needs and desires of working-class consumers while they at the same time actively and creatively appropriate the signs and practice of naming the myriad imitations in *Shanzhai* that, in turn, expand the range of objects and activities that it can signify. Therefore, the *Shanzhai* phenomenon nurtures a sort of collectivity that replenishes the copying practice. The collectivity corresponds to the organic and interactive mode of creativity that is practiced not only through the remaking of fashion products but also through the way of conducting business to seek marketing advantages.

As mentioned, in order to advertise a dress on Weibo, a designer needs to pay a considerable fee to ensure that the message reaches all of her followers. Sina Corporation, which owns Weibo, designs the algorithms that manage user interactions on the site, highlighting some bits of news while excluding others. In other words, these media corporations accumulate wealth from women designers' and *Shanzhai* fashion consumers' participation in as well as from their interactions with these platforms. Furthermore, relatively advanced *Shanzhai* business owners may form a digital cluster using media platforms, intentionally or unintentionally, to guard their business's advantages in terms of online traffic, fanbase-clientele, resources, and networks and to exclude newcomers that are weak and merely seeking support. The Weibo account *Shanzhai Master Groupon* (山主团, SMG thereafter), for example, is both a team working to promote *Shanzhai*-related business opportunities and products and a union of established but not yet top-ranked *Shanzhai* shops. SMG serves as a venue for consumers to view a collection of *Shanzhai* products made by a variety of designers who are experts in specific types of fashion imitation; therefore, many other designers want to avail themselves of SMG's benefits in terms of advertising, promotion, and marketing.

The women designers utilize the algorithms made by the media platform creatively in order to maximize their business outreach. Since SMG pays an enormous amount of fees to Weibo in order to ensure that every tweet reaches every follower, its members can afford to garner attention and attract business in ways that would not be possible on their own. They utilize such algorithmic tools as tagging, cross-posting, commenting, forwarding, and sharing each other's promotional information to enhance their marketing efforts. As Gillespie (2014) argued, algorithms represent the key logic governing the flow of information on social networking sites, providing "a means to know what there is to know and how to know it, to participate in social and political discourse, and to familiarize ourselves with the public in which we participate" (p. 167). By working collectively and being complicit in their own subordination to the media platforms, SMG and its members reshape their practices so as to conform to media corporations' hegemony through algorithmic inclusion and selected presentation and to facilitate their own politics and entrepreneurial activities. The collaboration is simultaneously repressive, on the media corporations' side, and progressive, on the women designers' side.

However, in order to gain the favor of SMG and its members, a shop must already demonstrate considerable productivity, a sustainable business model, increasing revenues, and a loyal fanbase-clientele. Illustrative in this context is the story of a woman designer whom I shall call Josie operating a *Shanzhai* shoe business in Chengdu, Sichuan. Her business was small in scale, usually releasing less than a dozen new products quarterly, with a collection consisting of factory knockoffs and self-modified copies of established brands. During one of our exchanges on WeChat, Josie complained about the fierce competition in the industry of fashion imitation. When I mentioned SMG to her as a potential means to advertise her merchandise, she responded, with a note of sarcasm, "I tried [to contact the owner of the Weibo account] but no one bothers to reply. They only respond to huge stores but not a small one like mine." With the facilitation of Weibo, it is easy to mobilize consumers and gather business resources, for, in order to enforce a kind of protectionism and on the basis of complementary advantages, members of SMG combine assets to enlarge their enterprises. In this respect, the digital space, rather than democratizing the online public sphere of fashion production-consumption, has been colonized by corporate hegemony in terms of both its own logic of capital accumulation and a hierarchy that is intensified and aggravated by well-established *Shanzhai* entrepreneurs.

In many ways, women designers practice *Shanzhai* as both a meaning-making process—producing a form of culture in a de-centered, participatory process—and also as a value-making process—deploying multiple, hierarchical marketing strategies and business tactics to maintain commercial dominance to maximize profits. The designers consider themselves to be engaging in a widespread form of copying, and in doing so they offer a kind of legitimation of *Shanzhai* as a manifestation of individuals' desire to create their own versions of the things that enter their own social lives. The legitimacy of *Shanzhai* is in a paradoxical opposition to the practice of copying. As shown at the beginning of the chapter, the success of some women designers' *Shanzhai* businesses has inspired further copycats who aspire to similar popularity by copying *Shanzhai* items. This is the phenomenon of the *Shanzhai* of *Shanzhai*, in the context of which copies of copies are highly contested among the designers and consumers of the "original" copy.

A case in point is the woman designer Grape-Lee, a maker of high-end shoes. In 2016, she posted a short video on her Weibo account featuring a shoe OEM with which she had collaborated to copy luxury shoe brands such as Jimmy Choo, Roger Vivier, and Manolo Blahnik (Grape-Lee, 2016). Unlike a sweatshop, the factory shown in the video featured clean floors, modern machinery, a combination of skilled workers and white-collar staff, and careful organization, with separate departments for research and design, storage, production, and quality control. Grape-Lee described the facility as one of China's top-tier shoe OEMs and her contract with it as being exclusive so that her shoes would not be copied. Numerous re-tweets of and comments on the post made clear that designers and their customers alike have serious concerns about being "*Shanzhai*-ed" by others. In the case of this particular designer, the concern about protecting the StudioLee brand had both economic and cultural components.

In this context, a pair of copied shoes has the power to deconstruct and to rebuild the aura of uniqueness and exclusiveness, or fetishism, that conflates two distinct perceptions of creativity. The meaning-making process of *Shanzhai* fashion transforms individuals' aesthetic expression into folk knowledge production and value-making in specific market situations, and it fits into the notion of individual creativity as well as the global system of IPR relating to the creative industries (Pang, 2012). On the one hand, women designers copy in order to rearticulate aesthetic expression collectively, thereby generating different meanings and creating, again, fashion folk knowledge, but they condemn those who would do the same to them by copying their creative fashion imitations. On the other hand, their vision of collectivity, unlike that of the ICT workers producing pirated cellphones, explicitly incorporates the individuated notion of property promoted in the modern West and symbolized by the IPR system. These designers embody both a collaborative mode of cultural production and a neoliberal framing of consumer-citizenship; information-rich, they appreciate both global and local brands; they participate in culture as meaningful practices but also pursue profit therefrom.

From this perspective, these *Shanzhai* of *Shanzhai* not only rewrite the story of mimesis but also reflect an autonomous mode of modern technological reproduction (Appadurai, 1986; Pang, 2008) that situates creativity in the precarious elaboration of transnational consumer culture, of the state, of fashion imitations, and of the women designers as individuals. The *Shanzhai* of *Shanzhai* is dynamic and rhizomatic, and it is for this reason that its birth and evolution create opportunities to liberate cultural production—even as the practice acknowledges the precarity within these opportunities with regard to the obligation to churn out ways and means to express creativity and earn profit without any guarantee of success. The widespread nature of this phenomenon in China's post-socialist cultural landscape reflects the cultural dilemma (Yang, 2016) that it faces: the state attempts to establish for itself a brand consistent with the globalized discourse and norms (i.e., IPR as a rational system of creativity) to counter global hegemonic forces of cultural expressions, but it simultaneously encounters resistance (i.e., *Shanzhai*) which appropriates the very global hegemony of transnational mass culture to disseminate its power.

As for the women designers, faced with the threat of the *Shanzhai* of *Shanzhai*, they seek creative ways to discourage copying of their products. The creation of an appealing social media personality, which seems largely responsible for the success of many *Shanzhai* businesses, represents one such response, since it requires, as has been seen, an enormous investment in terms of time and resources and so cannot easily be imitated. The practice and activity of self-fashioning as a unique icon, therefore, has taken on a vital importance in the ever-expanding industry of online celebrity. The creation of fashion icons thus multiplies the capacity of *Shanzhai* and generates the potential for a new form of class division between fashion icons and fans.

A NEW CLASS DIVISION IN THE FORMATION: FASHION ICONS VERSUS FANBASE-CLIENTELE

Celebrity endorsement is a time-honored marketing practice for brands; companies around the world have for decades paid top dollar to popular names in entertainment, sports, fashion, and so on as a means to establish a connection with celebrities with the expectation that their fame and popularity will boost sales (Bradic, 2015). As China emerges as the world's largest economy and home to a significant portion of the world's consumer class, brands around the world have become eager to gain access to this lucrative market. Transnational fashion power-houses have since the beginning of the century been partnering with

Chinese celebrities, including such A-list women actors as Fan Bingbing, Zhang Ziyi, Zhou Xun, Gong Li, and others have been retained by Louis Vuitton, Gucci, Chanel, Omega, Miu Miu, Chopard, and Christian Dior in campaigns designed to create demand by Chinese consumers for global brands. Such campaigns are most successful when the celebrities actually do use and appreciate the fashion products that they promote. The proliferation of social media has accelerated greatly these celebrity branding efforts, with the result that celebrity styling is increasingly driving e-commerce generally and *Shanzhai* businesses specifically.

Celebrity styling refers to the phenomenon in which a product, or, less often, a service, is endorsed by a celebrity with or without an official announcement of a partnership with the corresponding brand. It can be considered a form of social commerce practice, "the employment of social networking technologies and their capacities (such as online posting, linking, sharing, following, and commenting) as tools for buying and selling products online and offline" (Pham, 2015, p. 55; see also Barnes & Lescault, n.d.). Although the practice is by no means a recent innovation, it has spread with the proliferation of digital mobile media and social networking sites such as eBay, Amazon, Facebook, Pinterest, Twitter—a good example being the aforementioned Instagirls fad (Okwodu, 2016)—or, in China, Weibo, WeChat, and Taobao, where the Great Firewall dutifully blocks the majority of foreign social media sites. In addition, the practice of celebrity styling also benefits from platform algorithms created and dominated by media corporations to maximize the visibility and profitability of certain content over others. Celebrity styling establishes a direct link between consumers and beloved fashion brand ambassadors, encouraging an interactive consumption experience through the continuous feeding of consumers' appetites for glimpses of their idols. Celebrities may, for example, post selfies of themselves at home in silky pajamas, captured in a chic look by the paparazzi, or in a television drama wearing a trendy outfit. While a number of issues have arisen with respect to the practice, including the pay-to-wear controversy mentioned in Chapter 3, it is nonetheless not considered to have a significant impact on counterfeiting (Kaur, 2017). When celebrity styling goes viral among the fashion-forward public, *Shanzhai* fashion makers look for ways to monetize it, fueling growth in the copying of celebrity-endorsed items and the sale of imitations.

For example, the Chinese woman actor Yang Mi has been described as "the queen who drives sales" (带货女王), for every item that she owns, wears, or shares becomes highly sought after by her fans and replicated by numerous Taobao sellers. The popularity of the Moschino bear sweater, Miu Miu belted ballerina flats, Coliac loafers, 99Bunny letter socks, and Michael Kors Mercer bags among Chinese fashion consumers around the world is largely attributable to her look, which is sophisticated and relaxed with a hint of vogue. A quick search of "styling as Yang Mi" (杨幂同款) on Taobao generated the maximum allowable pages (100) for a Taobao search, with 44 items per page, but judicious use of filters and refined keywords made clear that the actual available products exceeded the search results—the search engine having been designed so as to optimize the user's experience by limiting the range of available options. According to the trendy fashion commentary WeChat account gogoboi, the "styling as Yang Mi" phrase was searched over 170,000 times in 2015. The large volume of searches and subsequent sales of both name-brand products and counterfeits is indicative of this actor's importance for brands and Taobao sellers (Ye, 2016).

Shanzhai women designers are by no means late to the game of reproducing celebrity stylings, for many of the recommendations that they receive from their fanbase-clientele concern styles and looks endorsed by their favorite celebrities. As proprietors of customer-centered businesses, women designers perform the lion's share of the work necessary to "translate" a celebrity style—sometimes fancy, impractical, luxurious—into an affordable and attractive look for their customers.

As seen in Chapter 3, these designers strive to balance exclusivity and affordability. Their products need to be *au courant* and to tap into their customers' desire for a particular look while retaining the exceptional quality, competitive pricing, and limited quantities that customers expect. Designers train themselves to be effective fashion psychologists when it comes to bridging the gap between the desire for high-end goods endorsed by internet sensations and the goods available in their own collections. They are honored, "proper" intermediaries of fashion trends and tastes, representing a much more accessible kind of fashion icon than the celebrities who engage in comparatively few personal interactions with their fans, let alone form the sort of one-on-one, individualized relationship that *Shanzhai* designers often form with the customers who are enthralled by their lifestyles.

From celebrity styling to *Shanzhai* production, the making of a fashion replica is a process of multiple interpretations and recreations in which information, interactions, competition, discussion, and disputes circulate among fashion powerhouses, celebrities, women designers, *Shanzhai* products, fanbase-clienteles, market niches, and other participants in a spontaneous and temporary manner. Created in the process are the multiple copied versions of a given popular product, myriads of *Shanzhai* of *Shanzhai*. As discussed, *Shanzhai* can hardly be viewed as a liberating force that empowers women designers to participate in a democratized space for cultural expression, but the copying in *Shanzhai* is collectively imagined as a meaningful practice for both the women designers and their customers. It is in this respect that the *Shanzhai* of *Shanzhai* phenomenon conflates the meaning-making and value-making perspectives on and mechanisms of copying and creativity, thereby giving rise to ostensibly oppositional viewpoints between women designers who earnestly support the expansion of *Shanzhai*, on the one hand, and those who concentrate on entrepreneurial breakthroughs geared toward capital accumulation, on the other.

Some women designers are attracted to the spirit of *Shanzhai* because it offers the possibilities of reproducing, recreating, and challenging established cultural production and of opening-up alternative space to express themselves and seek success. VIAN, for example, was committed to the *Shanzhai* fashion industry and certain of its "bright prospects," embodying in this respect the ideology of the free market. She practiced the idea of *Shanzhai* in her business, making replicas of the looks favored by her customers. At one point, another woman designer, Tutu, accused VIAN of plagiarizing her *Shanzhai* products (Figure 4.2).

Conversely, woman designers like Tutu and the aforementioned Grape-Lee have reacted with alarm to the *Shanzhai* of *Shanzhai* phenomenon. Tutu shared her thoughts on the subject in a WeChat post:

Some sellers are unintelligible. … Am I obligated to watermark all my original images to prevent counterfeiting? I have always been against following the masses and producing junk and kitsch that is everywhere on Taobao. I insist on reproducing aesthetic niche designs in small batches. Many of my inspirations, such as collections from Miu [Miu] and O'2nd China Only, were purchased from franchise stores at high cost. I expect my efforts to be rewarded by providing unique collections second to none, whereas some sellers rip them off right away. I am not eager to have my selected styles be so brutally ripped off, but my devotion to produce a proper imitation, my girl's enduring of extreme heat in summer to model the sweater, and all of

This image is Tutu's original photograph of her *Shanzhai* outfit production, with her signature bunny plush alongside.

Figure 4.2   Tutu's WeChat post commenting on a screenshot in which VIAN presented a set of nine images of outfits and solicited consumers' suggestions for products to imitate

our not-yet-reaped fruits are stolen by someone effortlessly! I don't want to see my production become the junk and kitsch on Taobao! I hope my fans have a unique outfit and will not run into someone else on the street and feel embarrassed! How I wish it!

Many other women designers can appreciate Tutu's emotional testimony, which gives voice to their anxiety about and vulnerability to their competitors and their investment in managing their relationships with their customers.

These conflicting views—for and against *Shanzhai* of *Shanzhai*—converge at one point, however, namely, recognition that the guiding principle of the *Shanzhai* industry is the extraction of all potential value from the market so as to maximize profits. The logic that underlies the power of celebrities' endorsements on social media to drive sales and win fans both on- and offline parallels that of the *Shanzhai* of *Shanzhai* phenomenon. A style, once it has been popularized by some designers, becomes enchanting to others eager to copy it and thereby captivate their own fanbase-clienteles.

Women designers and their customers differ among themselves with respect to demographics, economic capacity, and tastes, but their choices regarding what they produce and consume are mainly informed by their social status or class standing. In the fashion world, however, class has been finessed into a loose division between fashion icons and fan-clienteles, a process again facilitated by the performance, narrative, and sensations prevalent on social media. In the context of the transformation of society into a factory without walls, the neoliberal language of entrepreneurship, such as market segmentation, niche creation, and branding strategies, taps into the governmentality of self-discipline. This form of class division increasingly involves subordinating identity to difference, commodity to brand, and the symbolic to the real (Lash & Lury, 2007).

While, as documented in previous chapters, most women designers operate their online shops through Taobao and strive to maintain their popularity through performances and interactions with their fanbase-clientele on social media sites, these platforms are extracting a huge amount of value from them because they contribute to referral traffic on the internet, pay high fees for advertising, and have no real alternatives for setting up their shops. The fragile class boundary between these designers as fashion idols, on the one hand, and *Shanzhai* fans, on the other, and the interconnectivity among actors in the broader *Shanzhai* fashion industry combine to intensify the precariousness embedded in it and to drive the constant and intense pressure to perform digital labor.

To be clear, precarity has a distinct character in the context of China. Keane (2016b), in a critical investigation of China's creative industries, asserted that cultural production remains under the control of the state's ideology but that the freedom to create and produce coexists with the system of regulation and control. Rather than viewing precarity as an entirely negative material constraint on workers and their creativity, Keane suggested that precarious creativity in practice increases the knowledge capital of China's creative industries. The point that regulation is not always effective is well taken, the implication being that the situation is far too complicated to be explained in terms of the inability of the regulatory apparatus to protect the interests of every participant in the market, especially when consumers are complicit in their own paradoxical servitude to the freedom of consumption. Though the state has tightened control of copyrights and coordinated high-profile efforts by e-commerce companies such as Taobao and by fashion houses to combat counterfeiting, consumers are eagerly exercising their freedom to choose, which exceeds the reach of consumer protection laws. Cici, introduced above in the context of her internship with Taobao's Department of Risk Management, insisted based on that experience that counterfeiting was an issue only with name-brand products and that Taobao had significantly improved its system for filtering keywords associated with luxuries and thereby preventing the marketing of products by unauthorized individuals as authentic goods. According to her, *Shanzhai* products, in the form of copies and knockoffs of established brands, are not part of Taobao's effort to regulate and clean up the market environment.

> It is very obvious that they [individuals or firms involved in *Shanzhai* production] are not protected by the laws that protect name-brand products. That is, the shops selling these products are not protected by either laws or Taobao. If you purchase something somewhere that claims to be a Chanel, and if you believe it is, then it is real. However, if you find out that it is a fake, it has nothing to do with us. What you can do is to negotiate with the seller. Taobao is not responsible for such a situation, because when you buy it, you know it is not protected by laws that protect brands. But if the seller sells something with a Chanel logo, it is up to the Chanel company, rather than an individual consumer, to file a lawsuit against the seller. Or, because Taobao has an agreement with Chanel, it will clean up all the counterfeits on its platform. Although Taobao has promised to oppose IPR infringement, it is only responsible for monitoring behaviors and inspecting products sold by authorized franchisers of a particular brand ... it is not a quality control institution.

These arguments in any case favor the market, the idea being that consumers have both the right to be protected and the obligation to be responsible for their own preferences and choices. The fine line between authentic and copy also distinguishes the profitability for industrial practitioners from the proliferation of choices and rights for consumers. Observing celebrity styling and inspired by the prospect of a celebrity economy fueled by social media and e-marketing companies, women designers tend to keep silent about the multiple copies of fashion imitations while cultivating fanbases with the potential to elevate them from fashion icons to the more glamorous rank of *wang hong*, the self-made online celebrities. In the latter case, they are selling, not the product itself, but a whole lifestyle package, an imaginary possible life, to their fanbase-clientele.

A CELEBRITY PHENOMENON:
FASHION ICONS AS *WANG HONG*

Dressed in fashionable clothing, pictured in fancy cafes and restaurants, having traveled to cosmopolitan cities as well as beautiful countryside worldwide, Zhang Dayi has become a leading Chinese internet celebrity and influencer, or *wang hong* (网红) by curating a picture-perfect life on social media. Zhang is of the fashionista-type of *wang hong*, with more than 11 million followers on Weibo, and she has reaped considerable financial rewards by turning this fervent fanbase into loyal customers for her online shop, Jupe Vendue. Zhang used to be a model in *Rayli Fashion and Beauty*, China's most popular fashion magazine. She soon rode the wave of booming e-commerce and online shopping bonanza, earning some 300 million yuan in sales in 2015 from her Taobao shop, largely exceeding that of some Chinese A-list female stars such as Fan Bingbing, who topped the 2015 Forbes' China Celebrity List with a revenue of 128 million yuan in 2014 (Flannery, 2015; Tsoi, 2016).

Zhang has claimed that she not only models her own clothing but is deeply involved in the supply chain and after-sales support, selecting styles and fabric, arranging pattern-cutting and prints, overseeing the production process and copywriting, cultivating fan relationships, building trust, and facilitating customer service. She is practicing what Senft (2013) called micro-celebrity, "the commitment to deploying and maintaining one's online identity as if it were a branded good, with the expectation that others do the same" (p. 346). Emphasizing the performance and activities bound up with one's identity, Senft described the internet as an intricate grid in the context of which individuals interact with media in order to understand themselves. In the marketplace of the internet, micro-celebrities shift among and assume simultaneously various identities as sellers, buyers, and commodified goods that at times cannot be described even by such flexible terms as the portmanteau of "prosumers."

The upsurge in the *wang hong* economy in today's China illustrated in the example of Zhang is also manifest in various online shopping holidays, such as the sales that are offered yearly on November 11. The tradition traces back to November 11, 2009, when Alibaba's B2C (business-to-customer) shopping website Tmall.com debuted a 24-hour online sale offering a wide range of merchandise at a 50 percent discount (Lee & Wang, 2014; Sawhney, 2014). That year, just 27 merchants took part, and the sales value was 50 million yuan. The sale transformed into an annual holiday with Alibaba's 2014 declaration that it was "going global" and its ongoing expansion since to extend its reach across the entire map of e-commerce. A quite conspicuous feature of the 2016 iteration was the marked increase in the participation of online celebrities' stores and their capacity to monetize their online content, and the fervor for e-commerce in China was clear when Alibaba announced 120.7 billion yuan sales for the day (Qiu, 2016). According to the statistics analyzed by ebrun and Nascent (2016), in that year, 32 stores owned by *wang hong* racked up sales of over 10 million yuan, representing a 220 percent increase over 2015; three of these stores reported sales in excess of 100 million yuan.

Shanzhai women designers also rely heavily on these shopping holidays to boost sales and win over customers, which makes fall to winter very busy for them. When I asked two of my informants in Guangzhou if they would be willing to sit for face-to-face conversations and interviews during the winter of 2016, both of them declined, citing the large volumes of sales and short-handed staffing with which they were dealing. Business began to pick up for the women designers whom I observed around October 1, China's National Day, with the season extending from the aforementioned November 11 to December 12, another shopping festival, dating to 2016 and known as the Lovely Festival, and on through Christmas, New Year's Day, the Lunar New Year, Valentine's Day, wrapping up on March 8, International Women's Day. All of these holidays (or pseudo-holidays) take the form of spectacles in China's economic, social, and media landscapes, and *Shanzhai* designers and other Taobao sellers alike seize every opportunity to expand their businesses and profits.

For example, returning to November 11, 2016, the *Shanzhai* store PuffD.J. posted an announcement on its public Weibo account providing its customers with specific guidelines regarding sale items and giveaways, benefiting from discounts, the mechanism of its lottery, and so on. A post on the account on the following day indicated that the online customer service staff had received more than 10,000 inquiries, far exceeding expectations, and announced an encore sale the next day offering the same range of discounts. Though official statistics are not available for the *Shanzhai* fashion stores, their profits seem to be comparable to those of stores associated with online celebrities. The November 11 sale and the revenue that it generates provide a glimpse into the potential of online shopping and e-commerce in China.

To be sure, not every woman designer can be described as *wang hong*, and not every *wang hong* offers *Shanzhai* products. The overlap, however, is considerable; *wang hong* usually promote their products by modeling themselves through live streaming and interactions with their fans, just like many women designers-cum-fashion icons. The garments that *wang hong* sell are for the most part variations on global name-brand clothes and accessories. For example, the design of a popular bag sold by the *wang hong* Shirley was identical, except for the logo, to a mini studded "Drew" bag sold by Chloé that had been popularized by celebrities and pop stars through social media (Figure 4.3).

Wang hong offerings tend to sell well, often in the thousands. They also appear in celebrity stylings, while their release of many *au courant* items has led to numerous complaints from consumers of clashes on the street over supposedly exclusive outfits. In numerous ways, then, the social media-associated production of fashion by *wang hong* represents an alternative to the *Shanzhai* business model; these entrepreneurs not only copy designs and styles but also create appealing and distinctive

Figure 4.3   Shirley's "It Bag" (left) and Chloé's mini studded suede and leather "Drew" bag (right)

personalities that allow them to dominate a large share of the profits to be made in China's fashion industry.

Equally clear is the overlap of *wang hong* with the practice of celebrity endorsement discussed above, with the difference being that celebrities have the capacity to advertise themselves. Rather than such conventional figures as movie stars, singers, and royalty, however, *wang hong* resemble more closely YouTube personalities, vloggers, and Instagirls in terms of their self-presentation online. Further, while *wang hong* have been accused of the same kind of pay-to-wear practices that have been alleged in the context of celebrity endorsements, those women designers who present themselves as *wang hong* are largely immune from the branding of others since they are styling for themselves, managing themselves as the brands under which they sell their copies.

Wang hong are more approachable than celebrities to ordinary people in the age of digital media and online social networking. The de-centered process of cultural production and consumption, accompanied by the widespread usage of social media, invite ordinary people to showcase, interact, create, and deconstruct, to oppose the traditional top-down, hierarchical nature of the high-end fashion couture houses that organize and guard a specific set of tastes and values, though the latter have quickly caught up in the game of social media and real-person advertising. More often than not, the aspirations of the global fashion industry have been revitalized by the glamor and fantasy of flexible and creative work that, again, is propagandized by the state as part of the effort to increase its cultural power, thereby hailing *wang hong* and *Shanzhai* women designers into a makeover project associated with a particular lifestyle.

This lifestyle is woven and interwoven not only from such normative categorizations as age, body type, skin tone, and economic capacity but also from emotions, tastes, and information. The various aspects differentiate one another, representing as they do real-life situations and constructing a familiar feeling to the audience even when they encounter such a lifestyle for the first time. Nonetheless, as Pham (2015) argued, "The real women in fashion media are generally not represented by, for example, disabled women, obese women, or women whose gender presentation is nonnormative" (p. 57). The discursive and embodied construction of *wang hong* in the fashion industry remains, therefore, discouragingly narrow, so that the linguistic component of *wang hong* shrinks into a particular cultural imagination of beauty that prizes slimness, long legs, porcelain skin, a tapered face, large eyes with cosmetic contacts, youth, cuteness, innocence, and, sometimes, a bit of vogue and sexiness (Kane, 2016). This is the imagery of look and style that generates the trends in selfies and beauty standards and is reinforced by the advancement of technological gadgets and apps offering facial and bodily enhancement (Kong, 2016).

It is within the context of the range of various lifestyles that the fanbase-clienteles for various *wang hong* organically and spontaneously become an imagined and bounded audience for their performances. Useful here is Alice Marwick and danah boyd's (2011) conceptualization of celebrity "as an organic and ever-changing performatic practice [sic] … involv[ing] ongoing maintenance of a fan base, performed intimacy, authenticity and access, and construction of a consumable persona" (p. 140)—a notion of celebrity that, increasingly, involves strategic use of social media. Framing celebrity practice as performance in a manner in keeping with Erving Goffman's dramaturgical metaphors, these researchers analyzed tweets from 237 Twitter users to explore how celebrity performance and practice create debatable, authentic, and intimate images that cater to fans' expectations and buttress interactive relationships between celebrities and fans.

The lucrative nature of the *wang hong* market has encouraged numerous media companies to try to act as "*wang hong* incubators" (网红孵化器), that is, as generators of online fame for self-branded online celebrities, especially for those who have established fervent fanbases through their social media activities and celebrity practice. The Hangzhou-based company Ruhnn, for example, successfully launched the online persona of the aforementioned Zhang Dayi.[19] An executive manager in Ruhnn in charge of branding Zhang and her online shop told me that e-commerce was increasingly being driven by personalities rather than brands. To cater to those who dream of *wang hong* status and of monetizing their social media production, Ruhnn provides an enormous and stable supply chain for the development of a uniquely charismatic persona as conveyed through fashion taste and relational interactions with the fanbase-clientele. My informant explained that the majority of Ruhnn's founders had backgrounds in IT; they had developed their own enterprise resource planning (ERP) system to manage the core business activities, such as purchasing materials, managing inventory, logistics, finance, production, and marketing, that rely heavily on databases. ERP nurtures in turn the entire supply chain from materials selection and product delivery to the cultivation of *wang hong* status and building the reputation of an online shop.

As a rapidly expanding sector of the fashion industry and economy, *wang hong* represent, not a random response to the internet as a marketplace and neoliberal governmentality of the branded self, but rather, as Kim (2013) argued with respect to the globalization of K-pop idols, "a systematically planned, monitored, manifestation of 'entrepreneurial self'" (p. 8). Young women are enticed by the lives and glamor of *wang hong* promoted by e-commerce companies, who recruit and sort them to create a market niche. The *wang hong* incubators provide them with resources only if they consider these apprentices could be profitable. My informant in Ruhnn recalled that her company had signed a Korean model two years previously for a trial period of a couple of months as she sought to develop her personal appeal as a cosmopolitan traveler while the company prepared to present her as a commodity across various media platforms. This model, like other would-be *wang hong*, received the backing of a team to work on her online image, personality and behavior, clientele management, and social commerce strategies, again with the support of the products, logistics, finance, and other resources made available by Ruhnn's supply chain. The *wang hong* wannabes certainly need to perform an enormous amount of unpaid digital labor in self-fashioning and self-branding, constantly investing in and reinventing themselves to garner attention and maintain popularity—this work approximates that of women designers' *Shanzhai* production in being simultaneously aspirational and precarious.

These practices nevertheless raise the issue of how *wang hong* maintain the appearance of realness and accessibility to their fans, these characteristics being selling points and part of the enchanting trick of *wang hong* performativity, as many interactions between them and their fans can in practice be performed by their agents, team members, company representatives, or individuals hired for the purpose (Marwick, 2013; Marwick & boyd, 2011). When consumers can easily identify their products as more or less exact copies, in terms of official status, the question arises regarding where the trustworthy, reciprocal relationship between them and their customers actually resides that—they and e-commerce companies claim—remains bound up with their performances, personality, identity, subjectivity, and potentiality, all of which are inherently unstable and lacking in inner coherence. The *wang hong*

Shirley introduced earlier in this chapter, for example, was caught by her fans purchasing from a wholesale market rather than designing and producing her merchandise in her own factory, as she had claimed. At issue was a product marked as a copy and the sincerity and authenticity of the persona performed by Shirley.

There is no magic formula for success among *wang hong*, though workshops, seminars, courses, and training are offered by new media companies to young women with dreams of being the next fashion idol and internet sensation. And, unlike company-backed *wang hong*, some women designers with whom I spoke had turned themselves into *wang hong* and established a persona as a means to accumulate capital, on the one hand, and to fulfill their insatiable desire to be perceived as unique, creative, glamorous, entrepreneurial, and successful in life, on the other. Viewed in this light, *Shanzhai*, both the practice and production, represents only one piece of the *wang hong* persona, which includes various other pieces associated with the unstable, temporary, and constantly changing set of circumstances that characterize the Chinese fashion industry.

The discussion so far has explored how *Shanzhai* both embodies and challenges the existing understanding of copying as making money and making culture. The potential represented by *Shanzhai* to inspire women designers to differentiate themselves in terms of both product offerings and other aspects of the whole lifestyle package is particularly evident in *wang hong* styling and branding. This potential is made available for consumption by the designers' fanbase-clientele, which, in turn, transcends the challenge posed by the *Shanzhai* of *Shanzhai* phenomenon. This potential is a possible threat to the designers in terms of being ripped off, deprived of their "authenticity" and "originality" in creating niches for copies. No matter that the copies are material *Shanzhai* products or immaterial personas as women designers' *wang hong* performativity, they are relatively automatic and unpredictable for their event-like characteristics in a culture of circulation. As will become clear, *Shanzhai* operates like a fluid entity and without a fixed form, allowing various actors to engage and disengage with its processes; it is constantly moving, adding to or subtracting from itself, shifting from one transient shape to another, indeterminate and unpredictable in its multiplicities.

THE *SHANZHAI* OF *SHANZHAI*: SIMULACRUM
AND THE POWER OF THE COPY

Furthermore, while the spread of the *Shanzhai* of *Shanzhai* phenomenon has pushed women designers to shift their online personas and fanbase-clienteles to more of a *wang hong* style, the booming online celebrity economy has intensified the competition among women designers and led to an exponential increase in the production of multiple fashion imitations that display reverence for existing copies. This state of affairs is well illustrated by the story of a hunter green check-pattern chiffon dress released in the summer of 2016 by Zhang Dayi (Figure 4.4, #1). Since the piece sold well, she remade it and released it again in spring 2017, and it is in fact quite common for *Shanzhai* designers to recycle a popular design in several versions (e.g., short- and long-sleeved, mini, midi, and maxi, cotton, polyester, and chiffon, bright red, chrome, and baby blue). In this way, they significantly expand the range of selections for their customers.

Zhang was not the only one to roll out the popular design, however. In the summer of 2015, the woman designer Bunny had already listed this dress for sale in her online shop Sgirl (later renamed SleepyBunny; Figure 4.4, #2). She offered both the hunter green version and a navy blue one with light orange and yellow stripes. In addition, her versions of the dress came with two black ribbons—one silk and the other velvet—for collar decoration. Scrutiny of her Weibo post and her back-and-forth communication with consumers regarding the *Shanzhai* process revealed that

Figure 4.4 (from left to right) 1. Zhang Dayi summer 2016/spring 2017 collections; 2. Sgirl summer 2015 summer collection; 3. Korean brand Milkcocoa spring-summer 2015 collection; 4. Polo by Ralph Lauren autumn/winter 2014 ready-to-wear collection

her dresses were copies of products by the Korean brand Milkcocoa, and, indeed, Bunny contrasted that brand's original long-sleeved version with her short-sleeved version in the product description.

Interestingly, Milkcocoa (Figure 4.4, #3) did offer a short-sleeved version of both colors that Bunny copied in the summer of 2015, but she had purchased for copy the long-sleeved version released earlier in the spring and proceeded to modify into her short-sleeved one. Then, in the fall of 2015, Bunny produced a batch of long-sleeved dresses with the same design in two colors and put them on sale, informing her customers through Weibo that it usually took several months to arrange the production of a new item and that, by the time she had acquired the long-sleeved version from Korea through a purchasing agent, she had already missed the chance to produce it for the spring and ended up delaying the release until the fall. Therefore, she had made some modifications, mainly reducing the length of the sleeves, to create the summer version.

In point of fact, Milkcocoa was not the first to release the dress either; on its website, the Korean brand posted promotional images of Korean stars, including Tiffany Hwang from the band Girls' Generation, who wore the dress for events and commercial images. Owing to this celebrity styling, Milkcocoa quickly put it on the rack, creating two versions and two colors (for both spring and summer) simultaneously. The dress initially appeared, however, in Ralph Lauren's autumn/winter 2014 ready-to-wear show as part of a new line of womenswear with a youthful, urban feel (Figure 4.4, #4). The check-pattern dress traveled, then, from a New York runway show to a Korean celebrity's public display, was modified by a Korean online retailer, then modified further by a Chinese *Shanzhai* designer, and then reproduced, presented, and commodified by a *wang hong*. These multiple versions of the dress demonstrate the power of the copy of a copy.

Milkcocoa's version of the hunter green check-pattern garment was clearly inspired by Ralph Lauren's. Multiple Korean stars' endorsements of it then attracted the attention of the online fashion brand Milkcocoa. Both dresses can be seen as the "object" in Baudrillard's terms (1988), that is, a thing of a sign in a system of signs of status. In such a value system, a hierarchy of objects is established primarily based on the sign-value that individuals buy into when they consume the object. From this perspective, it is possible to differentiate the sign-values of Ralph Lauren's dress as the original and of Milkcocoa's *Shanzhai* as a copy, with the former establishing a totality of meanings over a period of time for consumers to endorse and the latter seeking merely to partake of the aura of the former.

By way of background, the Ralph Lauren corporation was founded in 1967 and launched the Polo brand the following year, specializing in men's sportswear; it then grew into one of the world's most widely recognized consumer brands, with numerous stand-alone shops and department segmentations. Polo's womenswear line, launched in early 2014, inherited the fame and aura of its parent brand. Unlike haute couture, the intention behind this ready-to-wear collection was not to distance producers and consumers; on the contrary, mass consumption has been the engine for production and the motor of capital accumulation for Polo. From Baudrillard's perspective, the sign-value of the brand rests not only on its object-form of clothes, accessories, and other consumer items but also on the customer's authentic experiences in relationship to the brand.

The creation of such an authentic experience is multi-faceted but socially bonded, a sophisticated and oft-used means to bridge the gap between the knowledge of production and that of consumption, to make the consumer consume in a way that is consistent with how these products and knowledge were produced and how they were intended to be consumed (and of course, consumers play a role in the construction of the aforementioned aura). Through the process, media, in a variety of forms, largely present in either a positive or negative light the spread of brand images and signs. One fashion observer commented on the Polo womenswear line at the 2014 Ralph Lauren autumn/winter show in New York,

> It was broken up into different sartorial stages of a young woman's life. There she was in her mignon schoolgirl attire (with a matched slanted beret). Out on the city street in her day glow puffa jacket and beenie, trying out the whole Native American look with fringe bags, Navaho blanket coats and arts and crafts carpet motif dresses. And finally a bit of rebellious cool via "Nirvana" lumberjack plaid tops and vests and a patch covered leather biker jacket to top it all off. A look for an everyday occasion. (Michault, 2014)

Commentaries and critical reception of the brand as such are countless since the establishment of the brand itself. Apparently, Ralph Lauren's dress in the show possessed greater sign-value compared to either Milk-cocoa's or Bunny's reproduction in terms of what their customers sought after and yearned for. Thus, Milkcocoa sought by reproducing the dress, not to dispel the mystery of Ralph Lauren's ostensible originality, but rather to partake in its sign-value. However, Bunny's reproduction of Milkcocoa's imitation complicates the notion of the copy: her Taobao product description and the multiple conversations between her and her customers through social media make clear that her dress was, again, modeled on Milkcocoa's rather than on Ralph Lauren's.

This sequence of events can be seen as an effective simulation from a typical Baudrillardian reading, a view that opposes the concepts of authenticity and simulacrum in the context of postmodern consumer society. Milkcocoa's counterfeiting dress successfully destructed and replaced an original reality, that is, Ralph Lauren's dress, in a process of simulation that changes the referential system of the signs through which value is both negated and rebuilt (Baudrillard, 1988). The great reliance on images that are constructed by multiple forces that is characteristic of postmodern society diminishes individuals' contact with the reality, the authentic, and the so-called real world, which are supposed to precede the images. Reality itself has begun to simulate the images, which now precede and determine the real. Under these circumstances, the world of economics is no longer separate from that of ideology, culture, and images owing to the mediation of the media, so that history "is our lost referential, that is to say our myth" (Baudrillard, 1994, p. 46).

Still more insight into the *Shanzhai* of *Shanzhai* phenomenon can be gained by viewing it from another perspective, Gilles Deleuze's (1994) theorization of simulacrum, which I use here to define the *Shanzhai* of *Shanzhai*, the multiplicity of fashion imitations in Shanzhai practices. In *Difference and Repetition* (1994), Deleuze defined simulacra as "those systems in which different relates to different by means of difference itself. What is essential is that we find in these systems no *prior identity*, no *internal resemblance*" (p. 299, emphases in original). Deleueze's approach is consistent with that of Baudrillard in that the simulacrum deconstructs the world of reality by depriving it of its referential system. But whereas Baudrillard saw nostalgia for a lost original, "the Real," Deleuze argued that the world is only made real through the simula-crum, leaving the original, the model, and with it so-called Reality, no longer relevant, thereby subverting a Platonic worldview.

In his reading of Nietzsche's effort to bring about the "overthrow of Platonism," Deleuze (1983) described Plato's philosophical motive as seeking to "distinguish essence from appearance, the intelligible from the sensible, the Idea from the image, the original from the copy, the model from the simulacrum" (p. 47) by dividing "the domain of the image-idols in two: on the one hand the *iconic copies* (likenesses), on the other the *phantasmatic simulacra* (semblances)" (pp. 47–8, emphases in original). According to Deleuze, the Platonic philosophical view of the world is about sorting out iconic copies that best represent the original, the model, the Idea in their external appearance and internal similarities, a model of the world that is well founded on the same, the likeness, and the similarity. From this perspective, the proper evaluation of a copy is founded on how much differential quality it possesses to represent the pre-existent model in both appearance and internal likeness. A simula-crum—being in this sense a copy of a copy—is degraded because it only approximates the external appearance of a model and fails to retain the internal similarities that identify the model or original. Hence, Deleuze argued that the Platonic model is Sameness and the Platonic copy is the Like. The existence of the simulacrum only decreases a copy's represen-tational power of the original, therefore challenging the Platonic idea that the world is founded on sameness, likeness, and similarity (Deleuze, 1983, p. 50). Deleuze called for an upside-down approach to understand a world of simulacrum in which similarity exists only as a product of pure differences. "The simulacrum is not degraded copy, rather it contains a positive power which negates *both original and copy, both model and reproduction*" (Deleuze, 1983, p. 53, emphasis in original).

From a Deleuzian perspective, then, Milkcocoa's dress is not merely a beautiful rip-off of Ralph Lauren's sign-value and aura. To begin with, if the ostensible authenticity of a garment in theoretical and method-ological terms resides in its "original" design, then embodied in Ralph Lauren's runway dress is profound reverence for the time-honored check and tartan pattern in fashion—the originality of which pattern has been lost through repeated modification and appropriation. Further, Milkcocoa has long been defined by its mix-and-match of rich color, flowery fabrics, plaid knits, and simple or elaborate compositions. Milk-cocoa's imitation of the dress is consistent with and lends sophistication to its brand image of delicacy, youth, sweetness, and naive optimism. In addition, the Korean pop star's endorsements kindled the vision of a celebrity lifestyle that is associated with pretty dresses in general as much as it is with the Ralph Lauren brand. In other words, the sign-value of the brand is no more significant than that of the product itself. The value in Milkcocoa's dress, no longer residing in signs as a communication of meaning, is actualized through the learning of affects, perceptions, and experiences to which consumers can be subject.

The actualization of virtual value in images as signs in this manner, or, to borrow Lash and Lury's (2007) theorization, the "thingification" of images, is taken further in the *Shanzhai* of *Shanzhai* that is Bunny's reproduction of Milkcocoa's copy of Ralph Lauren's dress. Lash and Lury (2007), inspired by the Deleuzian notion of internal difference as constitutive, argued that today's global culture industry works through brands in a logic of difference. Because brands are relational, they have history and memories, and the products in a brand actualize it, relying for their operation less on representation and interpretations of meaning than on a way of doing, making a brand a matter of use and exchange rather than merely the sum of its symbolic values. What is at stake in theoretical and methodological terms is that images as media become things, and in so doing they move away from sign status toward the real. What Baudrillard conceived as hyperreality—a system of signs in which referentials are liquidated that maintain an ideological grip on postmodern consumer society—is, then, "thingified," so that the images and signs are operational and capable of entering into the circulation of culture. The simulacrum internalizes the difference between any claims of original and copy and renders them indiscernible, leaving the fundamental internal disparity, without prior identity and representation, as the only way to communicate and measure our sense of sameness.

Bunny's reproduction of the check-pattern dress based on Milkcocoa's is, I suggest, a testimony to the power of the simulacrum, which, in the case of Milkcocoa's dress, is so perfect that it is no longer clear where or what the original is. Bunny's expertise is in recreating Milkcocoa's collections—that is, in imitating in order to construct her own brand as one that is similar to Milkcocoa's but has a more narrowly defined niche including teens, college students, and office workers in their mid-20s—so she creatively modified the design for her own purpose and reduced the production cost and the price for her well-developed fanbase-clientele. There are also numerous copies that, unlike Bunny's *Shanzhai* version of Milkcocoa's copy, provide no clear indication of their origins on Taobao (a quick search by uploading the image generates a plethora of results). While the dress is still being assessed by consumers in terms of its symbolic meaning, its ability to signify a certain fashion status, and its representation of a particular identity are merely the external effects of the internal differential machinery of the simulacrum. The copy of the copy is, then, an image without resemblance to a prior original; rather, it possesses affective and immanent differences as the very condition of thinking of similitude and similarity. More often than not, these multiple copies of the copy form an actualized singularity that pivots around the logic of DIY and the *Shanzhai* spirit in an operational and playful but immanent and immediate way without the possibility of hierarchy. The pleasure in *Shanzhai* relates more to the doability of the object and less to the extensive substance of a particular product.

The multiplicity of *Shanzhai* can be seen materialized vividly in another simulacrum in the form of a dress offered by the *wang hong* Zhang Dayi that resembled those of Ralph Lauren, Milkcocoa, and Bunny all at once in a superimposition of designs behind which stand no originals. The only illusion is that, as Deleuze will agree, every act of ripping off a design rests on the presumption of a prior model. The power of the *Shanzhai* of *Shanzhai* assumes a positivity of its own when the world is experienced as it is produced through simulacrum alone. *Wang hong*, like *Shanzhai*, operate like a brand, differentiating themselves by providing relational experiences with their fanbase-clientele that create differences. The product that a customer receives is an object, but the experience is non-objectual; it is a feeling, an emotion, an attachment, or an affect. Products can be diversified without altering the experience; this is the intensive quality of the brand. Yet the same experience is experienced and actualized only through internal differences with respect to interactions, communication, and meaning-making in the relationships between consumers and *wang hong*, consumers and products, *wang hong* and products, and so forth, without prior similarity and identity as a starting point from which to branch out.

The *Shanzhai* of *Shanzhai* phenomenon demonstrates the object-event and conviviality of copying and creativity. It is precisely the eventful quality of *Shanzhai* that proclaims its organic, connective, and emergent becoming. The singularity, difference, and disjuncture of *Shanzhai*, emerging especially in the thing itself, are conditioned by its ability to be copied, multiplied, and heterogenized. *Shanzhai* functions as intensities, instead of extensities. It is Gilles Deleuze and Félix Guatarri's (1987) rhizome, a model of culture in which any point can and must be connected to another, with qualitative differences as multiplicity;

the rhizome can be broken up at any point and start over again as an always-open map to be entered at any point.

Both copying and creativity are enlivened through immanent actions that create difference by means of difference, as in the *Shanzhai* industry, where a fashion imitation is a singularity different from another through multiplicity. In other words, recognition of the irrelevance of the originality/authenticity dichotomy, combined with a notion of sameness founded purely on differences, can serve as an opening to a becoming with the potential to overturn a privileged position of cultural expression. Infinite negotiation and differentiation can be made between abundance and scarcity, in-between-ness and stability, or indeterminacy and predictability. *Shanzhai* is the very condition of creativity, a context in which the copy of the copy lives a life in itself and for itself.

CONCLUSION

Fan Yang (2014a), in analyzing the 2011 "fake Apple Store" controversy in Kunming, Yunnan, that attracted the attention of both domestic and international news media, problematized the power relations and subject positions with respect to the copy and Apple's hegemony. For her, Apple is a brand in what Lash and Lury (2007) called, building on Adorno and Horkheimer's (1997) notion of the culture industry, the global culture industry. As she put it:

> Apple products exemplify "the thingification of culture" characteristic of the global culture industry, even appearing to have perfected its "extension of intensity," the "outering" of the human sensorium, in Marshall McLuhan's sense of the term … and these goods have to attach themselves to "openings, competitions, launches, visits and performances" to present the brand name through object-events. (pp. 78–9)

This chapter showcases an articulation of *Shanzhai* parallel to those of global brands like Apple, a spectacle of "Chinese fakery" that resulted from Chinese officials' efforts to conjure a "Chinese reality" based on real social conditions (Yang, 2014a, pp. 81–7). Yang (2016) later suggested that *Shanzhai* as a brand for "the people" is later expropriated by the nation-state. I agree with Yang in seeing *Shanzhai* fashion as a brand that provides qualitative differences in its ability to be copied, multiplied, and heterogenized. Yet, at the same time, I part company with her argument that refers to *Shanzhai* as both a culture for the people and a nation-specific phenomenon corresponding to the global capitalist hegemony. In my reading, *Shanzhai* fashion explicates a cultural domain of imitation that is relatively autonomous and organic. Although bound up with heterogeneous temporalities within China's post-socialist environment, *Shanzhai* is nonetheless evolving in unexpected ways so as to elude the ideological grip of discourse about IPR, national innovative capacity, and political reading of mimesis. The events of *Shanzhai*, in its performance of the *Shanzhai* of *Shanzhai*, *wang hong*'s *Shanzhai*, to name but a few, extend media into things that can do with and play with, as the actualization of *Shanzhai* is not only part of people's body decoration but also their sensorial extension to feel the vibe as well as rejoice in it. At the same time, the things materialized and actualized from *Shanzhai* are touted as if they are able to offer idiosyncratic experiences of singularity in their heterogeneous multiplicity. In these senses, *Shanzhai* is both the real and the virtual (Lash & Lury, 2007).

I have argued in this chapter that if a culture is always open and heterogeneous, if it can be entered at any point and can start over when attacked, the individuals who form one part of that culture are thereby guaranteed the possibility of an exit from it or an alternative to it by advancing their digital labor, their production, and their contingency in the temporary conjuncture of space, time, and power. I have also pointed to the possibility within the precarious creativity that characterizes women's digital labor.

Ernesto Laclau and Chantal Mouffe (2001), in their critique of pluralist democracy and advocacy of radical democratic politics, astutely observed that the new political frontier requires acceptance of the ineradicability of antagonism. This acceptance recognized the conceptual impossibility of a non-exclusive public sphere for rational argument and foreclosed any possibility of a final reconciliation of an all-inclusive "we" to reach rational consensus. Laclau and Mouffe urged acknowledging "that any form of consensus is the result of a hegemonic articulation, and that it always has an 'outside' that impedes its full realization" (p. xviii). From this perspective, conflicts and discrepancies, rather than disturbing or hindering progress, are the very engine of a possible democratic project that opens from within and in the context of which the hegemonic struggle can and should be recognized, grasped, and combatted.

Following their lead, I propose here that precarious creativity be viewed, not as something that determines *Shanzhai* women designers' futures or undermines their wholesomeness or threatens the prosperity of the fashion industry, but as the very condition of possibility. Women's precarious creativity is their means of living and fighting against what limits them fully blooming. It is enlivened through practice and at the same time fuels the passion of practice.

5
Shanzhai Dreams and the Chinese Dream

Early in the Chinese film *MBA Partners* (梦想合伙人, 2016; thereafter *MBAP*), the main character, a young woman from a small town in southern China named Lu, is arrested in New York City in connection with her business selling counterfeit bags, which she is doing to support herself while studying English; earlier, her boyfriend leaves her because of his unhappiness with this line of work. While temporarily behind bars, she thinks to herself, "My American dream has floundered." Eventually returning to China, she and two other women whom she meets at business school start their own e-commerce firm selling women's luxuries, and, when it proves successful, another character congratulates Lu by saying, "Finally, you have realized your dream." Notably, the literal translation of the film's Chinese title is *Dream Partners*.

In recent years, "dream" has become a popular buzzword in China, featuring in the mass media and in numerous state-sponsored campaigns, particularly on propaganda posters that have been ubiquitous throughout the country. Government-run "Chinese Dream" websites have proliferated on the internet, and conferences, speeches, photography competitions, talk shows, popular songs, and even dances devoted to the topic have been disseminated through various state institutions and organizations through print, television, and digital media, even in foreign countries where the state-sponsored Confucius Institute has a presence (China.org.cn, 2013; CNTV, n.d.; Guo & Li, 2017; Liu & Zeng, 2015). The Dream discourse has become a lexicon of first, government-driven projects and second, miscellaneous folk activities designed to guide the search for prosperity and confidence.

MBAP was produced in a time of "dreaming." Apparently conceived as a feminine version of the 2013 film *American Dreams in China* (中国合伙人; hereafter *ADIC*), it directly evokes *ADIC* in featuring a trio of leads and the message that the Chinese Dream is superior to the "American Dream." Nonetheless, the actualization of dreams in *MBAP* has met with a cold reception from critics. In any case, the film provides an informative glimpse into the complex relationship among the state's ideology, digital commerce, the fashion business, and women's work in the broader context of the Chinese Dream.

As discussed in Chapter 1, President Xi in late 2012 articulated a vision of what he called the Chinese Dream as part of the ideology of national rejuvenation as the state sought to establish China's place as a "great cultural power" through the cultivation of creativity and innovation (Keane, 2016a, p. 40). This aspect of the Dream discourse has coincided with a heated discussion within China's business and IT sectors of the value of the grassroots creativity manifest in *Shanzhai* culture for inspiring innovation (Tse et al., 2009). That is, while the Chinese Dream is a top-down project designed to establish structural and systematic channels for innovation, it has also sought to co-opt *Shanzhai* culture, especially in the IT sector, in order to harness the bottom-up flow of creativity and foster innovation nationwide. The rise of such domestic IT companies as Xiaomi is one example of the state's effort to fabricate *Shanzhai* as a counterfeit subaltern culture that recalibrates nationalism under the name of innovative capacity (Keane & Zhao, 2012). Viewed this way, the Chinese Dream is an ideological construct that, among other things, allows the state to rework *Shanzhai* so that it furthers the goal of increasing China's global cultural power by leveraging its citizens' creativity and capacity for innovation.

In this chapter, I document the collision of women designers' *Shanzhai* dreams with the state's Dream. Women designers' multiple dreams, like their practices of *Shanzhai* of *Shanzhai* discussed in the previous chapter, began to take shape long before Xi articulated the grand narrative of the Chinese Dream. The Dream discourse has captivated these women by consolidating their imitative business tactics into an aspirational entrepreneurial lexicon and a set of practices. The Dream discourse appropriates the *Shanzhai* spirit of creativity and mobilizes the human capitals of the grassroots, a process that seemingly opens a space for women designers to dream a Chinese Dream of their own and seek success promised in post-socialist China. However, the uncertain legal status of their mode of fashion production leads to the social and ideological tendency to deny the designers recognition for their labor, creative and otherwise. Notwithstanding they are called to become Chinese Dreamers to fulfill desires and aspirations, it is exactly such aspirations of entrepreneurship, flexibility, creative autonomy, and the promise of prosperity that marks the impossibility of them ever actualizing a Chinese Dream. Instead, however, they are actively seeking out their own spaces in which to live their own *Shanzhai* dreams. These dreams originate and are practiced in the precarious work that women designers conduct in the social factory, but they are not based on an appeal to patriotic duty. Various in their articulations and imaginations, these dreams are becoming an emergent common, a *Shanzhai* common to which all of these women are aspiring. Their experiences mirror those of other cultural workers in China, making them representative of a much larger terrain of precarious labor.

The official Chinese Dream discourse creates a post-socialist covenant between individual citizens and the nation-state to collaborate in conceptualizing China's future. The Dream encourages personal pursuits while taking away the safety net that used to be provided by the state to its citizens. The Dream discourse attempts to synthesize top-down (nation-branding) and bottom-up (grassroots creativity) processes, while people are privatized and left precarious. Nevertheless, such precarity, or precarious creativity, is packaged in the context of the cultural creative industry as another neoliberal facet of the Chinese Dream. It is in this respect that the film *MBAP*, as a form of popular culture, is particularly instructive. Specifically, the film focuses on the allure of the Chinese Dream discourse while attempting to give due attention to women's work and lives, especially those involved in the creative industries who are looked to as a source of the state's cultural power. My analysis of *MBAP* sheds light on the manner in which the aspirational Chinese Dream discourse hails women into the position of nationalistic subjects by tapping into a postfeminist sensibility centered on the glamor and fantasy of a global fashion industry that feminizes the workplace and daily life.

I conclude this chapter with a reading of the politics of the Chinese Dream as a neoliberal promise for a post-socialist future in which, for women like those described in this book, the experiences of precarity and the very act of copying reveal the simultaneous possibility and impossibility of the Chinese Dream.

DREAMING MULTIPLE DREAMS IN *SHANZHAI*

I asked each of my informants about their dreams, though they themselves rarely raised the subject. In Chinese, the concept can be translated as *mengxiang* (梦想), "something to be dreamed of," or *lixiang* (理想), "an ideal or goal to be actively pursued." But it is important not to become preoccupied with terminology here. When they were not forthcoming about their dreams, I asked the informants about their plans and goals for their lives or businesses, about where and who they expected to be in five or ten years. In the course of these discussions, the women elaborated multiple visions of possible futures.

Each of them spoke of the ability and autonomy to do something that they loved as a key consideration when they thought of their fashion careers and *Shanzhai* businesses. For some, *Shanzhai* seemed a natural path to follow; as mentioned in previous chapters, a number of the designers had family or social connections to garment factories, the fashion industry, or import/export businesses that kindled their interest and facilitated the establishment of their shops. Other designers started their *Shanzhai* businesses on their own, without the support of family and with scarce financial resources, being driven by the entrepreneurial spirit.

Illustrative in this context is the account told to me by Mey, the former fashion buyer, of turning down a stable government job to start her fashion business:

After graduation from university, I didn't want a routine job, spending every day in the same way and knowing that what I do in my 40s will be identical to what I do in my 20s. So I just started my own business. I have liked fashion since I was young and wanted to major in fashion design multiple times in my life, but my parents never agreed because they thought I was too good a student to waste my talent on fashion. … I went to a military university to study radar communication and did well in my major. But I started to prepare [for my fashion business] when I had an internship as an undergraduate, ignoring my parents' wishes. I was supposed to work in institutions that build spacecraft like Shenzhou 7 and 8. But those places are no different from military universities, like prisons. I didn't like it. There is one [state institute] on the shore near my hometown, with a good environment, and [it offered me a] handsome salary. [I just couldn't imagine spending] every day only monitoring satellites and welding circuit boards. I feel that there is more to living than breathing. We need to have a goal to pursue … so that we can say we have not lived in vain.

Mey and her parents clearly had very different views with regard to the significance of the talent that she displayed in school, her individual interests and passions, and how these factors should figure in her choice of career and purpose in life. For Mey's parents, personal choice was less important than a talent that could lead to a secure job; considerations of one's purpose in life was of much less importance to them than the stable, secure, and prosperous existence guaranteed by Mey's good grades and which could be found by working in the iron rice bowl.

For Mey herself, the purpose of life was not a given but something to be explored, sought after, and realized on one's own, and she followed her passion instead of following the life promised to her if she were to pursue a traditional career. Born in the 1980s, Mey belonged to the generation that reaped the fruits of China's economic leap and opening-up. The difference between her and her parents' understanding of life was typical of her peers and other women designers. In her case, the state's promised reward for employment in a military institution was economic security and social status, but that promise seemed hollow and the way of life dull. She asserted her individuality when she followed her heart for a life devoted to fashion rather than submitting to an arranged marriage with the iron rice bowl.

Accounts like these document the Dream discourse's distinct generational aspect as a result of social transformation and the shift in ethos from socialist to post-socialist China. Thus, "I want to do something," "passion for fashion," "get busy," "do something I love," "not ambitious but happy with life," and "bittersweet business" were among the expressions that I heard during my interviews with the designers profiled in this book. Like Mey, many eschewed the iron rice bowl jobs to which the educational system entitled them and that their families arranged for them, jobs that were recognized in social discourse and the hierarchy of occupations. Instead, they actively searched for their purpose in life in their own ways, which, though distinct, fell under the umbrella of *Shanzhai*, desiring alternative, creative approaches to achieving their business goals and envisioning the multiplicity of possible futures in work and life.

As discussed earlier, one important factor in making women designers' *Shanzhai* dreams possible is the loose copyright regime in China that gives them license to copy fashion products to suit their customers' wishes. *Shanzhai* exists in a legal gray area, and this path to empowerment can be risky if designers attach the original brand names to their copies as a selling point, leaving them open to litigation from legal teams retained to defend the trademarks held by transnational fashion powerhouses. In addition, competition is fierce; while a given designer usually produces only a limited run of a copied piece, there is a constant stream of new designers looking to carve out niches for themselves in the *Shanzhai* industry. As a consequence, the market is being flooded with multiple copies of the same designs, prices are falling, and the quest for attention, loyalty, and profit is becoming more arduous.

These challenges have forced women designers to experiment with their business strategies, remaining open to new ideas about marketing, attracting consumers, and inviting them to participate in the *Shanzhai* process. For example, as mentioned earlier, some designers have adapted the time-honored practice of using a down payment to secure a purchase and have begun asking customers for a pre-payment of 10 to 20 percent of the final price when they start to produce a new item. The pre-payment—usually solicited after a sample is available for comparison with the original so that customers know what they are buying—serves as an estimate of demand and also to lock in customers without forcing them to pay the full price immediately.

A further example is that of the designer Bunny using the then new Taobao crowdfunding platform in early 2015 to raise funds for her imitation of a red wool-blend overcoat, again by her favored Korean brand Milkcocoa. Crowdfunding involves raising money for a project from a large pool of contributors; being a non-traditional means of financing, it often takes place on internet-mediated platforms. The practice in China dates back to an effort by Chinese celebrities in December 2013 to fund some pet projects; Taobao's crowdfunding platform was officially launched a few months later, in March 2014. To the best of my knowledge, Bunny's was among the first *Shanzhai* fashion crowdfunding projects initiated by a woman designer. Her copied coat, in a boyfriend style, was priced at ¥220; the funding target was the amount that Bunny estimated would be necessary to produce 200 pieces in two weeks. Her initiative was a success, and the final products were sent to consumers before the Lunar New Year holiday. However, Bunny had not tried crowdfunding again at the time of my conversations with her, and only rarely have other women designers made the effort. Part of the problem seems to be that the turnaround time for crowdfunding is too long for the dynamic and highly competitive world of *Shanzhai* fashion.

Alternatively, or in addition, financing a copycat project in this way may leave a designer particularly exposed to legal efforts to crack down on counterfeits and imitations on e-commerce platforms. Though Taobao serves as the hub for the women designers' shops and for digital transactions of orders, payments, and cash flows, it is quite sensitive to social pressure and government regulation when it comes to protecting IPR and policing copyright infringements. In comparison, regulation is less rigorous on Weibo and WeChat, the other sites where women designers simultaneously conduct their business. An example of the kind of trouble that designers can run into with Taobao was described by the woman designer Shiny in a post on her Weibo Moment about her attempt to market a product called a Gigi hoodie:[20]

A sad story: The Gigi hoodie was declared a copyright infringement. The shop has been shut down by Taobao. We are making an appeal now. If they sustain the original ruling, we have to open a new shop. The logistics department is working, and we can still ship out the packages. For the time being, we will turn to the new shop for orders and transactions. You do not have to pay the down payment for the Gigi hoodie again if you have already done so in the old shop; just take a snapshot of the deposit transaction and send it to our customer service staff. (November 23, 2016, 12:47)

Other women designers have had similar experiences; one, Suansuan, was cited for copyright infringement and as a result her shop was shut down a couple of times. Like Shiny, when their shops are shut down for this reason, the designers usually notify their fanbase-clientele immediately through Weibo and WeChat and direct them to place orders and to complete existing transactions at a new shop bearing the same or similar name.

Again, Weibo and WeChat offer much greater freedom of expression than Taobao, particularly for *Shanzhai* fashion businesses. However, these social media sites are used less often for cash transactions and direct commercial activities and more to solicit *Shanzhai* styles, document the copying process, and share promotional images from the brands being copied. Together with their fanbase-clientele, women designers build up their own fashion communities on social media sites, where they are free to discuss their hobbies and common interests—provided that they avoid politically sensitive content and blacklisted keywords.

There is, however, a hierarchical structure to business conducted through social media. Weibo, for example, positions itself as a platform devoted to relationships, sharing, and information exchange through its users' contributions of tweets, which are held to a certain word limit and a maximum number of pictures (nine) per post; the site also automatically screens out any commercial links embedded in a post.[21] Evasion of this limitation involves converting and shortening the long Taobao URLs using a third-party application in order to conceal its Taobao identification codes. Similarly, on WeChat, in order to share a link directing customers to a Taobao shop where a product can be purchased, a seller must convert the link into a format such as a barcode, again using a third-party application, in order to evade the filters, since the mobile payment systems of WeChat and Taobao are in competition.

It is in these respects that, as mentioned in previous chapters, the various media platforms represent a kind of double-edged sword for women designers. The women are themselves heavy media users and, along with their businesses, rely on these digital technologies, which, for their part, have made them complicit in their own subordination to corporate hegemony. At the same time, *Shanzhai* designers are constantly searching for alternative spaces and practices so as to make the platforms complicit in their individual politics. In addition, the policies and management of the various media platform providers and e-commerce companies reflect the priorities of the state regulatory apparatus and the dominant social discourse regarding *Shanzhai* and the cultural industry in general. The promise and precarity alike of *Shanzhai* are fully manifest in women designers' e-commerce entrepreneurship and their business of fashion imitation.

Precarity, then, is also inherent in women designers' activities as a collective and individualized life situation. It is precisely through their aspirational *Shanzhai* businesses that these women designers are exposed to great uncertainty and challenges within the gray market of fashion copying. The *Shanzhai* space that these designers inhabit is a liminal one where they are dreaming their own dreams and striving hard to fulfill them while at the same time their lives hang by a tenuous thread. In the precarious creativity that characterizes *Shanzhai* fashion, the power of copying is in tension with the power of policing. The gray market of *Shanzhai* is precarious by nature, sustaining an alternative micro-economy while being an anomaly in a field where the norm is large-scale production dependent on the neoliberal apparatus of global capitalism. However, the *Shanzhai* designers are not competing with corporate giants in the mass production of fashion commodities; rather, they embrace neoliberal entrepreneurism in the precarious space between danger and promise, crisis and hope, survival and success.

Each woman's dream is singular amid a multiplicity of other unique dreams. Their dreams are not the high tide but the foam atop the wave of the state's Chinese Dream discourse. The aspirational, neoliberal Dream of China was once an abstract interpretation of the history of women's endeavors to find prosperity in the private sector as they explored the possibilities and actualized the potentiality of the *Shanzhai* fashion industry. Strikingly, unlike the sprawling, multiple dreams of women designers, the grand, universal Chinese Dream discourse, disseminated through multiple media outlets, says nothing to women specifically, despite the fact they have long participated in the social life and workplace and have contributed enormously to China's rapid economic development and social transformation. *Shanzhai* dreams and women's entrepreneurship long preceded the state's ideological attempt to co-opt them and to consolidate a language of entrepreneurship, intentionally pointing out an inspiring future pathway for people to keep yearning and fighting for. In the following discussion, I survey women's entrepreneurship and business pursuits in China's creative sectors in order to contextualize the women designers' entrepreneurial spirit and historicize the Chinese Dream in a gender-specific way.

CHINESE WOMEN AND ENTREPRENEURSHIP

On May 20–21, 2015, the world's largest e-commerce company, Alibaba Group, hosted the first "Global Conference on Women and Entrepreneurship" in Hangzhou, China. In his opening speech to the attendees, on the theme "The Era of 'She'," Alibaba's founder Jack Ma proclaimed that "If there are any secrets to the success of Alibaba, the foremost of these secrets is women," to whom he also credited the spirit and energy of the younger generation on e-commerce and Alibaba's careful attention to small businesses. The acknowledgement of women included not only the female consumers who often shop at Taobao, Tmall, and other shopping platforms controlled by Alibaba but also women shop owners who have started their businesses on Alibaba platforms and contribute significantly to the digital economy through their entrepreneurship. One of my informants, Josie, rephrasing a famous piece of internet slang, joked that "Behind the great man Jack Ma there are great women like us" (我们都是马云背后的女人).

Attended by such famous names as author and businesswoman Arianna Huffington, Jessica Alba, actor and founder of the Honest Company, Liu Qing, president of the Uber-like app company Didi Kuaidi Dache, and actor and director Vicky Zhao, the conference emphasized the importance of women as the driving force in the service industry and the internet economy owing to their distinctive "imagination" and "natural edge in the feeling world," and due attention was given to the benefits of the work-life balance made possible through the flexibility of online entrepreneurship (Jones, 2015). Another speaker was Alibaba's co-founder and senior partner Lucy Peng, one of Forbes' Asia's 50 Power Businesswomen, who asserted that "One characteristic of women is that they are fond of having dreams. When I have a new business to start, I often dream of changing the world a bit."

While it is unclear how "imagination," "natural edge," and "dreams" eventually translate into business initiatives, market strategies, digital product development, and a beneficial balance of productivity and profitability, the significance of start-ups founded by women for ushering in the era of digital space and online commerce cannot be denied. Alibaba reported during the conference that women owned 50.1 percent of the shops on Taobao, a figure significantly higher than that for women start-ups in traditional industries around the world (46.5 percent; Wu, 2015). Also informative in this context is a white paper titled "Gender Equality and Women's Development in China" issued by the Information Office of the State Council that provided a comprehensive overview of the country's policies and efforts for women's development on the 20th anniversary of the United Nation's 4th World Conference on Women held in Beijing. According to this white paper, women at the time accounted for a quarter of China's entrepreneurs and about 55 percent of the country's new internet businesses (The State Council Information Office, 2015). A report by AliResearch, a research center affiliated with Alibaba, estimated the number of women shop owners on Taobao at close to 6 million, or about 49.4 percent of all Taobao sellers (AliResearch, 2016).

The e-commerce shops owned by women are concentrated in the service and retail sectors and in a manner, as already observed, that conforms largely with conventional female roles. In 2016, women dominated or held their own in start-ups in Chinese e-commerce in the categories of beauty and cosmetics (64.5 percent of businesses), garments (50.8 percent), and bags and shoes (49.5 percent; AliResearch, 2016). The same report indicated that the women who set up shops online were significantly younger than those who did so in offline contexts (31.4 compared to 47.6 years of age, respectively) and that women aged 18 to 29 made up 57 percent of all online female entrepreneurs—that is, women born in the 1980s and 1990s had the strongest entrepreneurial spirit and made the most use of digital technologies and e-commerce.

Such statistics are insufficient, however, to represent accurately the full range of leadership, equality, and diversity that characterizes online fashion retailing in China. The *Shanzhai* designers described in this book are part of the legion who eagerly joined the booming internet economy, which is, arguably, a fulcrum of the post-socialist promise to women since the reform era. The shifting conditions reshape and construct female subjects and the subjectivities that condition women's endeavors in the digital economy. Modern images of Chinese women have been largely defined in relation to production and consumption in a manner consistent with the prevailing scholarly tendency to understand Chinese womanhood through the construction of the female body (Barlow, 1994). In Maoist socialist China, the ideal female subject was the gender-neutral model worker who "holds up half the sky"—women were liberated from feudal bonds, guaranteed employment, housing, and social services like their male counterparts, and required to devote themselves to social construction in the workplace (Anagnost, 1989; Hanser, 2008). This China was animated by the spirit of grassroots, bottom-up transformations, and the spontaneity and autonomy of the People, while gender was subsumed within class struggle. China's claim that it was overcoming the class problem could not compensate for the political cruelty, economic stagnation, and social turbulence that characterized the Cultural Revolution. Subsequent reform and the opening-up policy announced in the late 1970s began a new era.

Two parallel waves of feminized labor, in the form of the emerging urban consumer and service sectors, have been mobilized by the state's embrace of an export-oriented and labor-intensive manufacturing economy. At first, female peasant girls were drawn to the outskirts of large cities to take manufacturing jobs in transnational factories, thereby helping to make possible China's rapid economic development by serving as the "cheap labor" that has been associated with the Made-in-China label worldwide. Pun's (2005) analysis of women migrant factory workers (*dagongmei*, 打工妹) in southern China showed how the disciplinary techniques and discursive practices of the factory reshaped the rural and fleshy female body for productive industrial labor. The low wages, poor conditions, long hours, rapid turnover, and temporary status all contributed to these workers' precariousness (Fan, 2004) but did not dampen their longing for modernity, sophistication, and upward mobility (Rofel, 2007).

Second, many young women have also joined the newly formed urban service industry and taken jobs in the consumer sector selling beauty products or modeling clothes, in the entertainment industry, or as flight attendants that conform to an active but often hyper-sexualized image of womanhood. This wave of feminized labor has contributed to the emergence of a distinct urban "pink-collar class" that typifies the market-driven, post-reform feminization of work in China. Both waves of labor have boosted women's consumption power, spawning a flourishing consumerism in urban settings that has tended to target, rather than factory workers, urban female professionals as part of the rising middle class with high-end shopping malls, beauty clubs, and fashion salons. The rise of consumerism and service businesses created historically unique opportunities for women to start their own businesses, and the ground was made more fertile for women to experience the benefits of creative work and consumption choices with the development of new technologies and of the cultural industry. So it is that women's entrepreneurship has emerged and boomed in consumer sectors; it is an entrepreneurship that reclaims gender and sexuality from Maoist asceticism and class struggle and marks a retrenchment from radical socialist equalitarianism (X. Wu, 2009; Zhang, 2000). Furthermore, the seemingly empowering potential of entrepreneurship and consumer society has been tempered by the growing urban gender gap and urban-rural divide since the mid-1990s (Hanser, 2008).

A striking feature of gender relations in modern China is that women contribute directly to both the economic productivity of society and to the reproductive work within the family on which society inevitably rests (Ye, 2010). Instructive in this context are the decennial surveys of women's social status that have been conducted jointly since 1990 by the All-China Women's Federation and the National Bureau of Statistics (2001, 2010). According to these surveys, at the end of 2000, 87 percent of women aged 18–64 years were employed, compared with 93.6 percent of men. While Chinese women have long worked outside the home, as mentioned in Chapter 2, the 1990s witnessed massive layoffs, especially from state-owned enterprises, during which time women workers faced significant discrimination in the job market. In order to support their families financially, in addition to performing reproductive and house work, many of these laid-off women, lured by the promise of flexibility and autonomy, opened small businesses as food vendors and proprietors of clothing shops and hair salons; my informant Cho, for example, belonged to this cohort of entrepreneurs.

By the end of 2010, the employment statistics for women and men had dropped to 71.1 and 87.2 percent, respectively; the numbers in the countryside were lower (60.8 and 82.0 percent) and those in the cities higher (80.5 and 93.6 percent). Of unemployed urban women, most (69.3 percent) were taking care of their families at home. Unsurprisingly, Chinese women spent more time than men on household chores and tutoring their children, thereby providing another indirect contribution to men's productivity by freeing more of their time and energy for other work (Ye, 2010). The recovery and gradual transformation of China's economy in the early twenty-first-century structure depended increasingly on consumption and the creative cultural industries, in which jobs and work are often temporary, flexible, and insecure, has led to an economy characterized by self-employment, start-ups, and venture companies. Although it is unclear how many of the women in China classified as unemployed are in fact self-employed, the significant decrease in women's formal employment in the two decades combined with reports that a quarter of Chinese entrepreneurs are women suggests a tendency among Chinese women to retreat from formal, stable jobs and embrace the risks of entrepreneurship.

Not every woman designer whom I encountered would call herself an entrepreneur (女性创业者). Some of them insisted to me that they were only doing what they loved and that allowed them to achieve financial independence while having time to take care of their children. However, as observed earlier, the concept of entrepreneurship has no precise parallel in Chinese, in part because work for profit was discouraged before the reform era. Vendors, hawkers, and street sellers all display the entrepreneurial spirit, in that they are willing to take economic risks and seek to maximize profits—it is perhaps for this reason that Taobao still to some extent resembles a bazaar more than a department store. China's increasing involvement in globalized economic, political, and socio-cultural exchanges has led to the state's appropriation of a new set of languages and practices, including that of entrepreneurship, as it seeks to fit new ideologies into old vernacular activities.

If the state's appropriation of a new language for entrepreneurship is to inspire entrepreneurs' self-confidence in operating small businesses, delicate maneuvers are required in the spaces of work and life alike where the neoliberal ethos of privatization and self-reliance is a triumph in the new media environment. Building on the argument, presented in Chapter 3, that the language of a work-life balance serves to disguise the gendered nature of digital labor in the social factory, here I further emphasize that new technologies, digital platforms, and e-commerce, rather than heralding a new form of women's digital entrepreneurism and business endeavor, are part of the neoliberal practice of risk-taking, individualization of responsibility for employment, and embracing of uncertainty. So it was that, in the 1990s, prior to the e-commerce boom in China, women who had been laid off poured into the self-employment and service start-up sector in order to create greater family wealth and then, when online shopping and e-commerce took off, these women leveraged the practices that they had learned to create fashion businesses, seeking as always to manage economic risks and maintain a work-life balance, in this case in a manner defined by flexibility, autonomy, upward mobility, and middle-class imagery.

This account echoes in large part Gina Neff's (2012) observations about employment risk and transformation in high-tech industries in the twenty-first-century US. Contrary to the conventional understanding that entrepreneurial behavior and start-up culture have changed significantly since Silicon Valley's dot-com boom of the late 1990s, Neff held that the earlier era's discursive entrepreneurialism, as expressed in its emphasis on self-reliance, risk-taking, adventure, and insecurity, became the cultural frame well before high-tech companies began to experience exponential growth. For example, workers in the news media appropriated the prevailing entrepreneurial spirit in the development of high-risk labor market strategies, with behaviors such as job-hopping and joining firms not tied to known commodities. Workers deployed these strategies as a means to exert a semblance of control over conditions that were evolving rapidly.

Following this line of argumentation, I seek to demonstrate in this book that women's gendered precarious experiences are tangible but remain largely invisible under the surface of the booming digital entrepreneurism and the sloganeering of "do what you love" (Tokumitsu, 2014). Much of the existing literature on precarity has accordingly focused on men, with male factory workers serving as the iconic precariats with regard to their temporary status, long working hours, mechanized work patterns, and profound feelings of insecurity and anxiety. Unlike factory work, the beauty business, as largely the province of women, manifests such feminine characteristics as caring, patience, and emotional intimacy. The prevailing sensibility of consumer culture fosters many gendered codes and cultural icons that construct and reify prevailing notions of femininity in the beauty and fashion industry, thereby echoing a post-feminist climate that uncritically celebrates individual choice, openness, and pleasure. What is striking in this respect is that the construction of femininity and normality functions as the starting point for some women's retreat from formal and regular jobs to embrace fashion work, with its appeals of initiative, freedom, and modernity, while the choice at this socio-historical conjuncture actually limits these women's potential in work and life. The fantasy of neoliberal aspirations and the reconfiguration of femininity in work, along with the pleasure associated with consumer culture and individual freedom of choice, have transformed and concealed the precarity that working Chinese women experience in their own socially constructed domains, in the household as well as in the fashion business. The Chinese Dream offers a dreamscape that is partial and uneven in its geographies. These women's *Shanzhai* dreams engage each in its own way with the official Dream discourse, which enables them with digital work and social and economic capital. Paradoxically, such an enabling power is also the source of their confinement to a system of patriotic and patriarchal capitalism.

THE CHINESE DREAM AND THE POST-SOCIALIST PROMISE

The Chinese Dream, as a hegemonic project that attempts to manufacture a social consensus and rebuild/rebrand the nation in a transnational space, represents President Xi Jinping's governmental response to the contemporary conjuncture of the social, cultural, political, and ideological contradictions that together exert a profound influence on individuals' lives at various points, particularly in leveraging *Shanzhai* culture in the service of the state's goals. At one point in Xi's well-known speech in 2012, he asserted

Everybody has an ideal and pursues his or her own dream. Now people are talking about the Chinese Dream. I believe that realizing the rejuvenation of the Chinese nation has been the greatest dream of the Chinese people since the beginning of the modern era. This dream concentrates a long-cherished expectation of many generations of Chinese people and encapsulates the overall interests of the Chinese nation and its people. It is the common aspiration of every Chinese individual. (Huang & Luan, 2013)

Here, Xi referenced an ongoing discussion in which "everyone" was engaged rather than offering something entirely new, as would have been usual for a newly appointed president expecting to lead the country for some time.[22] The catchphrase was already in use before Xi's speech in published books and articles, in both English and Chinese, such as Helen Wang's *The Chinese Dream: The Rise of the World's Largest Middle Class and What It Means to You* (2010), and a piece by *New York Times* editorial writer Thomas Friedman (2012) titled "China needs its own dream" that appeared just a few weeks before Xi's Chinese Dream speech. Indeed, The Economist (2013a) even went as far as to suggest Friedman as Xi's main inspiration and, based on the apparent echo of the cliché "American Dream" in US culture, suggested that Xi's speech should be read as an official response to the West's view of China's development.

In any case, besides encouraging the Chinese people to think about such traditional moral concepts as filial piety, diligence, persistence, and fighting for the greater good and the ultimate goal of nation-building, the Chinese Dream has served an ideological purpose for Xi as he positioned himself and his leadership in the Communist Party. The currents of marketization and privatization have exacerbated social inequality and China's urban-rural divide so that the socialist promise of equality, freedom, and justice has become increasingly hollow for ordinary people. As a consequence, each generation of leaders in China has searched for new promises to legitimize its leadership and mobilize the population for economic productivity, social advancement, and political stability. As the definitive slogan of Xi's leadership thus far, the Chinese Dream has over time taken on a broad range of meanings. Xi himself has repeated the phrase on multiple occasions in various contexts; at times, it has been a dream of national revival, of a strong military force, of ecological civilization, of contemporary Chinese values, of giving to the world, and of peace; at another, it has also been a dream of young people, of each

Chinese person, of those living overseas, in Hong Kong, Macau, and Taiwan, and of people in the many countries touched by the "One Belt One Road" initiatives (Wang & Feng, 2016).

In his first Dream speech, Xi stated that

> History informs us that the future and fate of every one of us is closely connected to the state and the nation. Only when the state and nation are well can everyone be well. To achieve the historical mission of the revival of the Chinese nation is arduous but honorable; it requires unremitting efforts of Chinese generations one after another. (Xi, 2012)

It is not at all clear who or what—the state, the nation, or individual Chinese citizens—is the subject that dreams the Chinese Dream in Xi's speeches. The situation has been well analyzed in Yang's (2016) theorization of the "split-subject" status of the state, "whereby the interpellation of the citizenry is itself subject to the ideological hailing of a global imaginary—in this case, the American Dream" (p. 178)—a condition that results in incongruent articulations regarding the identity of the dreamers. According to Yang's critical reading of the aforementioned film *ADIC*, such cultural artifacts have come to participate in the construction of an American imaginary that explicitly provokes Dream signifiers in China. In other words, Yang argued that the Chinese Dream, as a global-national ideological formation, causes the vision of "Made-in-China" to conform to the global discourse of IPR and attempts to secure the state's subject position in the cultural context of globalization and national development (see also Yang, 2014b).

At the same time, while the Chinese Dream is a grand narrative and framework promoted by the government, it is also evident in the material conditions of each individual Chinese citizen's attempt to grasp the multiple and polymorphous possibilities of the post-reform era. The Dream discourse involves a variety of actors, or "dreamers," who dream a dream of their own; the women designers are dreamers but their dreams are hardly captured by the state's Dream discourse (Callahan, 2013). The Chinese author Yu Hua (2014) once spoke of a friend who had a lifetime dream of voting in an election for China's head of state and concluded that the Chinese Dream should be "a dream dreamed in China," even if the form that it took, like that of his friend, fit poorly with Xi's vision of national rejuvenation.

Individual sentiments regarding the government-initiated Dream discourse, especially on the internet, have taken a variety of forms, from contempt, cynicism, and criticism to praise, gratitude, and reflection. Marquis and Yang (2013) argued that Chinese netizens' expressions of individualistic and fragmentary dreams through social media tend to focus on domestic affairs rather than on the country's international status. Based on an analysis of views of the Chinese Dream discourse on Weibo posts from November 2012 to May 2013, these scholars concluded that netizens were, again, concerned less about China's position on the global stage and more about such domestic problems as social and economic inequality, environmental pollution, and food safety—all issues that have a large impact on individual livelihood and quality of life and require collective effort to solve. Interestingly, the comparison of and distinction between the American Dream and the Chinese Dream in that study echoes Yang's (2016) elaboration of the state's imagination of China's future through the globalized ideology from the US.

There is a parallel between women designers' *Shanzhai* practices that often copy trends set and inspired by global/Western luxury brands and the Chinese Dream imagined through globalized ideology rooted in the West. Recent versions of the Chinese Dream are also noteworthy for embedding the notion that it can be realized on Chinese soil, thereby departing from earlier representations in the media of intrepid Chinese citizens traveling abroad to realize their dreams, especially to the US, where, at least according to some observers, the call of the American Dream has, paradoxically, lost its allure in terms of the fulfillment of the promises of freedom, democracy, individual rights, and wealth (Zhang et al., 2013). This is where the universal dream pales for Chinese people and is replaced by the Chinese Dream discourse. The Dream consolidates a post-socialist promise to unfetter productivity, the imagination, and individuality in the context of an ongoing debate worldwide about social development, improving systems that serve the public, values, and the meaning of life, making it a kind of universal discourse about a new superstructure of culture, social systems, values, and ideals based on new modes of production that is deeply rooted in China (H. Zhang, 2013).

While the Dream discourse sounds appealing in its opening-up of space for individual pursuit that inspires women designers' fashion business described elsewhere in the book, it has certainly been short on specifics regarding its fundamental nature and how it may be achieved. While this discourse has to some extent proved to be an effective marketing device for the Chinese government in its efforts to invoke powerful narratives about the past in pointing the way to an optimistic future, the post-socialist promise of the Chinese Dream resides on the margins of a neoliberal governmentality that promotes self-reliance. In this way, the discourse shifts social and economic responsibility from the state to individuals and masks imbalances, inequalities, and injustices with respect to individuals' potential to pursue personal growth, wealth, and the promise of middle-class consumer status. In forging and selling a sanguine story of national revival and individual prosperity, the Dream discourse has obviously differed from Mao's collectivism by reinforcing the capitalist mode of production since the reform era. As the writer and news commentator Einar Tangen declared in a special CCTV program on the subject, the Chinese Dream is both "individual and aspirational" (Cheng, 2013). Such a malleable and multi-dimensional interpretation of the Dream discourse allows it to mean something to everyone, just not a specific something.

As has been seen, one crucial oversight in accounts of the Dream discourse is attention to gender, which is clearly of critical importance for any study of women entrepreneurs. As discussed earlier in this chapter, while women play large roles in Chinese social life and work and contribute significantly to economic productivity and social advancement, their status and livelihood remain bound up with precarity and their lack of proper recognition. It is in this respect that the Dream discourse acts as a double-edged sword for women, facilitating their attempts to express and explore their potential while at the same time inscribing them within the state's ideology and mode of precarity. This double form of precariousness is most palpable in representations in popular culture in which the state attempts to define the discursive field of the Chinese Dream. With these considerations in mind, in the following I explore a little further the manifestation of the Chinese Dream discourse in popular culture as a means to reinvigorate the ideological apparatus of the state, looking in particular at the iconography of the *Mengwa* girl. This gendered construction of the Dream lends less inspiration to women designers in terms of their creative *Shanzhai* production but serves as a powerful ideological grip on family and gender ideals that nonetheless constrain women to dream their little dreams. I then focus on one artifact, returning to the film *MBAP* to delineate how the popular culture and the state's ideology feed each other in the construction of women's ideals and aspirations in their performance of creative work and social entrepreneurship. The manifestation of the Dream discourse in the film sheds light on how women designers in *Shanzhai* fashion imagine and practice their creativity.

MANIFESTING THE DREAM IN POPULAR CULTURE: PROPAGANDA AND MEDIA REPRESENTATIONS

Figure 5.1 presents propaganda posters from two very different periods in Chinese history. The one on the left dates from the 1950s; it features a woman at a construction site dressed in a typical primrose men's working suit with a towel tied around her neck, wearing a protective helmet with the face shield up and her hands in heavy gloves holding an electric welding rod. The caption under the image reads "We are proud to participate in the nation's industrialization." The poster presents the model socialist woman for the Mao era, defeminized and represented as equal to her male counterparts, a diligent worker in socialist construction whose aim is to "hold up half the sky." This is, then, the image of the woman's place in the early days of the People's Republic of China, when the state held firm to a socialist and communist dream of centralized planning and a relentless revolution against capitalism.

The poster on the right in Figure 5.1 picks up this story more than half a century later in 2013, with a national campaign of public service

Figure 5.1 A comparison of propaganda posters from the 1950s (left) and the 2010s (right)

posters on the theme of what the Chinese Dream means to ordinary people. These images appeared on fences around construction sites, bus stops, subways, newspaper stands, and billboards. The images, provided by well-known folk art institutions, depicted traditional clothing, mannerisms, games, and values (Johnson, 2013). One such image, shown on the right in Figure 5.1, is that of a young girl called *Mengwa*, literally "Chinese Dream baby," who sits pensively next to a caption reading "The Chinese dream is my dream." The figure is based on a representative piece of Clay Figure Zhang, a well-known pottery style and folk art form from Tianjin in northern China. The poster also includes a prose poem composed by a pro-government blogger named Yi Qing that describes an innocent girl running barefoot through a land of hope and ending with the refrain, "Ah, China, my dream, my sweet dream."

Taken together, these two posters document the evolution of the state's dream narratives. During the Mao era, the state hailed its citizens into national ideologies of industrialization, modernization, and socialist construction and forced gender equalization in what was described as an effort to liberate women from the domestic sphere and to augment the nation's workforce. It is this process that is celebrated in the "iron women" images such as the one reproduced here, reflecting a time when women began to participate in such sectors as farming, industrial production, construction, and defense.

Xi's catchy Chinese Dream quickly became the subject of successive media campaigns in an effort to consolidate his ideological grip on the party and state. This effort has involved the old propaganda techniques of "coloring the media outlets red" and striving to recover "some of the psychological power" that the party "once enjoyed under Mao" (The Economist, 2014). The apple-cheeked *Mengwa* in the poster was further appropriated for a series of videos on the subject of the Chinese Dream produced and released by the Bureau of Propaganda and Education under the aegis of the Publicity Department of the Communist Party of China (CCPPD) and the national web-based Chinese Network Television (CNTV), a division of the state's mouthpiece CCTV. The *Mengwa* image was made into an animated character for a series of propaganda productions that was broadcast repeatedly during prime-time programs on provincial, municipal, and county channels and appeared on major internet portals at the time of the 2015 Spring Festival.

Titled *Mengwa Brings You Good Luck and Virtue* (梦娃送吉祥, 梦娃送美德), the series presented viewers with a robust girl with chubby cheeks and a side ponytail in a bright maroon daisy-print suit. Unlike the emphasis on socialist and communist values and rejection of such traditional Chinese moralizing philosophies as Confucianism typical of Mao-era imagery, the *Mengwa* videos and posters referenced certain pre-communist moral doctrines as driving forces behind the aspirational Chinese Dream. Categorized as public service announcements, the series consisted of a 45-second introductory video elaborating seven moral doctrines and seven 13-second videos dedicated to each.[23] At the beginning of the first video, two animated magpies fly over plum blossoms that symbolize the return of spring. The magpies fly from the blossoms toward *Mengwa*, who awakes and stands up. Soon the magpies fly away, each carrying a string of traditional paper lanterns imprinted with two Chinese characters, *ruyi*, "as one wishes," and *jixiang*, "good luck," that frame the screen and *Mengwa*. Other images in the video include a sheep, symbolizing the year in the Chinese zodiac, and two children skating, sledding, and flying kites, traditional activities representing the transition from winter to spring. A cut-paper gate appears and draws *Mengwa*'s attention; she turns her back to the audience and toward the slowly opening gate while a young girl's voice chants a sing-song rhyme, "*Mengwa* awakes, the sun is smiling. The Chinese Dream is so glorious." The melody continues as the gate opens; *Mengwa* stops singing and interprets the Chinese Dream in terms of seven moral doctrines, each represented by three Chinese characters that fit with the meter of the song: "The nation is the family," "Goodness is in the soul," "Diligence is the fundamental virtue," "Frugality cultivates virtue," "Integrity makes a man," "Nothing is greater than filial piety," and "Harmony is precious."

The song then resumes: "A century-long dream is realized in the spirit of our times. Together, let's work hard to reach the same goal. Together, we wish our motherland to be prosperous and strong. May it enjoy harmony, happiness, good luck, and continual progress." The song is accompanied by iconic Chinese images depicted in cut paper, including the CCTV Headquarters, Beijing National Stadium (where the 2008 Summer Olympics were held), high-speed rail, the Oriental Pearl Tower, the Gate of Heavenly Peace, the Great Wall, pandas, figures in ethnic costumes, swallows, and firecrackers. The video ends with *Mengwa* opening her arms to the sky and sending out New Year's greetings: "May good fortune bless myriads of families. Together we fulfill the Chinese Dream."

The magpie, plum blossoms, Chinese zodiac, fireworks, the color of red, the background music played in Chinese string, wind, and percussion instruments, and the stylistic folk art form of paper-cutting are all traditional elements of the Chinese Lunar New Year celebration. Their deployment in propaganda promoting the Chinese Dream and the state's vision of morality represents an explicit return to Confucian values that, as alluded to earlier, had been harshly critiqued and repudiated during Mao's era.

These images of *Mengwa* have permeated daily life in China, for the videos and posters have been widely dispersed through mass media as described above. According to a report by the news agency Xinhua, as of the end of March 2015, the *Mengwa* overview videos had been downloaded from CNTV by over 1,000 local television stations, and central news portals and major commercial websites had reported that the *Mengwa* specials got 42.26 million hits (Shi, 2015). By the end of 2015, the video series had been viewed more than 100 million times (CCTV, 2016).

Comparing Mao's propaganda with Xi's, it is obvious that the state has exchanged a hard-sell approach for a friendly, subtle soft sell. Little, cute, and chubby, *Mengwa* represents the innocence of children who are both less gendered than adults and the future of the country. With her singing and dancing, the animated and girly figure is appealing and non-threatening. Possibly, the choice to feature a young girl symbolizes the state's intention to groom its citizens while they are still docile, but it is in any case clear that the ads are intended to target strategically the younger population using its preferred means of communication. The party-state has adapted its propaganda to the times by integrating elements of popular culture into a subtle form of psychological manipulation. Its message is also abundantly clear. The Chinese Dream is not about equality, class struggle, labor, gender, or the socialist system promoted in the arts from the 1950s through the 1970s. Rather, it is about aspiration, about the future, about pride and strength, notions that require a more nuanced and finely tuned propaganda machine.

Alongside the top-down *Mengwa* campaign, many local media outlets have also co-conspired in their own servitude to the grand narrative of the Chinese Dream. A prime example is *My Chinese Dream: An Interview with Prominent Public Figures in their Pursuit of Dreams*, a weekly talk show featuring the lives of public figures—such as sports stars Yao Ming, pianist Lang Lang, and IT entrepreneur Zhou Hongyi—and their aspirations for success in their respective fields and in so doing provided a set of mainstream, top-down Dream narratives. While the aim was clearly to provide a comprehensive but individualized vision of what the various interviewees called "My Chinese Dream," the connection with the official Dream discourse was at times fairly tenuous. Also noteworthy is the strong gender bias among the interviewees, who included only two women, the actor Hai Qing and the dancer Yang Liping, a bias that implicitly calls into question whether women can or should aspire to be Chinese Dreamers.

While the state propaganda machine co-opts popular media to disseminate its ideological construct and strives to master the art of psychological manipulation, studies have shown that the Chinese public, such as women designers, have in fact been widely engaged in articulating their own versions of the Dream. Meng and Sun (2013) found, based on an analysis of more than 160,000 Chinese Dream-themed posts on Weibo, that the Dream discourse has been contested, serving to construct not only a national identity but also a range of self-expressions. They concluded that Weibo was functioning in this case as a socialization platform for public participation that empowered ordinary people to engage in the process of producing, circulating, and consuming information in ways that were semi-autonomous and pushed back against mainstream interpretations of the Dream discourse.

Individual Chinese citizens do, I suggest, exercise a certain autonomy and flexibility by expressing their own understanding of the Dream, whether partisan, ambivalent, oppositional, indifferent, or otherwise, on social media and digital technologies. One example is the "dancing grannies" who choreograph their square dancing (广场舞) to songs about the Chinese Dream and post the results on video portals and social media accounts. This form of dancing is a popular exercise regimen for middle-aged and retired women, who gather for the purpose at dawn and dusk in public spaces (BBC, 2013). The hobby has become quite popular across China, with an estimated 100 million practitioners according to CCTV (Hu, 2013). The "grannies" (or "*damas*," 大妈) dance to various kinds of music, mostly Chinese popular songs, constantly coming up with new routines for new pieces. A recent search (May 6, 2017) using the keywords of "the Chinese Dream" plus "square dance" on the popular video portal Youku.com generated over 400 videos, the majority of them providing instructions for dancing to a song called "The Chinese Dream" by Zhuang Ni, a folk-style singer. Other popular videos reveal a theme when it comes to these songs, with titles such as "Most Beautiful is the Chinese Dream" (最美中国梦), "Together We Fulfill Our Chinese

Dream" (共圆中国梦), and "Beautiful Chinese Dream" (美丽中国梦), the last having been posted on YouTube by a group from San Francisco (sfguangchangwu, 2016).

Notwithstanding the popularity of this square dancing, and the noise that it creates, its public performance in this manner could be said to reflect women's working out of a sociality and social participation based on women's sharing of common experiences and desires (ChinaDaily, 2014; Wang, 2014). The state, not surprisingly, recognizes such vernacular forms of cultural activities and appropriates them to serve its political and ideological purposes. In Hunan, for instance, the government, specifically the Hunan Culture Department, has promoted twelve "Core Socialist Values" through a campaign called "Let's All Dance" that involves teaching the citizens 20 song-and-(square)-dance routines (Zhao, 2016). More than 15,000 teachers have been trained to provide instruction in schools, factories, businesses, and community centers in a conspicuous gesture of responding to President Xi's call to "make them [Core Socialist Values] all-pervasive, just like the air" ("Xi stresses core socialist values," 2014). Also unsurprisingly, netizens have expressed mixed feelings about this campaign on social media.

Square dancing perhaps is one of the most prominent cases that engender public discussions of the life of grassroots women. It demonstrates the neglect of gender in the national propaganda and popular discourse, on the one hand, and the state's swift appropriation of such a vernacular cultural expression for its ideological agenda, on the other. This is where the *Shanzhai* women designers find their resonance. For one, while women designers embrace entrepreneurial initiatives and practice precarious creativity in the pursuit of their dreams, the popular cultural production of Chinese womanhood nonetheless overlooks their endeavors and the praxis of their dreaming. For another, the discursive field of the Dream discourse is reflected in the reinvention of model citizens in popular culture, which has been particularly evident in the case of the idealization of women, for example as model entrepreneurs aspiring to and working hard to achieve their goals, navigating the national-transnational dreamscape, and generally investing in the construction of post-socialist China. The simultaneous neglect and construction of women as Chinese entrepreneurs captures the increasing sophistication of the state's propaganda in terms of appropriating popular culture. The tensions are embodied in the discursive formation of the Chinese Dream in relation to gender. The film *MBAP* and its critical reception are particularly instructive in this regard and accordingly merit further attention, for the film lends clear if subtle support for the notion of a female version of the mainstream Dream discourse.

MBA PARTNERS, A CHINESE DREAM FOR WOMEN, AND POSTFEMINIST SENSIBILITIES

As mentioned, *MBAP* was dubbed by critics a women's version of the earlier *ADIC*, but in fact the similarities between the films are limited to the trio of leading roles (in that case, male) and engagement with the Chinese Dream discourse. *MBAP* is more of a glossy soap opera celebrating love, friendship, (women's) inspiration, personal growth, and success in business; it has relatively little to say about the social transformation of China in the post-reform era, the specific experiences of this generation of Chinese entrepreneurs, or the naivete of the obsession of the American Dream—all of which were significant aspects of *ADIC*. Set in the first decade of the twenty-first century, *MBAP*'s depiction of the development of the dot-com industry seems more obvious than inspired. Set against the backdrop of the growing internet economy and China's entrepreneurial boom in the wake of the economic restructuring, the massive layoffs of the 1990s, and the growing venture mentality of embracing risks in the pursuit of prosperity, *MBAP* was itself a transnational business venture, having brought together Korean-drama veteran Jang Tae-yoo as the director with Chinese financiers (as it happens, the venture was not a success, with, a mediocre 81 million yuan in box office receipts for a film that cost 90 million yuan to make and was expected to bring in 300 million yuan).

A striking feature of the film is that it catered to the popular conception of entrepreneurship, that is, from a decidedly gendered perspective. Further, the very novelty of the scenario contributed freshness and a down-to-earth perspective to the representation of Lu's dream as a blend of romance, entrepreneurship, and participation in the digital economy and the fashion business. The film clearly invokes the dream theme at the outset by opening with images of the Statue of Liberty accompanying Lu's voiceover, "Someone said on a TV show, 'If you love him, send him to America, because it is heaven. If you hate him, send him to America, because it is hell.'" The portion of the film set in the US combines a glossy portrayal of the vicissitudes of love with realistic sequences of the highly racialized and marginalized world of counterfeit vendors who are sustaining that country's knockoff economy (Hines, 2016). Significantly, then, when Lu's boyfriend leaves her for a posh white American woman, he dismisses Lu as "a so-called 'businesswoman' selling fake bags." Moreover, while the film makes clear the boyfriend's reasons for coming to the US, it is less clear about Lu's own motivation apart from following him, revealing only that she imagines a life of "a youthful campus, romantic dinners, endless fashion parties like those in the *Sex and the City*, and a sleepless Manhattan." At the end of the film's opening sequence, Lu has lost her boyfriend, her temporary job as a street vendor, her temporary home in the US, and whatever amorphous American dream had led her out of China in the first place.

Having brought Lu back to China, the film is also unclear regarding why and how she decides on entrepreneurship as the path to fulfilling her grandest "dream" as it is realized in the finale. As this part of the story unfolds, Lu's dream is revealed to be one of self-actualization that also involves collaboration with the other two ambitious women and support, in terms of both finances and manpower, from two devoted male characters. The film insists that Lu's dream of success in business, friendship, and love is rooted in Chinese (not American) soil.

I find the film's lack of depth in exploring the potent message of women entrepreneurship especially significant. Specifically, rather than giving its audience glimpses of business tactics, market plans, supply chains, resources, and labor, *MBAP* emphasizes dreams and aspirations as the decisive factors in an entrepreneur's success. In this respect, the plot is consistent with the slogan that was part of many promotional posters for the film, "Let's share the joy and become wealthy together" (*tong gan gong fu*, 同甘共富), which twisted a Chinese idiom *tong gan gong ku* (同甘共苦), "to share life's joys and sorrows." The slogan turns the old-saying into a pun, playing on the film's title "the partners," with whom people can make business endeavors, enjoy the happiness, and reap wealth. Missing from the slogan, naturally, is any mention of the hardship, risks, and adversity associated with the reality of entrepreneurship in China. Even the treatment of the threat to the characters' business posed by counterfeit goods feels sloppily narrated, as the trio of entrepreneurs turn their nearly bankrupt firm into a Wall Street-listed company in a mere 18 months through the almost magical power of a shopping app. For all the film's flaws, however, its finale presents a dilemma that lies at the heart of contemporary China. For while the dream is actualized on the Chinese soil, in that the women find success in the domestic market, it is international recognition—specifically that of the US—that represents the climax of the women's business careers and of the film's dramatic arc. The incredible success that Lu achieves in the end is, of course, ironic given the lack of market success that the film itself experienced.

Some glimpses of real-world challenges intrude into the narrative, in particular with respect to gender bias in the business world. In one of the film's subplots, the trio attend a party in an effort to obtain funding for their business from a variety of investors, all of whom are men. For some reason Wen, a formerly successful businesswoman, fails to realize that the "barbeque" is in fact a semi-formal business meeting, and the women find themselves pitching their idea to serious-looking businessmen in suits while they are themselves clad in outdoor leisure clothing. A more obviously sexist moment occurs when Lu is delivering a presentation and a major investor interrupts by declaring "I like them [presentations] short, just as I like short miniskirts," marking a critical reflection on the sexualization of female bodies in the business world. In the end, this investor rejects their pitch with specific reference to the women's gender: "Ladies, if you dress up sexy for our club, we would have been much better entertained. But you failed to do so, which is a pity. As you see, this is a place for gentlemen to talk business." Although Lu counters that "gentlemen's business" has intentionally neglected the huge market represented by Chinese women, the sequence nonetheless speaks to the systematic structural barriers that make it difficult for women to enter and find success in the business world.

The film portrays a sympathetic and powerful business school professor, who sponsors the three women's business endeavor with his social network and cultural capital. Such a construction of genders poses the question of whether women who cannot count on the same kind of good fortune and male sponsorship that *MBAP*'s female leads enjoy can hope to find success as entrepreneurs. As might be expected, I see in *Shanzhai* women designers an affirmative answer to this question. The entrepreneurship portrayed in *MBAP* is obviously distinct from the real-world creative work of women designers, which is far more complex, nuanced, and most of all precarious than Lu and her partners find it to be. *Shanzhai* women designers, of course, enter the market for the specific purpose of selling fashion imitations and therefore cannot expect to achieve the kind of success that would give them standing within the well-established hierarchy of brands and their companies an entry into the NASDAQ.

The similarities between the women entrepreneurs depicted in *MBAP* and *Shanzhai* women designers are instructive as well. Both the real-world and the fictional women choose to start businesses devoted to women and fashion, focus their entrepreneurial efforts online, deal simultaneously with the ups and downs in work and life, and receive help from family and friends. Their dreams are rooted in the desire to share in China's booming consumer market and to enjoy the same respect and opportunities that men enjoy. Applying the film's promotional refrain to the women's version of the Chinese Dream, it could be said that all of these women figures, both in the film and in *Shanzhai* business, are dreaming within a broader framework of the state's ideology, which co-opts the language of entrepreneurship to serve as propaganda. The film is in these respects propagandistic, but actual propaganda from such government organizations as the All-China Women's Federation (ACWF) and its various branches is replete with such aspirations and ambitions as part of an effort to establish role models for women "from ordinary backgrounds who strive to realize their dreams and thus contribute to the Chinese Dream" (ACWF, n.d.). By conveniently sidestepping such gender issues as employment discrimination, social inequality, and domestic violence, the inspiring stories downplay the intense social debates and disputes relating to gender that are reflected in the growing number and intensity of feminist activities.

The disregard for gender in the explication of the Chinese Dream is consistent with the lack of explicit engagement with gender relations and subjectivities that has characterized the discussion of digital labor in cultural studies and in the media (Andrejevic et al., 2014; Duffy, 2015). The work and life of real women have changed dramatically in China in recent decades, but these changes are only dimly reflected in their representation in the media. The government-endorsed term *shengnu* ("leftover women") is one of a number of sexist terms for single urban professionals over the age of 25 or so. The unmarried status of these women has been pathologized as a Chinese social problem in the context of a traditionally patriarchal perspective (Fincher, 2014) and has inspired scores of television dramas, films, matchmaking campaigns on social media, and dating shows (L. Li, 2015; Zheng, 2015). In this regard, *MBAP* represents an effort to depict and envision an alternative possibility for women in work and life, though at the same time the film's representation of entrepreneurship in the digital economy and focus on feminized fashion work reaffirm social and historical constructions and expectations relating to gendered work. The narrative harnesses the contemporary ethos of postfeminist sensibilities in the service of the pre-socialist vision of the Dream discourse and presents individual aspirations, freedom, independence, and modes of self-expression as being rooted deeply in the consumer marketplace.

The fact that massage, beauty, and fashion are identified as feminine work is an indication that, while Chinese women today play a large role in the labor market, a significant portion of the work that they take on remains fraught with problematic gender associations. The discourse that work empowers women has become increasingly confounded with a postfeminist mentality of play, pleasure, and choice in a constellation of ideas and beliefs with the potential to explain away any differences between men's and women's experiences using the language of individualism (Gill, 2014). This sensibility of a femininity constructed in the workplace valorizes the supposed glamor and fantasy of beauty work in a way that fosters the growth of the female consumer market (McRobbie, 2009). The beauty and fashion industry provides women with ready-made aspirations to modernity, urbanity, and upward mobility interwoven with expectations regarding freedom, entrepreneurism, and individual satisfaction. In addition, just as the aspirational consumption of goods can serve as a mark of status, women are also called on to perform what Duffy (2016) labeled "aspirational labor," that is, "a forward-looking, carefully orchestrated, and entrepreneurial form of creative cultural production" (p. 446) in their search for future cultural and economic capital through the potentiality of such digitally enabled activities as fashion blogging, micro-celebrity, and social media modeling. Duffy additionally argued that the myths of amateurism, creative autonomy, and collaboration constructed in the aspirational labor process conceal the hierarchical, market-driven, and self-promotional aspects of creative digital production.

The digital labor performed by *Shanzhai* women designers is aspirational to the extent that they believe their future resides in their fashion businesses, in a field that they truly love and in which they feel competent to engage. The designers whom I interviewed frequently voiced such sensibilities and aspirations. One, known here as Tammy, told me that, before she started her *Shanzhai* business with her friends, she had hopped from one job to another without knowing exactly what she wanted to do. Around 2013, she came to the conclusion that her heart was in fashion and started her *Shanzhai* shop. For her, the business provided an urban, modern, and creative orientation to the business world, tapping into the allure of "Do what you love." Similarly, Cho at one point said that her dream was to dress each of her customers in fashionable and trendy clothes, bags, shoes, and other accessories from her shop. Still another informant, whom I call Brette, once worked at a big IT firm in Shenzhen; the work was financially rewarding, but she found it strenuous and tedious and eventually (in 2010) started a Taobao shop featuring Japanese-style socks "for fun." She had quit her IT job a few years later, still finding it to be physically and psychologically demanding, and was devoting herself full time to her fashion business. She had gradually developed her own niche by selling factory "extra" luxury bags—directly on WeChat so as to avoid Taobao's censorship regime; generally speaking, she used WeChat for selling high-end copies and the Taobao shop for off-brand stock. She told me that she had formed many friendships with the customers who frequented her shop and was convinced that she was better off running her fashion business than she would have been if she had remained in the IT industry, fashion being "more suitable for a woman … being pretty, sharing, and making friends."

These *Shanzhai* fashion narratives and the self-positioning that they describe are problematic, however, in their uncritical celebration of freedom and femininity, the potential limitations of new media technologies and e-commerce, and their reinforcement of such conventional dichotomies of gendered labor as production/reproduction, public/private, and work/family (Weeks, 2011). Women designers' experiences in their work and lives enact various modalities of the various material, tangible, visceral, and sensorial imaginations of urbanity, modernity, and a particular kind of femininity that fits perfectly with their self-identification and -branding. Nevertheless, the lack of attention to and denial of recognition for their specific, individual dreams in the ideological construction of China as an innovative, creative, and undeniably great cultural power is a measure of the hollowness of the post-socialist promise implied in the Chinese Dream discourse.

DREAM AND DREAMERS

In this chapter, I have elaborated on the brutal encounter between women designers' *Shanzhai* dreams and the Chinese Dream, arguing that their dreams expose from within the simultaneous possibility and impossibility of the larger Dream. Often compared to the American Dream, the

Chinese Dream draws attention to the rise of China "again" on a global scale. The currency of this Dream is elusive, and the paths to its fulfillment for individuals are tightly controlled by the government. Yet it is difficult for any entity to control imagination or the various inspirations for individual initiative, and it is this notion of freedom that is inscribed in *Shanzhai* culture and manifests in *Shanzhai* dreams. While the state seeks to instrumentalize the Chinese Dream as a top-down process of mainstreaming a sub-culture in the service of its nationalistic discourse, *Shanzhai* dreams capture a much larger terrain in which individuals grapple with privatized responsibility as the work to articulate their own dreams.

While the Chinese Dream downplays issues relating to gender, the multiple registers of *Shanzhai* fashion in women's digital labor and creative work indicate that the ethos of entrepreneurism, the promise of a more luxurious lifestyle, the criticism and resistance from the general public, and the state's hegemony are all gendered phenomena that relate to precarity. An exploration of women's practice in *Shanzhai* fashion therefore has the potential to reveal previously unrecognized facets of the situation and to complicate the picture further. As mentioned earlier, the women designers discussed here, as self-made entrepreneurs, have found their economic capabilities and cultural expressions to be greatly constrained by the state owing to its ability to silence and co-opt their attempts of recognition. Notably, the same government that advocates the Chinese Dream also provides its citizens the freedom to seek recognition, as was evident in the case of the *Shanzhai* of *Shanzhai* products discussed in the previous chapter.

Shanzhai fashion exemplifies the many dimensions of this type of production in China. In this respect, women designers are interlopers in the Chinese Dream: they are called to be the Chinese Dreamers, desiring individual prosperity through digital fashion work, nevertheless excluded and denied full entry into the very dream they aspire to achieve. In the context of the modern Chinese Dream, their creativity is illegitimate, their innovation irrelevant, and their collective production of knowledge and information excluded from estimates of the nation's prosperity. Nevertheless, it is precisely their precariousness that characterizes best the discursive formation and ideological operation of the Chinese Dream, in which the encouragement of private initiatives and growth coexists uneasily with limitations on individual political expression (Ong & Zhang, 2008; Rofel, 2007).

Further, because the Chinese Dream offers so little space for the women designers, their *Shanzhai* dreams overshadow it as they pursue their goals. A *Shanzhai* dream differs significantly from the Chinese Dream in being unique, one-of-a-kind, even as it coalesces and collaborates with other *Shanzhai* dreams in working to imagine a possibility, a potentiality, a becoming that has risen from internal differences to each other. Such a possibility renders a master narrative unnecessary, since the aim of the latter is to construct a new sameness and a community under the same construct of national identity, pride, and strength. Women designers are all dreaming distinct, affective, and tangible dreams; these dreams are their sprawling aspirations to a variety of things. The *Shanzhai* dream is, in the terms introduced in the previous chapter, a rhizomatic dream, and in this respect contradicts the purportedly universal Chinese Dream. Women designers' precarious creativity in *Shanzhai* fashion is evidence of the ambivalent relationship between the national affect of hope and promise, on the one hand, and the fragility of individual potentiality under the neoliberal ethos, on the other. The intricately bounded relationship between women designers' freedom to work and create and the state's regulation of compartmentalized dreams showcases the precarity that is pervasive in aspirational, post-socialist China.

6

Shanzhai Culture, National Ideologies, and Transnational Capitalism: A Double-edged Sword

My focus in this book has been on women's experience of precarious creativity in the shifting cultural domain of production and consumption in contemporary China. Specifically, I have examined the work and life of women who create fashion imitations and conduct *Shanzhai* business over digital platforms. Inspired by both transnational fashion trends and a creative, entrepreneurial ethos, these women are pushing the boundaries of the gray market of *Shanzhai* fashion while placing themselves at considerable risk of being regulated and policed by the state. Like many other cultural workers in China, they are striving to carve out a precarious space for individual expression and prosperity where they can articulate their aspirations, desires, and dreams in a post-socialist landscape.

As has been seen, these designers come from a variety of social backgrounds, have their own understandings of fashion tastes and trends, and engage with their fanbase-clientele in diverse ways. Their definitive characteristics are that they create their own versions of fashion and regard *Shanzhai* practice as the norm for fashion production. There is a historical continuity running through the development of the modern Chinese fashion industry as changes in socio-cultural values and the emergence of a market economy have combined to make China the world's top exporter of textiles, garments, and miscellaneous goods. As the state has struggled to implement a strict IPR system and strategically transform the country's productivity from "Made in China" to "Created in China" in the manner suggested by the Chinese Dream, women designers have aggressively seized the opportunity represented by the e-commerce boom to actualize their passion for fashion.

Only rarely, however, has the story of women *Shanzhai* designers been told in celebratory tones as one of creativity and rebellion. Instead, in mainstream media narratives and the public imagination alike, *Shanzhai* fashion culture has been associated with shoddy goods circulating in a legal gray zone. There is no hype around the buzzword *Shanzhai*, and no connection of it to the evils of global capitalism or Western hegemony. *Shanzhai* fashion has been marginalized in conventional discourse and portrayed in ambivalent terms, even (or especially) in the fashion industry.

Receiving little attention or discussion, at least of a positive or constructive sort, from academics or society at large, these women work in a conjuncture of shifting social ideals, increasingly subtle and nuanced political control, a booming economy and increasing living standards, flourishing if highly constrained media and digital cultures, and the intersectionality of transnational capitalism, national ideologies, and the *Shanzhai* ethos. Like their male counterparts working in other creative domains of the cultural industries, women designers' digital labor is being reconfigured within privatization and entrepreneurship with a neoliberal ethos, giving rise to a postfeminist sensibility reflected in such seductive terms as "gaining one's independence," "pursuing one's dream," and "maintaining a work-life balance." Most of my informants had achieved a certain level of success in terms of profits and fame in the *Shanzhai* fashion business, and most were convinced that they were living at the best possible time when it came to chasing their goals for success in work and life. Simultaneously, these women's struggles and endeavors as pioneers in the *Shanzhai* fashion industry were subject to the enchanting consumption power of global fashion trends and the regulatory as well as the ideological power of the state.

On the one hand, while women are able to produce fashion products by translating their sensibilities regarding transnational fashion tastes and chic looks into affordable quality copies, their choices of styles and designs are already trapped within the global fashion hierarchy. The transnational fashion consciousness, and, consequently, the status that is associated with the power of consumption, are discursively formulated and buttressed by powerful fashion houses and luxury brands, the majority of which originated in developed countries. The fierce competition among women designers has also accelerated the copying of any creative breakthrough with the potential to define a niche, as was apparent in the discussion of the *Shanzhai* of *Shanzhai* phenomenon in Chapter 4.

On the other hand, the state has ignored these women's contributions to both economic development and innovative capacity. To be sure, the state has not overlooked *Shanzhai* production, for, even as it has implemented numerous top-down efforts to foster innovation and creative cultural industries, it has at the same time expropriated the human capital harnessed by *Shanzhai* production in an attempt to integrate bottom-up practices of creativity into its technocratic development planning. However, men have been celebrated as the force behind *Shanzhai* production in particular and nation-building projects in general and therefore as symbolic of the future of a strong nation. The new entrepreneurial language that is emerging in this context also tends to be gender-blind and therefore unsympathetic to women designers, who have long struggled with patriarchal and patriotic morality that disciplines and polices them in the social factory.

My study of *Shanzhai* women designers has accordingly foregrounded women's digital labor in the precarious domain of the creative industries while also challenging the conventional notion that the rebellion and resistance characteristic of the *Shanzhai* ethos pose a challenge to the established national-transnational power structure. In the current economic, political, and cultural environment, the women who make fashion copies are treated as interlopers in China's cultural landscape, in transnational consumerism, and in the global culture industry. Their precarious creativity in creating the culture of *Shanzhai* fashion thus is both an individualized life situation and a specific socio-historical product that typifies contemporary digital labor. Represented in their experiences are "both the multiplication of precarious, unstable, insecure forms of living and, simultaneously, new forms of political struggle and solidarity that reach beyond the traditional models of the political party or trade union" (Gill & Pratt, 2008, p. 3; see also Fantone, 2007).

This is the double-edged sword of precarious creativity, which simultaneously serves as a form of oppression in the information society and stands to benefit from the new politics that it makes possible. In other words, while women's work and life in the *Shanzhai* fashion industry are marked by palpable precarity, it is, as argued especially in Chapter 5, also in *Shanzhai*—which is produced in a creative space by these women— that they aspire to chase their own unique dreams and achieve their goals in the broader dreamscape of China, albeit without guarantee.

CAN WE STILL DREAM IN *SHANZHAI*?
THE DOUBLE DENIALS OF SHANZHAI FASHION

Historically, *Shanzhai* culture originated in the flourishing imitation cellphone industry beginning in the mid-2000s, and for this reason has long been considered a sort of folk-oriented IT and working-class ICT (Wallis & Qiu, 2012). *Shanzhai* practice is associated with a celebratory ethos of creativity and ingenuity and has a distinctive class component, referring as it does to both the technological know-how of *Shanzhai* entrepreneurs and the migrant working class to which the main consumers of *Shanzhai* cellphones belong. The description of copying practices in the fashion industry as "*Shanzhai*" is simply a kind of self-designation of their work by women designers and their customers that places it in a positive light as a de-centered approach to garment-making combined with a snobbish disdain for rip-offs produced elsewhere in society or by outsiders.

The description of the overall contours of the *Shanzhai* fashion process presented in Chapter 1 and of the production chain in Chapter 3 makes clear that *Shanzhai* is a highly consumer-centered practice. Designers often maintain their customers' interest by documenting the details of the copying process and by comparing the original with the copy to show the similarities and the improvements featured in the latter. Figure 6.1 illustrates such a comparison; the coat on the left is from the 2015 winter collection of the brand Dizzit, and the one on the right one is the

Figure 6.1   A comparison of the original product and the *Shanzhai* copy made by the designer Wanzi

Shanzhai. The capital letter "Z" at the top of the image is used to indicate the original because it is the first letter of the Chinese pinyin for *zhengpin* (正品, "the original") and the "S" stands for *Shanzhai*.

This image also documents the fact that, early on, women who made copies of fashion products intentionally called their practice "*Shanzhai*." The term was and is considered apt because of the designers' motivation and desire to make their own versions. However, unlike the copies of cellphones and technological gadgets from which the *Shanzhai* phenomenon emerged, fashion imitations have rarely been celebrated as exemplary of grassroots creativity and resistance; nor have women designers been recognized as subjects who have established a new means of cultural production and consumption—even though *Shanzhai* is, first and foremost, a business strategy for earning a profit, whether in the fashion or the cellphone industry. The women designers are in fact outliers of the recognition of *Shanzhai* in its discursive formation to epitomize the power of the multitude and provide collective cultural imagination.

In recent years, some women designers have taken to using "Y"—the first letter of the Chinese pinyin for *yangpin* (样品, "sample")—instead of "S" (*Shanzhai*) to indicate the copy, or sample, in their pictorial comparisons of the products. Usually, a designer displays only the final version of the sample labeled with her own name next to the original branded

Figure 6.2   A comparison of the original and the sample by the designer VIAN

commodity. Figure 6.2 shows the designer VIAN's comparison of an original product from the 2015 summer collection of the local fashion label Cocoon (right) and the sample (left). She in this case removed the Y label and called her product "VIAN's version," assuring her customers in the description of the product on her online shop that it conformed to the design of the original and exceeded it in terms of quality.

The change in the naming of a fashion imitation does not, of course, change the imitative practice of *Shanzhai*. Numerous tweets featuring fashion imitations on Weibo and WeChat still use phrases such as "beg for *Shanzhai*" (*qiushan*, 求山) or "start to *Shanzhai*" (*kaishan*, 开山), indicating that the term retains its currency for describing the production, consumption, and circulation of imitated fashion. For example, in Chapter 4, I discussed the Weibo account Shanzhai Master Groupon, which maintained an up-to-date inventory of the latest *Shanzhai* fashion products produced by a wide range of designers and factories, providing links for consumers to purchase the recommended items.

The fact that the *Shanzhai* label remains attached to these fashion products may be indicative of attitudes in general toward fashion imitation and the control imposed on it. Public opinion regarding *Shanzhai* fashion has been ambivalent; on the one hand, the proliferation of copies has made high-end apparel accessible; on the other, celebrities' claims to have worn imitations "by accident" have incurred a backlash (Tencent Fashion, 2010). The implication is that *Shanzhai* in fashion contexts, rather than signifying grassroots ingenuity and creativity, remains more often associated with the inferiority of the "Made-in-China" label that has been discursively shaped by and freighted with concern about the cheap Asian labor that has contributed significantly to China's economic progress and to the transnational-national imagination of factory workers (Canaves, 2009; CNN, 2007; Lee, 1998; Pun, 2005).

The government in the past decade took a more proactive position with regard to reclaiming the quality of and rebuilding confidence in products manufactured in China by creating new and strengthening existing regulations pertaining to IPR, a move that has resulted in increased industrial self-policing as well. Taobao, for example, as the dominant shopping platform and the site where most fakes are offered for sale, has collaborated with a dozen e-commerce companies on numerous anti-counterfeiting campaigns (Taobao, 2010). In spring 2015, many webpages featuring a popular trenchcoat that imitated a product by the Korean fashion brand Imvely were censored and deleted by Taobao without any prior notice to either the sellers or buyers. I myself bought such a coat from Wanzi, who ended up notifying her consumers that her webpage had been deleted by Taobao for violating the copyright law by using Imvely's original promotional images of the coat. This was not a unique incident; most webpages that featured fashion imitations with copyrighted advertisements and images from the original brands were removed around the same time. This large-scale censorship of Taobao shops coincided with a nationwide crackdown on fakes sold online (Wong, 2015).

Shanzhai products are being renamed with increasing frequency in a manner that sheds light on the intricate relationship between *Shanzhai* culture and the state, and as a consequence of the intensification of both the social backlash and governmental regulations. According to Yang (2016), *Shanzhai* represents a collective conception of an alternative to the globalizing regime of IPR. Her analysis demonstrated that the state distinguishes the "*Shanzhai* economy," based on fakes as well as illicit products, from "*Shanzhai* culture," which is understood as a manifestation of the creativity of ordinary people. From this perspective, IPR functions as a state-legitimized system to profit from individual creativity while the "*Shanzhai* economy" stands in opposition to the value-making aspect of creativity involved in IPR. The state appropriates "*Shanzhai* culture," however, as part of its claim to represent the people and to authority over culture. In this way, the state recasts *Shanzhai* as a part of the national brand, one that is both compatible with global IPR demands and, presumably, representative of the people (Yang, 2016).

Extending this line of argumentation, the state's expropriation of *Shanzhai* can be seen to generate two intertwining effects. First, class loses the capacity as an analytical term to explain the current cultural regime, under which the state has sought to deprive the people of *Shanzhai* on the grounds that *Shanzhai* serves as an anti-authoritative culture of economic expression. The grassroots nature of *Shanzhai* is being subsumed into the mega-narrative of increasing innovative capacity and national branding. The *Shanzhai* spirit and its power to encourage rebellion and resistance to authority encounters suspicion on top of the ontological anxiety and insecurity caused by daily concerns of food safety, environmental pollution, and natural disasters (Bristow, 2008; Chai, 2015; Watts, 2007). It therefore seems to be safe to reinterpret *Shanzhai* as simply a consumer- and innovation-centered and business strategy that has particular resonance with the "Created-in-China" discourse (Keane & Zhao, 2012). A textbook example of the characteristics of this strategy is the smartphone maker Xiaomi, often described as China's answer to Apple (Lai, 2015; Linshi, 2015) owing to its "snazzy design, glitzy launches, and the cult-like fervor it inspires in its users" (The Economist, 2013b); its CEO Lei Jun is even represented in a trendy Steve Jobs-style outfit of jeans and a black shirt. Xiaomi borrows heavily from *Shanzhai* as a business model in terms of its relationship to Apple, but it can hardly be described as a *Shanzhai* brand or product. Rather, proceeding from imitation, Xiaomi has become a successful, legitimate, and innovative company in its own right, having transferred the extracted value of *Shanzhai* culture into its business strategies and technological breakthroughs for the purpose of profit. The firm projects an image of young men pursuing their dreams in China's creative industries, typifying the masculine technological space of *Shanzhai* and the gendered nature of economic development under the Chinese neoliberal and post-socialist state.

That state's expropriation of *Shanzhai*, particularly in the development of ICTs, was made official during the 18th National Congress of the Communist Party of China (CPC) in November 2012, when the Innovation-driven Development Strategy (IDS) was promoted as the means to transform and optimize China's economic structure (Hu, 2012). In contrast with this kind of top-down plan, the Chinese Dream discourse officially announced later in the same month delicately inserted the state's ideology into the everyday lives of its citizens by recognizing and encouraging personal pursuits that can bring prosperity to both the individual and the nation (Kuhn, 2013). The Dream discourse highlights the state's effort to implement a top-down campaign for promoting cultural power while at the same time appropriating the bottom-up capacity for innovation, which is evident in the transformation and success of domestic IT companies such as Xiaomi.

As the state has expropriated *Shanzhai*, women *Shanzhai* designers have been losing the language through which to seek an alternative space to express themselves. Again, it has been the case that, though women designers' work has not been acknowledged in the mainstream, male-dominated *Shanzhai* discourse, they have nevertheless been positioning themselves under the umbrella of *Shanzhai*, thereby leaving themselves targets of state policing and of social condemnation as ineligible to take part in this cultural meaning-making practice. Yet such name-claiming, as the Z-vs-S comparison foregrounds, is the political language through which women designers experience the impossibility of recognition yet explore the possibility to resist and challenge their conditions as unrecognizable.

This reading of the situation is consistent with Judith Butler's (2009) association of gender performativity with precarity in her analysis of an incident in 2006 in which undocumented immigrants sang the US and Mexican national anthems in English and Spanish during a street protest in Los Angeles. These people petitioned the government to allow them to become citizens by exercising the rights of protest and petition that only citizens can have. Specifically, Butler argued that precarity was manifest in the performance of asserting a right that the protesters did not possess as a means to claim that they should possess that right. The point of comparison here is that, with the reworking of *Shanzhai* to suit the nation-building agenda of the Chinese Dream, the women designers are gradually losing the precarious language, in this case, the language of *Shanzhai*, and its capacity to help them make themselves visible. More often than not, the Z-vs-Y comparisons of the type shown in Figures 6.1 and 6.2 signify a retreat from the effort to claim the recognition that continues to be denied to women designers. In this respect, they are placed in a double state of precarity by the state's co-optation of *Shanzhai*: on the one hand, they are excluded from "the people" whom *Shanzhai* culture supposedly represents; on the other, they are further deprived of the language to articulate their lack of recognition and with it the space to do so.

The women designers who practice fashion imitation and operate their *Shanzhai* businesses, then, are not only deprived of recognition as creative grassroots and anti-establishment cultural workers in *Shanzhai* culture and as constructive nation-building subjects, but they are also exploited as a labor force to sustain the country's economy and self-exploiting to provide themselves subsistence. Their creative responses to their precarious situation are manifest, and must be practiced, in every aspect of their daily lives; this is their best hope for making sense of their lived reality. Their individual *Shanzhai* dreams have been obscured by the greater Chinese Dream that threatens to overwhelm them.

Precarious creativity for these women, first and foremost, involves the entanglement of the top-down national "Created-in-China" initiative with the bottom-up practice of *Shanzhai* culture that is being packaged and sold as a version of the Chinese Dream. The designers' individual *Shanzhai* dreams invert the hegemony of the global fashion labels and their fetishization of commodity and class, in that their digital labor de-fetishizes the production process and de-mythologizes the class ideology embedded in fashion production and consumption. Nonetheless, as participants in the creation of a *Shanzhai* imaginary, the women designers struggle to claim for themselves the right to participate in the cultural process. On the one hand, the Dream discourse opens up possibilities for women designers to gain recognition for their participation in *Shanzhai* culture, for embracing entrepreneurship and the DIY spirit, for aspiring to the glamor and fantasy of transnational consumerism, and for seeking the status associated with fashion awareness and cosmopolitanism. When creating copies of fashion products through appropriation, modification, and innovation, the designers also must stay abreast of fickle global fashion trends, consume high-fashion products, maintain contact with factories, establish and network with their customer bases, sustain their popularity through social media, and stay alert to the political and economic climate, especially to policies and rules governing e-commerce. On the other hand, the very act of copying and the counterfeit nature of *Shanzhai* fashion products fall outside the rational system of creativity that legitimizes the state's expropriation of *Shanzhai* for the Chinese Dream. It is for these reasons that I have described contemporary women *Shanzhai* designers as impossible Chinese Dreamers kept ever at a distance from that Dream's promise.

THE ROAD AHEAD:
DOING *SHANZHAI* IN THE STATE OF THE DREAM

My argument here is not, however, that the Chinese Dream produces identities and alterities by imposing binary divisions between legitimate Dreamers and precarious dreamers on the cultural domain of China. Rather, I am suggesting that the multiplicity of individual differences that these women designers produce is symptomatic of a massive clash among cultural producers in China as the state and the *Shanzhai* producers seek in their own ways to control the manufacture of ambitions, aspirations, truths, and dreams. While China's economic domain has been unshackled from central planning, its political and social domains are increasingly policed and regulated, and it is in this context that the Chinese Dream and similar propaganda campaigns have been deployed as means to engineer and manifest a single identity for every Chinese citizen and to hail them into the subject of patriotism. Viewed this way, the Dream discourse is an abstract machine that functions to homogenize real social differences within one overarching narrative that pushes the differences to the absolute and subsumes the absolute under the identity of the Chinese Dreamers.

In the Introduction, I referred to the critical view of precarious labor and class struggle advanced by Italian theorists associated with the *operaismo* movement, in particular their valorization of "a multiplicity, a plane of singularities, an open set of relations, which is not homogeneous or identical with itself and bears an indistinct, inclusive relation to those outside of it" (Hardt & Negri, 2000, p.103). This notion of labor differs from those in which "the people" and the "working class" are conceptualized in respect to a homogeneous identity tied either to the modern nation-state or to industrial capitalism. This approach has intrigued many other theorists and writers in approaching power as something dispersed throughout capitalism rather than emanating from a single point, thereby making a democracy of the multitude a political possibility. In discussing the spontaneous, temporary, organic, and creative, yet precarious, phenomenon of the *Shanzhai* of *Shanzhai* in Chapter 4, I demonstrated that the power in copying subverts and overtakes the power of the icon, the original, and the model, debunking the notion of originality and serving as the locus for creativity in the women designers' *Shanzhai* practices—creativity in this case being defined as the ability to imitate and create various versions of a notional garment. In contrast with the globalized IPR system and the formal copyright protection mechanism, which juxtapose authenticity/originality with fake/copy in order to regulate capitalist production and profits, *Shanzhai* fashion production, especially the *Shanzhai* of *Shanzhai*, exposes the impossibility of a coherent identity as either "original" or "copy" owing to the multitude of distinct *Shanzhai* practices. *Shanzhai* fashion in this respect rejuvenates copying and creativity through the multiplicity that it introduces into cultural production and, in so doing, reveals that the collectivity is only imagined and practiced through the singularities and differences of the multitude.

In the contrast and contestation between the women designers' *Shanzhai* dreams and the Chinese Dream, the former must accordingly cope with a double denial, from both the state and from the broader society. Instead of seeking collectivity within *Shanzhai*, they increasingly internalize the precariousness of their fashion businesses and practice self-reliance. This tendency is reflected in the incorporation of the words *zizhi* (自制), "self-designed" or "self-produced," or *dingzhi* (定制),

"custom-made," into the names of some of their online shops. In Chinese, *zi* means something like "self" and suggests an anti-corporate position, while *ding* translates as "according to" and suggests a consumer-oriented mode of production. The popularity of these words in this context also reflects the development of self-accountability mechanisms in response to the prevailing political and socio-cultural atmosphere of the privatization of the self under post-socialist control (Ong & Zhang, 2008). In other words, these women designers are struggling over the production of themselves and their own politics, consciously or unconsciously, in their encounter with, as Foucault (1988) would put it, the biopower of the state. They are self-made designers in the context of *Shanzhai* culture and the Chinese neoliberal state apparatus occupying a liminal space in the creative economy.

Within this liminal space, they have been rewarded with profound precarity for their cultural work. As the Z-vs-S/Z-vs-Y and *zizhi* and *dingzhi* examples suggest, while women designers pursue their own dreams and prosperity through their *Shanzhai* businesses, the very nature of copying precludes their dreams from forming part of the Dream; their contributions to economic development, cultural expression, material abundance, and aesthetic expression have all been denied. In the face of the state's power to police and to regulate, women designers feel compelled to submit to the Dream narrative and to retreat from demanding recognition.

Nonetheless, a liberating aspect of this liminal space is that the women designers never stop dreaming within it. I discussed in Chapter 5 the diverse ways in which women operate their *Shanzhai* businesses, constantly experimenting with digital platforms, marketing tactics, and social networking, envisioning alternative future possibilities, and expanding their capacities to produce, consume, and circulate knowledge, images, codes, information, and affects. Their *Shanzhai* dreams, instead of being synthesized into the grand Chinese Dream, are enlivened by the impossible Chinese Dream. While the state strives to bring all resources, wealth, and cultural expression under its command—as manifest in the aspect of the Dream discourse that encourages privatization of all social domains for the public good—*Shanzhai* fashion, especially the *Shanzhai* of the *Shanzhai*, demonstrates how the process of post-socialist transformation in production, consumption, and accumulation also creates an entirely new social life in which the producers (i.e., the women designers), the forms of production (the de-centered fashion circuit, unrestricted information networks, and highly fluid social relations), and the products (fashion ideas, tastes, designs, patterns, fabrics, knowledge, information, codes, sensation, and affects) all demand a high degree of freedom and open access to a common.

A "common" in this context refers to the material and socio-cultural conditions for humanity, belonging to neither the private nor the public sphere but residing mainly in the becoming of the multitude, as Hardt and Negri (2009) have described it. These scholars elsewhere (2004) pointed out in this regard that "the challenge posed by the concept of multitude is for a social multiplicity to manage to communicate and act in common while remaining internally different" (p. xiv). Critiquing the standard view as composed of false alternatives that dichotomize social production as either private or public, capitalist or socialist, Hardt and Negri (2009) formulated the notion of "the common" as a new space for politics. The stories of women *Shanzhai* fashion designers have long been forced into similarly artificial dichotomies, so I have sought instead to flesh out the manner in which they, with their multiplicity of distinct dreams, communicate and act in "common"—which is to say, neither in ways that further capitalist accumulation and exploitation by privat-izing resources, wealth, and cultural expression nor in submission to the state's ideological grip and command over biopower in its effort to produce subjects and objects under the public reign. Instead, as a new space for politics composed by the multitude in the process of the pro-duction of subjectivities—a space that is internal to the social relations that are, in turn, geared toward capital—the common is, in this case, produced through the women designers' precarious creativity within the social factory, neither in forms of unionization nor privatization, but in the process of biopolitical production, in order to create the basis for an alternative social and economic order.

For all of these reasons, women's precarious creativity in the context of China's *Shanzhai* fashion industry remains a promising field for inves-tigations of spaces for the common and for politics in general within the modern neoliberal state. One intriguing area of the *Shanzhai* fashion industry in this regard is consumption. As observed in the discussion of prosumption, in many parts of modern economies, production and consumption are no longer distinct processes; rather, production has intruded into many aspects of life. This shift in the nature of labor has occurred with the facilitation of digital technologies and a rethinking of class values; for the women designers profiled in this book, this has meant being heavy consumers as well as producers of fashion products while their digital labor in the social factory never ceases. The consumption of *Shanzhai* fashion is accordingly most fruitfully viewed as immanent to the circuit of precarious creativity, which is distinct from production but makes possible the survival and prosperity of the producers. Consumers and customers, or what I refer to as a woman designer's fanbase-clientele, should also be treated as cultural producers of *Shanzhai* fashion; their interest in transnational fashion trends is what makes them consumers and then, according to the neoliberal state's ideology, patriots. *Shanzhai* consumers are also diverse with respect to their levels of spending, social status, involvement in the production of fashion knowledge, and so forth. Given that they have their own preferences, choices, goals, and purposes in keeping pace with *Shanzhai* fashion culture, the constructive power of this massive number of consumers as a potentiality, a becoming, is significant and remains to be quantified.

The story of *Shanzhai* women designers also needs to be viewed from broader perspectives, for instance through comparison with workers in other countries and industries. Also in need of further investigation are the stories of male designers, who in the present book have served mainly as a foil for the women's stories. I did observe that many domestic menswear firms have also practiced creative copying tactics in terms of both establishing brand image and designing garments; in fact, this tradition long precedes the use of *Shanzhai* to refer to such practices. My failed visit to China's "blue jeans capital" described in Chapter 2 provides a vivid glimpse into the ways in which men participate actively in *Shanzhai* fashion production—apparently mainly as bosses or pat-ternmakers. Men's work and life in *Shanzhai* fashion may tend to take different forms from that of women's, and their desires, aspirations, and dreams may likewise differ. An essential question in this respect is how the common can transcend gender while still being enlivened by a mul-tiplicity of gender-specific experiences.

I have throughout this book privileged the notion of the multitude, and this tendency points naturally to understand capitalism as a global phenomenon not only owing to its fundamentally synthetic nature but also because of the revolutionary aspect embodied in it. What I am sug-gesting is that, in the same way that empire, to again quote Hardt and Negri (2004), "spreads globally its network of hierarchies and divisions that maintain order through new mechanisms of control and constant conflict," the multitude benefits from "new circuits of cooperation and collaboration that stretch across nations and continents and allow an unlimited number of encounters" (p. xiii). Thus, I showed in Chapter 4 that the journey of a hunter green check-pattern dress from a New York runway and online promotion in Korea to Chinese *Shanzhai* shops and modeling by a *wang hong* involved diverse and heterogeneous producers, consumers, and objects, all with their own singularities. In network capitalism, it is imperative to understand how singularities differ as well as the commonalities that enable the cultural participants in whom these singularities reside to communicate and act out possible politics.

For women designers, the road ahead is not promised, let alone guaranteed, by the state's Dream. Their precarious creativity, exercised through their *Shanzhai* fashion businesses, exemplifies the affective structure of what Lauren Berlant (2011) called the cruel optimism of "a relation of attachment to compromised conditions of possibility whose realization is discovered either to be impossible, sheer fantasy, or too possible, and toxic ... [and to be] the condition of maintaining an attachment to a significantly problematic object" (p. 24). Perhaps the Chinese Dream may eventually reveal to these women designers the impossibility of a small *Shanzhai* dream as well as the becoming of a Dreamer. In any case, this investigation of their work and lives has shed light on the conditions in which they live: if their pursuit of or calling to a good life is built on the shaky foundation of cruelty, the cruelty of the Dream represents also the possibility of room for optimism in every little dream for which it is worth fighting. This is a political project that is already in becoming-the-common in *Shanzhai* fashion.

Appendix: Demographics of Informants

Name	*Shanzhai* Type	When started fashion business/*shanzhai*	Education	Age	Marital status	Location
Apple	Mid-range apparel	September 2014	College	Late 20s	Single	Shangqiu
Autumn	Low-to mid-range apparel	2008/2009	College	Early 30s	Married with two children	Hangzhou
Benxe	Mid-range apparel	October 2014	College	Late 20s	Married with one child	Quanzhou
Brette	High-end bags and mid-range apparel	August 2010/2014	College	Mid 30s	Married	Shenzhen
Cho	High-end apparel	1997/2009	Normal school	Late 40s	Married with one child	Shanghai
Ivy	Low-to mid-range apparel	April 2015	College	Mid 20s	Single	Beijing
Jimi	High-end bags	April 2012	N/A	Early 30s	Single	Wuhan
Josie	Mid-range shoes	2010/September 2012	Normal school	Late 20s	Single	Chengdu
Katie	Mid-range-high-end apparel	February 2014	College	Early 30s	Married	Shanghai
Lenka	Mid-range accessories	July 2006	College	Late 20s	Single	Shanghai
Lyn	Mid-range apparel	2016	N/A	Mid 30s	Married with one child	Hangzhou

Name	*Shanzhai* Type	When started fashion business/*shanzhai*	Education	Age	Marital status	Location
Maison	Mid-range apparel	March 2013	College	Late 20s	Single	Haikou
Mey	Mid-range apparel	June 2011/February 2014	Military university	Late 20s	Married with one child	Yantai
Moon	High-end bags and mid-range apparel	2011	N/A	Early 30s	Married with twins	Dongguan
Sami	High-end apparel	Early 2008	College	Late 20s	Single	Shanghai
Summer	Mid-range shoes	July 2014–January 1, 2017	College	Late 20s	Married with one child	Chengdu
Tammy	Low- to mid-range apparel	2013	N/A	Late 20s	N/A	Hangzhou
Vivien	Mid-range apparel	2010	N/A	Mid 30s	Married with one child	Hangzhou

Notes

1. Many name-brand phones nowadays have increased their features to cater to the growing Chinese market and global demands. For example, Apple brought dual-SIM support to its latest iPhone XS and XS Max.
2. OEM refers to Original Equipment Manufacturer. China's apparel OEMs or OEM services receive orders from transnational fashion houses and produce garments with the design, fabric, and other raw materials provided by them.
3. Fashion-forward means someone who is interested in fashion and has a forward-looking perspective on fashion trends. Persona is a role or characteristic adopted by a person to be perceived by others. Together and put into the context "fashion-forward persona" means that the woman designer created something for her consumers to be perceived as fashionable and perhaps trend-setters.
4. My informant Summer closed the Taobao shop and her *Shanzhai* business at the beginning of 2017, as she posted on the social media platform Sina Weibo (henceforth Weibo), indicating she had just become a mom and needed to take care of her baby and that she could not spare any time on operating the online shop. Although she is still active on Weibo, she no longer conducts *Shanzhai* business.
5. WeChat launched a new shopping function and related app WeChat Store, or Weidian, as a mobile marketplace in 2014, expanding the WeChat universe from instant messaging to e-wallet to social shopping. Interestingly, none of the women designers I interviewed and/or chatted with in this book had set up a shop on Weidian back in 2016. As of 2019, none has shifted their major business from Taobao to Weidian. This might be due to the different business models of Taobao and Weidian, and women designers' primary transaction platform is still Taobao.
6. The 14 cities were: Dalian, Qinhuangdao, Tianjin, Yantai, Qingdao, Lianyungang, Nantong, Shanghai, Ningbo, Wenzhou, Fuzhou, Guangzhou, Zhanjiang, and Beihai. And in 1987, Weihai became the 15th coastal city that enjoyed the preferential policies applied to those opened coastal cities.
7. "Iron rice bowl" refers to a secure occupation with steady income and benefits, usually in state-owned units. Initiated from the establishment of the People's Republic of China in 1949, the state became the main employer to provide jobs for its people. And as a job for life regardless of the effort workers put in, the term is sometimes used to describe unmotivated and unproductive workers. When Deng took power in 1978 and started to reform the labor market, the iron rice bowl jobs were among the first to be transformed to boost productivity.

8. A more recent discussion on the overtime working culture in Chinese IT companies known as 996 (working from 9 a.m. to 9 p.m., six days a week) gained a lot of attention. See www.nytimes.com/2019/04/29/technology/china-996-jack-ma.html (retrieved May 30, 2019).

9. Policies like *Provisional Rules of Management on International Networking on Computer Information Internet in People's Republic of China* (1996), www.scut.edu.cn/cwis/support/law1.html (retrieved December 5, 2014) and *Regulations of Security and Protection on International Networking on Computer Information Internet* (1997), www.gov.cn/gongbao/content/2011/content_1860856.htm (retrieved December 5, 2014) were common. An inventory of internet and telecom laws and policies issued before/on 2000 can be found at http://lawyer.20m.com/Chinese/internet2.html (retrieved December 5, 2014).

10. Alibaba started the B2C platform Alibaba.com in 1999.

11. The pilot FTZ is located in Shanghai. See http://en.shftz.gov.cn/ (retrieved November 25, 2014).

12. There are some women designers who work with their husbands or boyfriends to manage their *Shanzhai* business. Such a partnership generates interesting and unexpected outcomes in women's fashion practice and presentation, which will be given a full account in Chapter 3.

13. China employed its one-child policy from the 1980s; most of the internet generation/majority of the middle-class group are the only children in their families, which gave them lots of entitlements in their families.

14. A *hukou* is a record in the household registration system in China. Citizens are required by law to have a *hukou* in order to legally live in a place.

15. *Getihu* refers to people who are self-employed. It was commonly used during the 1990s, when the government largely promoted entrepreneurism.

16. *Haitao* is understood both as a noun, that is, international shipping-supported websites, and a verb, that is, to shop via those websites. It can also be used to refer to the group of people who *haitao*. For more information, see www.chinadailyasia.com/business/2015-10/07/content_15325632.html (retrieved October 27, 2016).

17. One the one hand, "leftover women" is a derogatory term in China referring to women who remain unmarried in their late 20s and beyond. The term has been widely used in news report, television series, reality shows, and other media productions that created a social discourse which attacks educated and professional women, and pressures young women into marriage. On the other, beginning in 1980, China strictly enforced a one-child policy, which allowed one couple to have only one child. After more than three decades, in January 2016, the national birth planning policy changed to a universal two-child policy to address the pressing aging issue in China. However, academic research and public debates have both pointed out that the loosening of a two-child policy might bring negative effects on gender roles and family duties, in which women are expected to bear more of the work of childcare at the expense of their career. Combined together, we can see a growing social discourse that pressures women to pull back from the

social and professional world and into family roles, reinforcing patriarchal gender roles that subject women to the domestic sphere.

18. WeChat Moments is a social networking feature embedded in the WeChat mobile app. Launched on April 19, 2012 in WeChat version 4.0, Moments allows users to share statuses, websites, and pictures with captions, creating private communication circles with close friends. Its function is similar to that of Instagram.

19. Ruhnn successfully listed its IPO (initial public offering) on Nasdaq on March 3, 2019, raising US$125 million on the day. See https://techcrunch.com/2019/04/03/ruhnn-ipo/ (retrieved July 7, 2019).

20. The Gigi hoodie is a remake of a hoodie worn by an American fashion model and online celebrity Gigi Hadid.

21. In February 2016, Sina fully canceled the 140-character limit for Weibo. Practically speaking, a user can write up to 2,000 Chinese characters in a single post.

22. As of March 2018, China removed the presidential term limits. Xi is poised to rule the country indefinitely.

23. A collection of the video series can be found on YouTube.com (retrieved May 4, 2017, from www.youtube.com/watch?v=rxpGU3DRW5w).

Bibliography

ACWF. (n.d.). *Our Chinese Dream*. Retrieved April 24, 2017, from www.womeno fchina.cn/womenofchina/html1/special/chinesedream/17/1222-1.htm

Adorno, T. & Horkheimer, M. (1997). *Dialectic of Enlightenment*. London and New York: Verso.

Airge. (2016, October 17). Here comes the Shenkuan, a salute to the successful launch of Shenzhou 11 [WeChat post]. Retrieved October 17, 2017, from https://mp.weixin.qq.com

AliResearch. (2016). *Research on Women Based on Alibaba Ecosystem* (Business). Hangzhou: AliResearch. Retrieved September 7, 2017, from http://news. dasinfo.com/archives/24738

All-China Women's Federation & National Bureau of Statistics in China. (2001). *1991–2000 Women's Social Status Report* (statistics) (pp. 1–22). Beijing: All-China Women's Federation and National Bureau of Statistics in China. Retrieved October 27, 2017, from www.stats.gov.cn/tjsj/tjgb/qttjgb/ qgqttjgb/200203/t20020331_30606.html

—— (2010). *2001–2010 Women's Social Status Report* (statistics) (pp. 1–19). Beijing: All-China Women's Federation and National Bureau of Statistics in China. Retrieved October 27, 2017, from www.wsic.ac.cn/staticdata/84760. htm

Anagnost, A. (1989). Transformations of gender in modern China. In S. Morgen (ed.), *Gender in Anthropology: Critical Reviews for Research and Teaching* (pp. 313–42). Arlington, VA: American Anthropological Association.

Andrejevic, M., Banks, J., Campbell, J. E. et al. (2014). Participations: Dialogues on the participatory promise of contemporary culture and Politics. *International Journal of Communication*, 8, 1089–106.

Appadurai, A. (1986). *The Social Life of Things: Commodities in Cultural Perspective*. Cambridge: Cambridge University Press.

Bai, S. (2009, August 26). China's online shopping comes to the tenth year. *Beijing Business Today*, A2.

Baidu-pedia. (n.d.). ochirly. *Baidu*. Retrieved November 9, 2016, from http://baike. baidu.com/view/166050.htm?fromtitle=ochirly&fromid=2439285&type=syn

Barlow, T. (1994). Theorizing woman: Funu, Guojia, Jiating (Chinese women, Chinese state, Chinese family). In I. Grewal & C. Kaplan (eds), *Scattered Hegemonies: Postmodernity and Transnational Feminist Practices* (pp. 173–96). Minneapolis, MN and London: University of Minnesota Press.

Barnes, N. G. & Lescault, A. M. (n.d.). Millennials drive social commerce: Turning their likes, follows or pins into a sale. *University of Massachusetts Dartmouth*. Retrieved September 25, 2017, from www.umassd.edu/cmr/ socialmediaresearch/socialcommerce/

Barton, D., Chen, Y., & Jin, A. (2013, June). Mapping China's middle class. *McKinsey & Company*. Retrieved from September 25, 2017, from www.mckinsey.com/industries/retail/our-insights/ mapping-chinas-middle-class

Baudrillard, J. (1988). *Jean Baudrillard: Selected Writings*. (M. Poster, ed.) (2nd edn). Stanford, CA: Stanford University Press.

—— (1994). *Simulacra and Simulation*. Ann Arbor, MI: University of Michigan Press.

BBC. (2013, December 12). China blog: Dancing grannies raise a ruckus. *BBC News*. Retrieved April 30, 2017, from www.bbc.com/news/blogs-china-blog-25330651

Benjamin, W. (1968). *Illuminations: Essays and reflections*. (H. Zohn, trans.). New York: Schocken Books.

Berlant, L. (2011). *Cruel Optimism*. Durham, NC and London: Duke University Press.

Blakley, J. (2010, May). Transcript of "Lessons from fashion's free culture." Retrieved February 25, 2017, from www.ted.com/talks/johanna_blakley_lessons_ from_fashion_s_free_culture/transcript

Bradic, L. (2015, September 30). Celebrity endorsements on social media are driving sales and winning over fans. Retrieved March 28, 2017, from https://socialmediaweek.or g/blog/201 5/09/brands-using-celebrity-endorsements/

Branigan, T. (2015, March 12). Five Chinese feminists held over International Women's Day plans. *Guardian*. Retrieved August 12, 2016, from www.theguardian.com/world/2015/mar/12/five-chinese-feminists-held-international-womens-day

Bristow, M. (2008, September 17). Bitter taste over China baby milk. *BBC News*. Retrieved May 3, 2016, from http://news.bbc.co.uk/2/mobile/asia-pacific/7620812.stm

Burkitt, L. (2012, February 13). LVMH fund takes stake in Trendy. *Wall Street Journal*. Retrieved February 1, 2017, from www.wsj.com/articles/SB10001 424 052970203646004577216084192457226

Butler, J. (2009). Performativity, precarity and sexual politics. *AIBR. Revista de Antropología Iberoamericana*, 4(3), i–xiii.

Cai, Q. (2007). Reflecting on internet egao culture. *Journal of International Communication*, 1, 57–8.

Callahan, W. A. (2013). *China Dreams: 20 Visions of the Future*. Oxford: Oxford University Press.

Canaves, S. (2009, November 27). A makeover attempt for "Made in China." *Wall Street Journal*. Retrieved May 3, 2016, from http://blogs.wsj.com/chinarealtime/2009/11/27/a-makeover-attempt-for-made-in-china/#:poiX4lTWV6paEA

Canaves, S. & Ye, J. (2009, January 22). Imitation is the sincerest form of rebellion in China: Copycat culture hits high point with Lunar New Year Show; Elvis in a pink wig. *Wall Street Journal*. Retrieved May 3, 2016, from www.wsj.com/articles/SB1232571389529 03561

Cartlege, S. & Lovelock, P. (1999). Special subject: e-China. *China Economic Quarterly*, 3, 19–35.

CCTV. (2016, January 14). CNTV's *Mengwa* animation series reached highest exposure rate. *CCTV*. Retrieved March 7, 2017, from www.cctv.cn/2016/01/14/ ARTIwRl4ivShGacK CVIwOsVc1 60114.shtml

CECA. (2016). *E-commerce Industrial Anti-counterfeit Big Data 2.0: 2015 Report on China's E-commerce Industry Anti-counterfeit Campaign* (pp. 1–131). The Policy and Lawmaking Committee of the China Electronic Commerce Association.

Chai, J. (2015, February 28). *Under the Dome: Investigating China's Smog* [Documentary]. China.

Chang, H. (2004). Fake logos, fake theory, fake globalization. (Y. Liao, trans.). *Inter-Asia Cultural Studies*, 5(2), 222–36.

Chen. F. (Director). (1980). *Spectre* (幽灵) [Motion picture]. China: Xiaoxiang Film Group.

Cheng, J. (2013, June 14). Chinese Dream [Mp4]. *CCTV Dialogue Special*. Changsha: China Central Television. Retrieved May 3, 2017, from http:// english.cntv.cn/2014/06/05/VIDE 1401920281045234.shtml

Cheng, L. (2010). Introduction: The rise of the middle class in the middle kingdom. In L. Cheng (ed.), *China's Emerging Middle Class: Beyond Economic Transformation* (pp. 3–31). Washington, DC: Brookings Institution Press.

Chew, M. (2010). Delineating the emergent global cultural dynamic of "lobalization": The case of pass-off menswear in China. *Continuum: Journal of Media & Cultural Studies*, 24(4), 559–71.

China.org.cn. (2013, December 7). Seminar on Chinese Dream convenes in Shanghai. *China.org.cn*. Retrieved May 7, 2017, from www.china.org.cn/ china/Chines e_dream_dialogue/2013-12/07/content_30828036.htm

ChinaDaily. (2014, July 24). Eight stories you want to know about square dance. *ChinaDaily*. Retrieved April 30, 2017, from www.chinadaily.com.cn/ china/2014-07/24/cont ent_17914368.htm

Chubb, A. (2014). China's Shanzhai culture: "Grabism" and the politics of hybridity. *Journal of Contemporary China*, 24(92), 260–79.

Clover, C. (2016, June 14). Alibaba's Jack Ma says fakes are better than originals. *Financial Times*. Retrieved August 9, 2016, from www.ft.com/content/6700d-5cc-3209-11e6 -ad39-3fee5ffe5b5b

CNN. (2007, July 26). *CNN Special: Made in China* [Documentary]. London.

CNTV. (n.d.). The "Chinese Dream" exhibition of new composed theme songs. Retrieved May 7, 2017, from http://ent.cntv.cn/special/zgmgqz/

Conor, B., Gill, R., & Taylor, S. (2015). Gender and creative labour. *The Sociological Review*, 63(S1), 1–22.

Curtin, M. & Sanson, K. (eds) (2016). *Precarious Creativity: Global Media, Local Labor*. Oakland, CA: University of California Press.

Davison, S. (2011, October 10). What Antonio Gramsci offers to social democracy. Retrieved January 25, 2017, from www.policy-network.net/pno_detail.aspx? ID=4064&title=+ What+Antonio+Gramsci+offers+to+social+democracy

Daxi. (2015, June 22). [Video file]. Retrieved July 2, 2015, from http://weibo. com/p/230444d4669a399 900 daea055ff4100f8d1294#146204743917

Deleuze, G. (1983). *Plato and the Simulacrum* (Vol. 27, pp. 45–56). Cambridge, MA: MIT Press.

—— (1992). *Postscript on the Societies of Control* (Vol. 59, pp. 3–7). Cambridge, MA: MIT Press.

—— (1994). *Difference and Repetition*. New York: Columbia University Press.

Deleuze, G. & Guattari, F. (1987). *A Thousand Plateaus: Capitalism and Schizophrenia*. Minneapolis, MN: University of Minnesota Press.

Denton, K. A. (2014). China Dreams and the "Road to Revival." *Origins: Current Events in Historical Perspective, 8*(3). Retrieved March 21, 2017, from http://origins.osu.edu/article/china-dreams-and-road-revival/page/0/0

Dong, B. (2015, December 14). Alibaba promoting "the Internet + Quality-Made in China." *China Youth News*, 03.

Dong, Z. & Peng, X. (1998). *Chronicles of Chinas Reform and Opening-up in 20 Years*. Shanghai: Shanghai Renmin Press.

Dongge Forum (2016, June 15). Jack Ma's comments on fakes [Video file]. Retrieved September 9, 2016, from www.bilibili.com/video/av4977302/

Douban. (2013, June 17). A dish of gossip of those camouflage foreign brands. *Douban*. Retrieved November 9, 2016, from www.douban.com/group/topic/4043161 9/?r=1

Duffy, B. (2015). Amateur, autonomous, and collaborative: Myths of aspiring female cultural producers in web 2.0. *Critical Studies in Media Communication, 32*(1), 48–64.

Duffy, B. E. (2016). The romance of work: Gender and aspirational labour in the digital culture industries. *International Journal of Cultural Studies, 19*(4), 441–57.

ebrun & Nascent. (2016). Reading into the data of 2016 Single Days' sale. Retrieved December 15, 2016, from www.ebrun.com/20161201/204447.shtml

Entwistle, J. & Wissinger, E. (2006). Keeping up appearances: Aesthetic labour in the fashion modelling industries of London and New York. *The Sociological Review, 54*(4), 774–94.

Fan, C. C. (2004). The state, the migrant labor regime, and maiden workers in China. *Political Geography, 23*, 283–305.

Fantone, L. (2007). Precarious changes: Gender and generational politics in contemporary Italy. *Feminist Review, 87*, 5–20.

Federici, S. (2008). Precarious labor: A feminist viewpoint. *In the Middle of the Whirlwind: 2008 Convention Protest, Movement & Movements*. Retrieved January 9, 2017, from http://inthemiddleofthewhirlwind.wordpress.com/precarious-labor-a-feminist-viewpoint/

—— (2012). *Revolution at Point Zero: Housework, Reproduction, and Feminist Struggle*. Oakland, CA: PM Press.

Fewsmith, J. (1999). China and the WTO: The politics behind the agreement. *NBR Analysis*.

Fincher, L. H. (2014). *Leftover Women: The Resurgence of Gender Inequality in China*. London: Zed Books.

Finnane, A. (2008). *Changing Clothes in China: Fashion, History, Nation*. New York: Columbia University Press.

Flannery, R. (2015, May 13). 2015 Forbes China celebrity list (Full list). *Forbes*. Retrieved February 2, 2017, from www.forbes.com/sites/russell flannery/2015/05/13/20 15-forbes-china-celebrity-list-full-list/#65faa 12a7d94

FlorCruz, J., Chang, E., & Ahmed, S. (2009, June 4). China's youth post-Tiananmen: Apathy a fact or front? *CNN.com*. Retrieved December 20, 2016, from www.cnn.com/2009/WOR LD/asiapcf/06/0 3/china.post.tiananmen. generation/index.html?eref=onion

Foley, B. (2017, February 23). Lagerfeld: Meryl Streep passed on Oscar dress when Chanel refused to Pay. *WWD*. Retrieved March 10, 2017, from http://wwd.com/fashion-news/fashion-scoops/karl-lagerfeld-chanel-meryl-streep-passed-on-oscar-dress-w hen-chanel-oscar-dress-10817502/

Fortunati, L. (2007). Immaterial labor and its machinization. *Ephemera: Theory & Politics in Organization, 7*(1), 139–57.

Foucault, M. (1988). *The History of Sexuality* (Vol. 1, An introduction). New York: Vintage Books.

Friedman, T. (2012). China needs its own dream. *The New York Times*, The Opinion Pages. Retrieved April 12, 2017, from www.nytimes.com/2012/10/03/opinion/friedman-china-need s-its-own-dream.html

gbtimes. (2016, May 19). Chinese netizens react to South China Sea dispute. Retrieved May 31, 2016, from http://gbtimes.com/china/chinese-netizens-react-south-china-sea-dispute

Gerth, K. (2010). *As China Goes, So Goes the World: How Chinese Consumers are Transforming Everything*. New York: Hill and Wang.

Gill, R. (2002). Cool, creative and egalitarian? Exploring gender in project-based new media work in Europe. *Information, Communication & Society, 5*(1), 70–89.

—— (2014). Unspeakable inequalities: Post feminism, entrepreneurial subjectivity, and the repudiation of sexism among cultural workers. *Social Politics: International Studies in Gender, State & Society, 21*(4), 509–28.

Gill, R. & Pratt, A. (2008). In the social factory?: Immaterial labour, precariousness and cultural work. *Theory, Culture & Society, 25*(7–8), 1–30.

Gillespie, T. (2014). The relevance of algorithms. In T. Gillespie, P. Boczkowski, & K. Foot (eds), *Media Technologies: Essays on Communication, Materiality, and Society* (pp. 167–94). Cambridge, MA: MIT Press.

Grape-Lee. (2016, April 29). [Video file]. Retrieved April 30, 2016, from http://weibo.com/1943171370/ DtaD yzFMV?type=repost#_ rnd1462205759257

Gregg, M. (2008). The normalisation of flexible female labour in the information economy. *Feminist Media Studies, 8*(3), 285–99.

—— (2011). *Work's Intimacy*. Cambridge: Polity.

Grossberg, L. (2010). *Cultural Studies in the Future Tense*. Durham, NC and London: Duke University Press.

Gucci sues Alibaba over "counterfeit goods." (2015, May 18). *BBC News*. Retrieved June 1, 2016, from www.bbc.com/news/technology-32781236

Guo, Q. & Li, D. (2017, April 25). Close-up: The Chinese Dream, My Dream—On the "Chinese Bridge" Chinese proficiency competition in Latvia. *Xinhua News*. Retrieved May 7, 2017, from http://news.xinhuanet.com/world/2017-04/26/c_1120 879486.htm

Hall, S. (1988). *The Hard Road to Renewal: Thatcherism and the Crisis of the Left*. London: Verso.

Han, B. & Dou, Y. (2009, January 12). Active consumption is patriotic. *Outlook Weekly*. Retrieved February 1, 2017, from www.chinanews.com/cj/plgd/news/2009/01-12/1524209.sht ml

Hanser, A. (2008). *Service Encounters: Class, Gender, and the Market for Social Distinction in Urban China*. Stanford, CA: Stanford University Press.

Hardt, M. (1999). Affective labor. *Boundary 2, 26*(2), 89–100.

Hardt, M, & Negri, A. (2000). *Empire*. Cambridge, MA: Harvard University Press.

——— (2004). *Multitude: War and Democracy in the Age of Empire*. New York: The Penguin Press.

——— (2009). *Commonwealth*. Cambridge, MA: Belknap Press of Harvard University Press.

Hartford, K. (2000). Cyberspace with Chinese characteristics. *Current History, 99*, 261.

Harvey, D. (2005). *A Brief History of Neoliberalism*. Oxford and New York: Oxford University Press.

Haute|Hot Couture News. (n.d.). What is haute couture. Retrieved May 12, 2016, from www.hautec outure news.com/what-is-haute-couture/

Hennessey, W. (2012). Deconstructing Shanzhai–China's copycat counterculture: Catch me if you can. *Campbell Law Review, 34*, 609–61.

Hesmondhalgh, D. & Baker, S. (2008). Creative work and emotional labour in the television industry. *Theory, Culture & Society, 25*(7–8), 97–118.

Hines, A. (2016, May 18). Knockoff: Another day at the office—on Canal Street with counterfeit vendors. Retrieved April 25, 2017, from www.villagevoice.com/news/knockoff-another-day-at-the-office-on-canal-street-with-counterfeit-vendors-8626379

Ho, J. (2010, June). Shanzhai: Economic/cultural production through the cracks of globalization. Paper presented at Crossroads: 2010 Cultural Studies Conference, Hong Kong. Retrieved March 24, 2015, from http://sex.ncu.edu.tw/members/Ho/20100617percent20Crossroadspercent20Plenarypercent20Speech.pdf

Hu, J. (2012, November 8). Keynote report at the 18th CPC National Congress. *China Xinhua News*. Retrieved September 26, 2019, from http://news.xinhuanet.com/english/special/18cpcnc/2012-11/17/c_131981259.htm

Hu, Q. (2013, November 13). Dancing with danger. *Global Times*. Retrieved July 7, 2016, from http://en.peop le.cn/90782/8455170.html

Huang, H. & Luan, J. (eds) (2013). *The Roadmap of the 18th CPC National Congress and the Chinese Dream*. Beijing: Foreign Languages Press. Retrieved June 7, 2015, from www.china.org.cn/arts/2014-03/26/content_31911187.htm

Huang, Z. (2015, January 29). The Chinese government has erased a damning report on Alibaba, but you can read it here. Retrieved February 2, 2015, from https://qz.com/335675/the-chinese-government-has-erased-a-damning-report-on-alibaba-but-you-can-read-it-here/

Hung, F., Lee, Y., & Blanchard, B. (2016, January 21). Chinese flood Taiwan president-elect's Facebook, demanding return to China [News]. Retrieved February 17, 2017, from http://uk.reuters.com/article/uk-taiwan-china-facebook-idUKKCN0UZ07Y

Huws, U. (2003). *The Making of a Cybertariat: Virtual Work in a Real World*. London: The Merlin Press.

iiMedia Research. (2018, February 6). 2017–2018 China cross-border e-commerce market research report. Retrieved May 9, 2019, from www.iimedia.cn/c400/60608.html

Jarrett, K. (2014). The relevance of "women's work": social reproduction and immaterial labor in digital media. *Television & New Media*, 15(1), 14–29.

Jenkins, H. (2004). Quentin Tarantino's Star Wars? Digital cinema, media convergence, and participatory culture. In D. Thorburn & H. Jenkins (eds), *Rethinking Media Change: The Aesthetics of Transition* (pp. 281–312). Cambridge, MA: MIT Press.

Ji, M. (2015, June). Science and technology in modern China: A historical and strategic perspective on state power. *The Yale Review of International Studies*. Retrieved July 7, 2016, from http://yris.yira.org/essays/1551

Jiang, Z. (2010). *On the Development of China's Information Technology Industry*. (Elsevier, trans.). Oxford: Central Party Literature Press and Shanghai Jiaotong University Press. First published in Chinese in 2009. Central Party Literature Press and Shanghai Jiaotong University Press.

Johnson, I. (2013, October 15). Old dreams for a new China. Retrieved May 4, 2017, from www.nybooks.com/daily/2013/10/15/china-dream-posters/

Jones, P. (2015, May 26). Alibaba hosts first "Global Conference on Women and Entrepreneurship" [News]. Retrieved April 23, 2017, from http://gbtimes.com/business/alibaba-hosts-first-global-conference-women-and-entrepreneurship

Kane, C. (2016, January 26). What selfies in American vs. China can tell us about beauty standards. Retrieved March 28, 2017, from https://mic.com/articles/133484/what-selfies-in-america-vs-china-can-tell-us-about-beauty-standards

Kaur, D. (2017, March 22). The unforeseen consequences of celebrity endorsements. *Luxury Lawyers Network*. Retrieved March 27, 2017, from www.luxurylawalliance.com/news-features/the-unforeseen-consequences-of-celebrity-endorsements/652843210

Keane, M. (2013). *Creative Industries in China: Art, Design and Media*. Cambridge: Polity.

—— (2016a). The ten thousand things, the Chinese Dream and the creative↔cultural industries. In M. Keane (ed.), *Handbook of Cultural and Creative Industries in China* (pp. 27–42). Cheltenham, UK and Northampton, MA: Edward Elgar.

—— (2016b). Understanding precarious creativity in China: "Knowing-how" and "knowing-to." In M. Curtain & K. Sanson (eds), *Precarious Creativity:*

Global Media, Local Labor (pp. 215–30). Oakland, CA: University of California Press.

Keane, M. & Zhao, E. J. (2012). Renegades on the frontier of innovation: The Shanzhai grassroots communities of Shenzhen in China's creative economy. *Eurasian Geography and Economics, 53*(2), 216–30.

Kersley, R. and Stierly, M. (2015). Global wealth in 2015: Underlying trends remain positive. *Credit Suisse.* Retrieved September 9, 2016, from www.credit-suisse.com/us/en/aboutus/research/research-institute/news-and-videos/articles/news-and-expertise/2015/10/en/global-wealth-in-2015-underlying-trends-remain-positive.html

Kim, Y. (2013). Introduction: Korean media in a digital cosmopolitan world. In Y. K. (ed.), *The Korean Wave: Korean Media Go Global* (pp. 1–27). London and New York: Routledge.

Klaffke, P. (2003). *Spree: A Cultural History of Shopping.* Vancouver, BC: Arsenal Pulp Press.

Klein, N. (2000). *No Logo: Taking Aim at the Brand Bullies.* London: Flamingo.

Kong, D. (2016, September 21). Unmasking East Asia's beauty ideals. Retrieved March 28, 2017, from www.businessoffashion.com/articles/global-currents/unmasking-east-asias-beauty-ideals

Kong, X. (2007). From export-oriented to domestic-demand dominant: Reflections and transformations of China's economic development strategy. *Journal of Shandong University, 3,* 50–6.

Kuhn, R. L. (2013, June 4). Xi Jinping's Chinese Dream. *The New York Times.* Retrieved September 7, 2016, from www.nytimes.com/2013/06/05/opinion/global/xi-jinpings-chinese-dre am.html?pagewanted=all&_r=0

Laclau, E. & Mouffe, C. (2001). *Hegemony and Socialist Strategy: Towards a Radical Democratic Politics* (2nd edn). London and New York: Verso.

Lai, R. (2015, January 1). Xiaomi mocks Apple with its very own premium phablet. *Engadget.* Retrieved December 3, 2015, from www.engadget.com/2015/01/15/xiaomi-mi-note/

Lash, S. & Lury, C. (2007). *Global Culture Industry: The Mediation of Things.* Cambridge: Polity.

Lazzarato, M. (1996). Immaterial labor. In P. Vimo & M. Hardt (eds), *Radical Thought in Italy: A Potential Politics* (pp. 133–48). Minneapolis, MN: University of Minnesota Press.

Le, Y. (2009, January 15). If active consumption can boost a country's economy, the poor are not qualified to be patriotic? Retrieved July 7, 2016, from http://view.news.qq.com/a/200901 14/000016.htm

Lee, C. K. (1998). *South China Miracle: Two Worlds of Factory Women.* Berkeley and Los Angeles, CA: University of California Press.

Lee, M. & Wang, S. (2014, October 31). China's Singles Day online shopping festival is going global. *Alizila.* Retrieved November 17, 2014, from www.alizila.com/china-singles-day-online-shopping-festival-going-global

Lessig, L. (2004). *Free Culture: How Big Media Uses Technology and the Law to Lock Down Culture and Control Creativity.* New York: Penguin Press.

Li, L. (2015). If You Are the One: Dating shows and feminist politics in contemporary China. *International Journal of Cultural Studies*, *18*(5), 519–35.

Li, L. N. (2017). Rethinking the Chinese internet: Social history, cultural forms, and industrial formation. *Television & New Media*, *18*(5), 393–403.

Li, P. (2015, July 1). Zhou Enlai and the "Four Modernizations." *The History of the People's Republic of China*. Retrieved October 9, 2016, from www.hprc.org. cn/gsgl/gsys/201 012/t20101221_1 16518.html

Lin, Y. J. (2011). *Fake Stuff: China and the Rise of Counterfeit Goods*. New York and London: Routledge.

Linshi, J. (2015, January 15). This is China's answer to iPhone 6 Plus. *Time*. Retrieved December 3, 2015, from http://time.com/3668994/ xiaomi-mi-note-iphone-6-plus/

Liu, F. (2010). *Urban Youth in China: Modernity, the Internet and the Self*. New York and Abingdon: Routledge.

Liu, H. & Zeng, W. (2015). Changsha host "the Chinese Dream" public-service advertisement exhibition. *Chinanews.com*. Retrieved May 7, 2017, from www .chinanews.com/cul/2015/11-04/7606210.shtml

Marquis, C. & Yang, Z. (2013, June 28). Chinese Dream? American Dream? Retrieved January 29, 2017, from http://people.hbs.edu/cmarquis/china dreamEN.pdf

Martinsen, J. (2009, January 20). Show your patriotism through spending. *DANWEI: Chinese Media, Advertising, and Urban Life*. Retrieved February 20, 2017, from www.danwei.org/financial_crisis/patriotic_spending_outlook. php

Marwick, A. (2013). Online identity. In J. Hartley, J. Burgess, & A. Bruns (eds), *A Companion to New Media Dynamics* (pp. 355–64). Chichester and Malden, MA: John Wiley & Sons.

Marwick, A. & boyd, d. (2011). To see and be seen: Celebrity practice on Twitter. *Convergence: The International Journal of Research into New Media Technologies*, *17*(2), 139–58.

McRobbie, A. (1998). *British Fashion Design: Rag Trade or Image Industry?* London and New York: Routledge.

—— (2002). From Holloway to Hollywood: Happiness at work in the new cultural economy? In P. du Gay & M. Pryke (eds), *Cultural Economy: Cultural Analysis and Commercial Life* (pp. 97–114). London: Sage.

—— (2009). *The Aftermath of Feminism: Gender, Culture and Social Change*. Los Angeles, CA and London: Sage.

—— (2011). Reflections on feminism, immaterial labour and the post-Fordist regime. *New Formations*, *70*(70), 60–76.

Meng, J. & Sun, X. (2013). Discourse interpretation and folk imagination of the China Dream: Data analysis based on more than 160,000 original posts on Sina Weibo. *Journalism and Communication*, *11*, 27–43.

Michault, J. (2014, February 12). Ralph Lauren ready to wear fall winter 2014 New York. Retrieved March 30, 2017, from http://nowfashion.com/ ralph-lauren-ready-to-wear-fall-winter-2014-new-york-6345

Ministry of Commerce. (2004). *Notice on Implement of National Standards of Retail Business Categorization.* Retrieved January 3, 2017, from www.mofcom. gov.cn/aarticle/b/g/200407/20040700246557.html

—— (2012). *Notice on the List of the First Batch of Demonstrative E-commerce Bases.* Retrieved January 3, 2017, from http://dzsws.mofcom.gov.cn/article/ dzsw/sftx/20 1204/20120408054220.shtml

Mintel. (2016, March 3). 58 percent of Chinese consumers purchase foreign products online from domestic shopping websites. *Mintel.* Retrieved November 8, 2016, from www.mintel.com/press-centre/retail-press-centre/58-of-chinese-consumers-purchase-foreign-products-online-from-domestic-shopping-websites

National Development and Reform Commission. (2011). *Conference of E-commerce Model Cities.* Retrieved November 19, 2015, from www.sdpc.gov. cn/xwzx/xwfb/201111/t201111 16_444879.html

—— (2014). *Notice on Agreement to 30 E-commerce Model Cities.* Retrieved November 19, 2015, from www.sdpc.gov.cn/zcfb/zcfbtz/2014 03/t20140325_ 604 195.html

Neff, G. (2012). *Venture Labor: Work and the Burden of Risk in Innovative Industry.* Cambridge, MA and London: MIT Press.

Negri, A. (1989). *The Politics of Subversion: A Manifesto for the Twenty-first Century.* Cambridge: Polity.

O'Reilly, T. (2005, October 1). Web 2.0: Compact definition? [Web log]. Retrieved September 7, 2015, from http://radar.oreilly.com/2005/10/web-20-compact-definit ion.html

ochirly. (n.d.). Brand story. *orchily.com.* Retrieved November 9, 2016, from http://ochirly. trendy-global.com/en/#

OIOatm. (2015, July 21). The memory of jeans: From sweep-the-floor to versatile cut. Enjoy. Retrieved November 11, 2016, from www.whyenjoy.com/ archives/14 881

Okwodu, J. (2016, December 19). Kendall, Gigi, Bella, and the year in Insta-Girls. *Vogue.* Retrieved March 27, 2017, from www.vogue.com/article/2016-insta-girls-instagram-fashions-new-normal-kendall-jenner-gigi-hadid

Ong, A. & Zhang, L. (2008). Introduction. In L. Zhang & A. Ong (eds), *Privatizing China: Socialism from Afar* (pp. 1–20). Ithaca, NY: Cornell University Press.

Pang, L. (2008). "China who makes and fakes": A semiotics of the counterfeit. *Theory, Culture & Society, 25*(6), 117–40.

—— (2012). *Creativity and Its Discontents: China's Creative Industries and Intellectual Property Rights Offenses.* Durham, NC: Duke University Press.

Pham, M. (2015). *Asians Wear Clothes on the Internet: Race, Gender and the Work of Personal Style Blogging.* Durham, NC: Duke University Press.

Pun, N. (2005). *Made in China: Women Factory Workers in a Global Workplace.* Durham, NC: Duke University Press.

Qi, X. (Director). (1984). *The Fashionable Red Dress* (街上流行红裙子) [Motion picture]. China: Changchun Film Group Corporation.

Qiu, J. L. (2004). The internet in China: Technologies of freedom in a statist society. In M. Castells (ed.), *The Network Society: A Cross-cultural Perspective* (pp. 99–124). Cheltenham, UK and Northampton, MA: Edward Elgar.

Qiu, L. (2016, November 12). 2016 Tmall Single Day's sale reached RMB$120 billion. *Guangcha*. Retrieved November 12, 2016, from www.guancha.cn/Industry/2016_11_12_380269. shtml

Ramli, D. & Chen, L. Y. (2016, June 14). Alibaba's Jack Ma: Better-than-ever fakes worsen piracy war. *Bloomberg.com*. Retrieved June 29, 2016, from www.bloomberg.com/news/articles/2016-06-14/alibaba-s-ma-fake-goods-today-are-better-than-the-real-thing

Raustiala, K. & Sprigman, C. (2012). *The Knockoff Economy: How Imitation Sparks Innovation*. New York: Oxford University Press.

Rofel, L. (2007). *Desiring China: Experiments in Neoliberalism, Sexuality, and Public Culture*. Durham, NC: Duke University Press.

Ross, A. (2008). The new geography of work: Power to the precarious? *Theory, Culture & Society*, 25(7–8), 31–49.

—— (2013). In search of the lost paycheck. In T. Scholz (ed.), *Digital Labor: The Internet as Playground and Factory* (pp. 13–32). New York and London: Routledge.

Ruan, K. (2016, August 9). Protecting fashion design: A copyright perspective. *China Intellectual Property Rights*. Retrieved November 16, 2016, from www.cnipr.com/sy/201608/t201 60809_198261.htm

Sang, Y. (2006). *China Candid: The People on the People's Republic*. (G. R. Barmé, ed.). Berkeley, CA: University of California Press.

Sawhney, M. (2014, September 22). Alibaba vs. Amazon: Who will win the global e-commerce war? *Forbes*. Retrieved November 15, 2014, from www.forbes.com/sites/forbesleadershipforum/2014/09/22/alibaba-vs-amazon-who-will-win-the-global-e-commerce-war/

Scholz, T. (ed.) (2013). *Digital Labor: The Internet as Playground and Factory*. New York: Routledge.

Senft, T. M. (2013). Microcelebrity and the branded self. In J. Hartley, J. Burgess, & A. Bruns (eds), *A Companion to New Media Dynamics* (pp. 346–54). Chichester and Malden, MA: John Wiley & Sons.

sfguangchangwu. (2016, October 8). Square dance team of San Francisco: Beautiful Chinese Dream [Video file]. Retrieved November 13, 2016, from www.youtube.com/watch?v= pqxSI6mchk8

Shao, H. (2015, January 29). What happens when a Chinese tycoon stands up against the government? Retrieved February 1, 2017, from www.forbes.com/sites/hengshao/2015/01/29/what-happens-when-a-chinese-tycoon-stands-up-against-the-government-oftentimes-you-fall-hard/

Sharkey, L. (2015, January 27). Naomi Campbell criticises new generation of Instagirl models. Retrieved March 10, 2017, from www.independent.co.uk/life-style/fashion/features/naomi-campbell-hits-out-supermodels-vs-instagirls-100058 37.html

Shawki, A. (1997). China: From Mao to Deng. *International Socialist Review, Summer*(1). Retrieved July 7, 2017, from www.isreview.org/issues/01/mao_to_deng_1.shtml

Shi, J. (2015, March 31). *Mengwa* videos become popular among audience. *Xinhua News*. Retrieved May 4, 2017, from http://news.xinhuanet.com/politics/2015-03/31/c_11 148262 23.htm

Sundaram, R. (2010). *Pirate Modernity: Delhi's Media Urbanism*. Milton Park, Abingdon, Oxon and New York: Routledge.

Tam, K. (2014). Dolce & Banana, a shanzhai creator's manual: Production and consumption of fake in contemporary Chinese art practices. In A. Hulme (ed.), *The Changing Landscape of China's Consumerism* (pp. 83–106). Oxford: Chandos Publishing.

Tan, H. (2016, December 21). Alibaba's Taobao website back in US list of "notorious marketplaces." Retrieved February 1, 2017, from www.cnbc.com/2016/12/21/us-puts-alibaba-taobao-website-back-in-its-list-of-notorious-marketplaces.html

Tang, R. & Ma, J. (2008). *30 Years of China's Economic Reform (1978–2008): Opening-up*. Chongqing, China: University of Chongqing Press.

Taobao. (2010). Taobao Marketplace collaborated with a dozen brand names to release anti-counterfeits campaigns. Retrieved July 2, 2016, from www.taobao.com/go/act/forum/315.php

Tencent Fashion. (2010, December 10). "Shanzhai fashion" in the circuit of fashion. Retrieved May 3, 2016, from http://luxury.qq.com/a/20101210/000004.htm

Terranova, T. (2000). Free labor: Producing culture for the digital economy. *Social Text, 18*(2), 33–58.

The Communist Party of China. (1978). *The Gazette of the 3rd Plenum of the 11th Central Committee of the Communist Party of China*. Beijing. Retrieved July 3, 2016, from http://cpc.peo ple.co m.cn/GB/64162/64168/64563/65371/4441902.html

The Economist. (2013a, May 4). Xi Jinping's vision: Chasing the Chinese dream. The Economist. Retrieved February 1, 2017, from www.economist.com/news/briefing/21577063-chinas-new-leader-has-been-quick-consolidate-his-power-what-does-he-now-want-his

—— (2013b, September 14). Taking a bite out of Apple. *The Economist*. Retrieved November 28, 2015, from www.economist.com/news/business/21586344-xiaomi-often-described-chinas-answer-apple-actually-quite-different-taking-bite-out

—— (2014, December 17). Propaganda: The art is red. *The Economist*. Retrieved November 3, 2016, from www.economist.com/news/china/21636783-propaganda-art-enjoying-new-lease-life-art-red

—— (2016, July 5). The new class war. *The Economist*. Retrieved October 30, 2016, from www.economist.com/news/special-report/21701653-chinas-middle-class-larger-richer-and-more-vocal-ever-threatens

The State Council Information Office. (2015, September 22). Gender equality and women's development in China. The State Council Information Office of the People's Republic of China. Retrieved January 3, 2017, from http://english. gov.cn/archive/white_pa per/2015/09/22/content_281475195668448.htm

Thomas, P. W. (n.d.). Haute couture: Fashion history. *Fashion-Era*. Retrieved May 2, 2016, from www.fashion-era.com/haute_couture.htm

Tokumitsu, M. (2014, January 12). In the name of love [Blog post]. Retrieved March 4, 2017, from www.jacobinmag.com/2014/01/in-the-name-of-love/

Tong, L. (2016, July 16). The social media "war" over the South China Sea [commentary]. Retrieved February 17, 2017, from http://thediplomat. com/2016/07/the-social-media-war-over-the-south-china-sea/

Tsang, A. (2016, June 8). Cross-border e-commerce: China policy update. *HKTDC*. Retrieved December 2, 2016, from http://hkmb.hktdc.com/ en/1XoA6AHP/hktdc-research/Cross-Border-E-Commerce-China-Policy-Update

Tse, E., Ma, K., & Huang, Y. (2009). Shan Zhai: A Chinese phenomenon. Beijing: *Booz&co.*

Tsoi, G. (2016, August 1). Wang Hong: China's online stars making real cash. *BBC News*. Retrieved September 30, 2016, from www.bbc.com/news/ world-asia-china-36802769

US Securities and Exchange Commission. (2014, June 16). *Amendment No. 1 to Form F-1 Registration Statement under the Securities Act of 1933. Alibaba Group Holding Limited*. Retrieved December 2, 2016, from www.sec.gov/ Archives/edgar/data/1577552/000119312514236860/d709111df1a.htm#toc 709111_17

US-China Economic and Security Review Commission. (2003). *SARS in China: Implications for Information Control, Internet Censorship, and the Economy*. Hearings. Retrieved from ProQuest database.

Virno, P. & Hardt, M. (eds) (1996). *Radical Thought in Italy: A Potential Politics*. Minneapolis, MN: University of Minnesota Press.

Vogel, E. F. (1981). *One Step Ahead in China: Guangdong under Reform*. Cambridge, MA: Harvard University Press.

Wallis, C. & Qiu, J. L. (2012). Shanzhaiji and the transformation of the local mediascape in Shenzhen. In W. Sun & J. Chio (eds), *Mapping Media in China: Region, Province, Locality* (pp. 109–25). London and New York: Routledge.

Wang, H. (1994). *The Gradual Revolution: China's Economic Reform Movement*. New Brunswick, NJ and London: Transaction Publishers.

—— (2004). The year 1989 and the historical roots of neoliberalism in China. *Positions: East Asia Cultures Critique*, 12(1), 7–70.

—— (2010). *The Chinese Dream: The Rise of the World's Largest Middle Class and What It Means to You*. Pasadena, CA: Pasadena, CA: Bestseller Press.

Wang, J. (2001). Culture as leisure and culture as capital. *Positions: East Asia Cultures Critique*, 9(1), 69–104.

—— (2006). The politics of goods: A case study of consumer nationalism and media discourse in contemporary China. *Asian Journal of Communication*, 16(2), 187–206.

Wang, L. & Feng, D. (2016, November 29). This is how General Secretary Xi Jinping describes the "Chinese Dream." *Xinhua News*. Retrieved April 18,

2017, from http://news.xinhuanet.com/politics/2016-11/29/c_1120016588. htm

Wang, L. F. & Li, X. (2014). *Jack Ma in Cloth Shoes: 27 Turning Points for Alibaba*. Beijing: Beijing Lianhe Press.

Wang, Q. (2014, February 21–23). Public dance: A sociality invented in individualizing China. Paper presented at the 17th Annual Harvard East Asia Society Graduate Student Conference, Harvard University, Cambridge, MA.

Watts, J. (2007, July 5). Made in China: Tainted food, fake drugs and dodgy paint. *Guardian*. Retrieved May 3, 2016, from www.theguardian.com/business/20 07/jul/05/china.in ternationalnews1

Weeks, K. (2007). Life within and against work: Affective labor, feminist critique, and post-Fordist politics. *Ephemera*, 7(1), 233–49.

—— (2011). *The Problem with Work: Feminism, Marxism, Antiwork Politics, and Postwork Imaginaries*. Durham, NC and London: Duke University Press.

Williams, R. (1985). *Keywords: A Vocabulary of Culture and Society* (revised edn). Oxford: Oxford University Press.

Wilson, H. W. (1995, January 7). China logs on to the internet. *The Economist*. Retrieved July 7, 2015, from www.hartford-hwp.com/archives/55/037.html

Wissinger, E. (2009). Modeling consumption: Fashion modeling work in contemporary society. *Journal of Consumer Culture*, 9(2), 273–96.

Wong, G. (2015, June 4). Chinese regulator announces new crackdown on online sales of fakes. *Wall Street Journal*. Retrieved January 15, 2016, from www.wsj. com/articles/chinese-regulator-announces-new-crackdown-on-online-sales-of-fakes-1433414502

World Bank. (2016). Data of China: GDP per capital (current US$). Retrieved December 9, 2016, from http://data.worldbank.org/indicator/NY.GDP.PCAP. CD?locations=CN

WTO. (2016). World trade statistical review 2016. Retrieved November 11, 2016, from www.wto.org/english/res_e/statis_e/wts2016_e/wts2016_e.pdf

Wu, A. (2015, May 22). Internet's "She-Era": Female e-entrepreneurs younger by 15 yrs. *All China Women's Federation*. Retrieved April 23, 2017, from www. women ofchina.cn/womenofchina/html1/1505/2087-1.htm

Wu, D. (2009, January 14). Beijing CPPCC members suggested to initiate patriotic shopping movement. *The Beijing News*. Retrieved February, 3, 2017, from http://news.qq.com/a/20090114/000120.htm

Wu, X. (2009). Changing gender discourse under marketization. *China Social Sciences*, 2, 1–13.

Wu, X. & Yu, X. (2003). Does the market pay off? Earnings returns to education in urban China. *American Sociological Review*, 68, 438–9.

Xi stresses core socialist values. (2014, February 25). *Xinhua News*. Retrieved May 7, 2017, from http://news.xinhuanet.com/english/china/2014-02/25/ c_126190257.htm

Xi, J. (2012, November 29). Xi Jinping's speech at the Road to Revival exhibition. *Ministry of Finance of the People's Republic of China*. Retrieved January 2, 2017, from www.mof.gov.cn/mofhome/liaoning/lanmudaohang/lianzheng jianshe/201408/t20140819_1128572.html

Xu, S. (1992). Computer development in China. *Computing & Control Engineering Journal, March,* 57–61.

Yang, F. (2014a). China's "fake" Apple Store: Branded space, intellectual property and the global culture industry. *Theory, Culture & Society, 31*(4), 71–96.

—— (2014b, October). The "Chinese Dream" in contemporary media culture. Paper presented at the 56th Annual Conference of the American Association for Chinese Studies, the George Washington University, Washington, DC.

—— (2016). *Faked in China: Nation Branding, Counterfeit Culture, and Globalization.* Bloomington, IN: Indiana University Press.

Yang, G. (2012). A Chinese internet? History, practice, and globalization. *Chinese Journal of Communication, 5*(1), 49–54.

Ye, S. (2016, November 14). Reflection: Why people love products of "Styling as Yang Mi?" *gogoboi.* Retrieved March 27, 2017, from http://mp.weixin.qq.com

Ye, W. (2010, March 8). Chinese women: A hundred year development and contribution [News]. Retrieved April 23, 2017, from www.mlr.gov.cn/wskt/wskt_syzs/ 201003/t20100308_710399.htm

Yi, D. (2014, April 8). The camera-wielding boyfriends behind fashion's most famous bloggers. Retrieved February 26, 2017, from http://fashionista.com/2014/04/fashio n-blogger-boyfriends

Yu, H. (2014, July 11). Voting in China, a distant dream. (A. H. Barr, trans.). *The New York Times.* Retrieved from www.nytimes.com/2014/07/12/opinion/yu-hua-voting-in-china-a-distant-dream.html

Yu, J. (2008). Internet egao: Carnival and resistance in ceremony. *Journal of Chongqing University of Posts and Telecommunications, 20*(1), 78–82.

Yuan, Z. (2006, March 27). The evolution of Chinese clothing after 1949. Retrieved July 29, 2016, from www.china.com.cn/chinese/zhuanti/gjszz/1166038.htm

Zhang, H. (ed.) (2013). The transformation of the "American Dream:" The American imagination in contemporary popular culture. *Literary Theory and Criticism, 5,* 43–52.

Zhang, H., Li, Y., Shi, Y. et al. (2013). Understanding China by reflecting on the "American Dream." *Red Flag Manuscript, 17,* 8–13.

Zhang, J. (2002). *Xi fu dong jian* (西服东渐). Anhui, China: Anhui Fine Arts Publisher.

Zhang, L. (2009). *"Carnival in cyberspace" or "site of resistance"? Internet egao culture as popular critique in postsocialist Chinese society.* (Master's thesis). New York University, New York City. Retrieved September 26, 2019, from www.academia.edu/download/3 4299540/Lin_Zhang_NYU_Thesis.pdf

——Zhang, L. (2017). Fashioning the feminine self in "prosumer capitalism": Women's work and the transnational reselling of Western luxury online. *Journal of Consumer Culture, 17*(2), 184–204.

Zhang, L. & Ong, A. (eds) (2008). *Privatizing China: Socialism from Afar.* Ithaca, NY: Cornell University Press.

Zhang, X. (2003). *Chinese Economy in the Storm of SARS.* Beijing: Economic Press China.

—— (2013, July 11). Zhang Xudong on the Chinese Dream: Finally it is time to talk of dreams [commentary]. Retrieved April 20, 2017, from www.guancha. cn /ZhangXu Dong/2013_07_11_156654.shtml

Zhang, Y. (2004). *Internet control in China: A digital panopticon.* (Unpublished MA thesis). University of Alberta, Edmonton.

Zhang, Z. (2000). Mediating time: The "rice bowl of youth" in fin de siecle urban China. *Public Culture, 12*(1), 93–113.

Zhao, K. (2016, September 1). China's "Core Socialist Values," the song-and-dance version. *The New York Times.* Retrieved October 9, 2016, from https:// nyti.ms/2cbzfEc

Zhao, Y. (2007). After mobile phones, what? Re-embedding the social in China's "digital revolution." *International Journal of Communication, 1*, 92–120.

Zheng, J. (2015). *Xiangqin: Matchmaking for Shengnü ("leftover women") in China.* (Thesis). University of Hong Kong. Retrieved July 1, 2017, from http:// hdl.handle.n et/10722/211139

Zhihu. (2015). How to evaluate the project "Quality-Made in China" under Taobao Marketplace? Retrieved November 11, 2016, from www.zhihu.com/ questio n/29756778

Zhou, X. & Qin, C. (2010). Globalization, social transformation, and the construction of China's middle class. In C. Li (ed.), *China's Emerging Middle Class: Beyond Economic Transformation* (pp. 84–103). Washington, DC: Brookings Institution Press.

Index

Page numbers in italics followed by an *i* indicates an image.

The Pluto Press Newsletter

Hello friend of Pluto!

Want to stay on top of the best radical books
we publish?

Then sign up to be the first to hear about our
new books, as well as special events,
podcasts and videos.

You'll also get 50% off your first order with us
when you sign up.

Come and join us!

Go to bit.ly/PlutoNewsletter